MacBook Pro®

PORTABLE GENIUS
5th EDITION

by Galen Gruman

WILEY

MacBook Pro® Portable Genius, 5th Edition

Published by
John Wiley & Sons, Inc.
10475 Crosspoint Blvd.
Indianapolis, IN 46256
www.wiley.com

Copyright © 2014 by John Wiley & Sons, Inc., Indianapolis, Indiana

Published simultaneously in Canada

ISBN: 978-1-118-67776-6

Manufactured in the United States of America

10 9 8 7 6 5 4 3 2 1

For general information on our other products and services or to obtain technical support, please contact our Customer Care Department within the U.S. at (877) 762-2974, outside the U.S. at (317) 572-3993 or fax (317) 572-4002.

Wiley publishes in a variety of print and electronic formats and by print-on-demand. Some material included with standard print versions of this book may not be included in e-books or in print-on-demand. If this book refers to media such as a CD or DVD that is not included in the version you purchased, you may download this material at http://booksupport.wiley.com. For more information about Wiley products, visit www.wiley.com.

Credits

Acquisitions Editor
Aaron Black

Project Editor
Martin V. Minner

Technical Editor
Paul Sihvonen-Binder

Copy Editor
Gwenette Gaddis

Editorial Director
Robyn Siesky

Business Manager
Amy Knies

Senior Marketing Manager
Sandy Smith

**Vice President and Executive
Group Publisher**
Richard Swadley

Vice President and Executive Publisher
Barry Pruett

Project Coordinator
Sheree Montgomery

Graphics and Production Specialists
Jennifer Goldsmith

Quality Control Technician
Jessica Kramer

Proofreading and Indexing
The Well-Chosen Word
Potomac Indexing, LLC

About the Author

Galen Gruman has written more than 35 books explaining how to use popular technology, incuding the iPad, OS X, Windows 8, iOS, Adobe InDesign, and QuarkXPress. He's the mobile columnist at the technology website InfoWorld.com, former editor of Macworld magazine, and both a Mac and PC user since 1985.

To my brother Stephen and his adventure, with MacBook Pro in hand, in China

Acknowledgments

It takes a team to make a book, and for this project I had the pleasure of working with the same crew that has helped me deliver the OS X Bible series for Wiley: project editor Marty Minner, copy editor Gwenette Gaddis, technical editor Paul Sihvonen-Binder, and acquisitions editor Aaron Black. And special thanks to Brad Miser, the author of earlier editions of this book, for setting the stage for the current act.

Contents

chapter 2

chapter 3

How Do I Take Advantage of iCloud? 172

How Do I Manage Contacts and E-mail? 192

chapter 8

How Do I Communicate
in Real Time?   228

chapter 9

How Can I Manage
My Calendars?   244

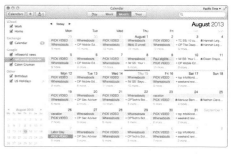

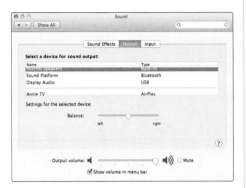

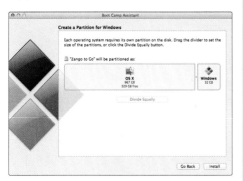

chapter 14

How Do I Solve MacBook Pro Problems? 348

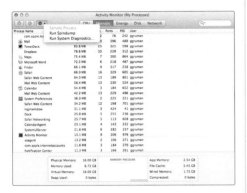

Introduction

From its distinctive metallic finish to its backlit keyboard, dazzling display, and inviting design, the MacBook Pro is amazing technology that looks as great as it works. Running OS X and including lots of amazing software, a MacBook Pro allows you to do more right out of the box more easily than any other computer. In fact, a MacBook Pro does so much that it's easy to overlook even more of the great things it can do. That's where this book comes in.

Although you probably already know how to turn on your MacBook Pro, you might not know how to create virtual working spaces on the desktop, so you can keep many applications and windows open at the same time and move among them easily. Although you likely know how to use the trackpad to point to objects on the screen and select them, you might not know how to create your own keyboard shortcuts for just about any command in any application you use. Although you have probably thought about how you need to back up your important data, you might not have actually done it. Also, although you've probably surfed the web, you may not have taken advantage of all the options that being connected can give you, from sharing files locally to communicating with people around the world, easily and inexpensively.

The purpose of this book is to provide a resource for you when you are wondering how to do something better, how to do it more easily, or even how to do it at all. Each chapter is organized around a question. In each chapter are answers to that question. These answers are task-focused so you learn by doing rather than just by reading. If you start at Step 1 and work through each one in sequence, you'll end up someplace you want to go.

The MacBook Pro Portable Genius is intended to be your companion, to guide you on your in-depth exploration of your MacBook Pro. After you've been through a topic's steps, you'll be prepared to go even further by extending what you've learned to other tasks.

This book is designed to cover a broad range of topics in which most MacBook Pro users are interested. There's no particular order to the topics in this book, so you can jump to any chapter without having read the preceding ones. To get started, I recommend that you look at the table of contents and decide which question you want answered first. Turn to the appropriate page, and off you go!

How Can I Use My Desktop Space Efficiently?

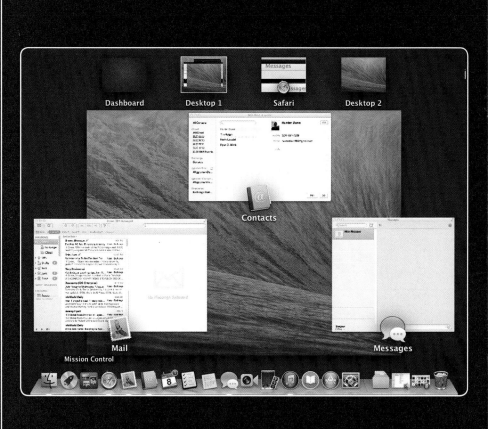

The MacBook Pro's Desktop is the area displayed on its screen. Like a physical desktop, you place things (in this case, icons and windows) on it to focus your attention on them and use their content. As you work, your Desktop naturally becomes cluttered with windows for applications, documents, and system tools. Keeping control of all these windows helps you make the most of your Desktop space. With all the great Desktop management tools that the Mac's OS X operating system offers, it's much easier to keep your MacBook Pro's Desktop neat and tidy than it is a physical desktop.

Setting the Finder Desktop's Icon Preferences

By default on a new MacBook Pro or in a new installation of OS X on a MacBook, icons for the MacBook Pro's hard drive, external hard drives, DVDs, CDs, and servers do not appear on the Desktop. This keeps the entire space on the Desktop clear for your files and folders. (If you upgraded to a new version of OS X or used the Migration Assistant to transfer the contents of another Mac to your MacBook Pro, the drive icons that display are whatever was previously set.)

To access drives, whether or not they appear on the Desktop, open a Finder window (choose File ➪ New Finder Window or press ⌘+N in the Finder, or double-click a folder or drive icon) and click them in the Sidebar to open their contents.

Note The folders and files you see on the Desktop are determined by the contents of the Desktop folder, which is located within your Home folder (choose Go ➪ Home in the Finder to see the Home folder's contents). If you don't want a folder or file taking up space on your Desktop, move it into a different folder within your Home folder. In addition to having a neater appearance, this also helps you work more efficiently because it's easier to find folders and files if they're here rather than scattered on your Desktop.

Perform the following steps to show or hide Desktop icons:

1. **Choose Finder ➪ Preferences.** The Finder Preferences dialog appears.

2. **Go to the General pane, if it isn't already visible.**

3. **Select and deselect the check boxes for the icons that you want to see and don't want to see, respectively, on your Desktop.** For example, to hide the icon for the MacBook Pro's internal hard drive or any external hard drive connected to it, deselect the Hard Disks check box. As you deselect the check boxes, the related icons disappear from your Desktop.

Note To set the size, grid spacing, text size, and other options for the Desktop, click the Desktop so no Finder windows are selected. Choose View ➪ Show View Options, and use the resulting panel to configure these settings for your Desktop. The title of this panel indicates the object for which you are configuring the view options, so it should be Desktop. You can use this same command with any folder to set its view options.

Working with Finder Windows

Much of the time that you are working on your Desktop will involve Finder windows. Two areas of Finder windows that you will use frequently are the Sidebar and the toolbar, in addition to the window itself. You can use these features as they are, but you can also customize them to make your Desktop space more efficient.

Using Finder windows

Finder windows are essentially lists of what's in whatever drive or folder you opened. Double-click a drive or folder to open a Finder window. If you open a drive or folder from the Desktop, a new Finder window opens for its contents. If you open a drive or folder from within a Folder window, the Finder window displays its contents in place of whatever it was previously showing.

A quick way to open a new Finder window in the Finder is to choose File ⇨ New Window or to press ⌘+N. That way, you can look at contents from different locations at the same time, and even copy or move items across them.

If you drag items from one Finder window to another, the items are moved if the Finder windows are showing contents from folders on the same drive. They are copied if the Finder windows are showing the contents of folders from different drives. Hold down the Option key when dragging to copy files on the same disk, and hold down the Option key when dragging to move files to a different disk; holding Option reverses the standard behavior.

Close unwanted Finder windows by clicking the Close button at the upper left of the window or by pressing Shift+⌘+W. Note that this shortcut is new to OS X 10.9 Mavericks and had been just ⌘+W in previous versions of OS X.

Mavericks introduces a new capability in Finder windows called Finder tabs that reduces clutter on the Desktop. It works just like a browser's tabbed panes do: Each pane has its own tab that you click to switch to that pane, as Figure 1.1 shows. Create a new tabbed pane by choosing File ⇨ New Tab or pressing ⌘+T. You can drag items from one tab to another: From the open pane, just drag the item to the tab of the other pane.

To close a tabbed pane, hover the pointer over its tab, and click the X icon that appears on the left side of the tab, or just press ⌘+W to close the active (open) pane.

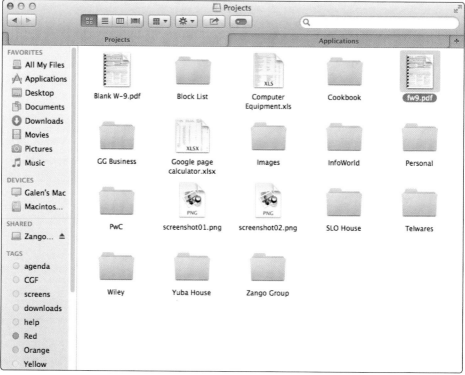

1.1 OS X Mavericks lets you have multiple tabbed panes in the same Finder window, to decrease Desktop clutter.

Using and configuring the Sidebar

The Finder's Sidebar makes it easy to get to specific locations, meaning folders, drives, and even files. It comes preloaded with a set of aliases (shortcuts) to common locations, but you can add items to, or remove them from, the Sidebar so it contains aliases to the items you use most frequently.

The Sidebar is organized into sections, as shown in Figure 1.2. You control which ones display by using the Finder Preferences dialog (choose Finder ⇨ Preferences). The process is similar to how you control which disk icons appear on the Desktop, except that you go to the Sidebar pane in the dialog rather than the General pane, and then check and uncheck the desired options to control what displays, as shown in Figure 1.3.

In the Sidebar itself, you can show or hide the contents of a section by hovering the pointer over a label, like Devices, and clicking the Hide or Show label that appears to its right to control if the section's contents appear.

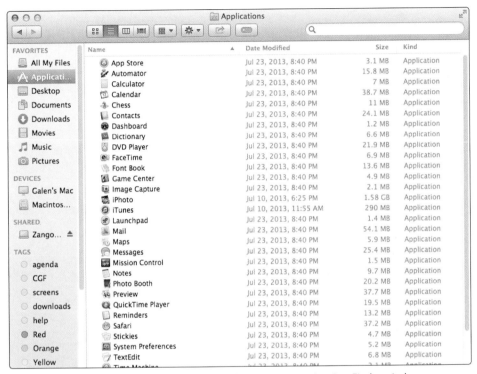

1.2 Use the Sidebar to quickly move to the items that you want to view in a Finder window.

So what are the sections? The Favorites section holds aliases to the folders on your MacBook Pro that Apple expects you open most frequently; you can customize it so it reflects the folders you open the most. The Shared section holds locations you are accessing on a network, such as a shared hard drive. The Devices section includes hard drives and disk images that are mounted on your MacBook Pro. And the new Tags section in OS X Mavericks shows files and folders that you tag with specific labels, such as those belonging to a specific project.

Using the items on the Sidebar is simple (which is why it's so useful). Simply click the icon with which you want to work. What happens when you click depends on the kind of icon it is. The following are the common items:

All My Files. When you click this icon, all the files you've worked with appear in the Finder window. You can use the view and browse tools to access any file you need.

AirDrop. When you click this icon, you can see other users connected to the same Wi-Fi network and have their AirDrop folder open—if they're using a Mac made in 2011 or later and running OS X 10.7 Lion or higher. You can send files to other users by dropping them on the person's icon in the AirDrop window, and they can share files with you in the same way.

Applications. If the icon is for an application, the application launches.

Documents. Clicking a document's icon opens the associated application, and you see and work with the document's contents.

Folder. When you click a folder, you see its contents in the Finder window.

Shared folder or drive. When you select a shared network resource, you see either the login dialog, or if your MacBook Pro is configured to automatically log in to the resource, you see its contents.

Devices. When you select a device, its contents are displayed in the Finder window.

Tags. If you click a tag icon, you see all files and folders using that tag—regardless of their location on the Mac— in the Finder window.

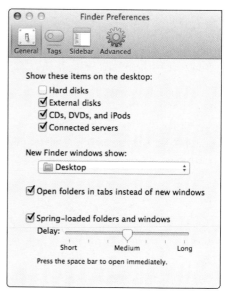

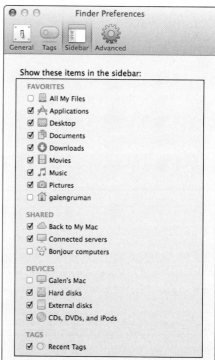

1.3 You can determine the kinds of resources available in the Desktop via the Finder Preferences dialog's General pane (top) and what appears in the Sidebar via its Sidebar pane (bottom).

Note Each type of Sidebar item has a distinctive icon, making what it represents easy to determine.

You can add an alias to a drive or folder to the Sidebar by dragging its icon from the Finder window into the Sidebar's Favorites section. To add an alias in the Sidebar to a file, select it and press Control+⌘+T. Drag any of these aliases out to remove them from the Sidebar (the original items are not deleted from the Mac, of course).

Note The Favorites section is the only one that you can manually configure. The content of the other sections is determined by the Preferences settings, what your MacBook Pro is connected to on the network, and the mounted devices or disk images. If you drag an icon onto something in the other sections, it may be copied there instead (for example, when you drag an icon onto a disk's icon).

To *copy* the file into a Sidebar location (rather than open that location in another Finder window), hold down the Option key while you move the file's icon onto a folder's or drive's alias in the Sidebar. But if you drag an item onto a *shared location* in the Sidebar, rather than to a folder or drive, it is copied to that location instead of moved; to *move* an item to a shared location via the Sidebar, hold down the Option key.

To change the order of items within the Sidebar, drag them up or down the list. As you move an item between others, they slide apart to show you where the item you are moving will be. (You can move items within their sections, as well as from the Devices section to the Favorites section (but not in the reverse direction, or to or from other sections).

Using and configuring the toolbar

The toolbar appears at the top of the Finder window and contains buttons and pop-up menus that you can use to access commands quickly and easily. You can configure the toolbar so it contains the tools you use most frequently. When you open a Finder window, the toolbar appears at the top.

Genius When viewing a Finder window in Grid view, you can change the size of the icons using the slider at the bottom right of the window. If you don't see it, choose View ➪ Show Status Bar.

The following default tools appear on the toolbar (as grouped from left to right):

- **Back and Forward buttons.** These move you along the hierarchy of Finder windows that you've moved through (just like the Back and Forward buttons in a web browser).

- **View buttons.** You can change the view of the current window by clicking one of the View buttons. For example, to see the window in List view, click the second button in the View group (its icon has horizontal lines). The four buttons (left to right) are Grid, List, Columns, and Cover Flow.

- **Arrange pop-up menu.** This menu lets you arrange the contents of the window. For example, you can rank items by name, date last opened, size, and so on. Choose None to remove the arrange settings.

- **Action pop-up menu.** This menu contains a number of useful contextual commands. These are the same as those that appear when you right-click an item. Options can include Move to Trash, Get Info, and Make Alias.

- **Share menu.** Use this menu to share a selected item; the options you see depend on the type of item you have selected. Options can include Email, Message, AirDrop, Flickr, and so on.

- **Tag button.** Use this new capability in OS X Mavericks to apply a tag to the selected item. A pop-up opens in which you can select an existing tag or type in a new one. Items can have multiple tags.

Note

Right-clicking opens a contextual menu showing options relevant to whatever was right-clicked. A right-click is also called a secondary click, because it's possible to have the Mac reverse the left and right sides of the trackpad (or external mouse if you're using one) to accommodate left-handed users. By default, a standard click, such as to select an item, is done on the left. Another way to do a right-click is to hold down Control and do a standard click.

- **Search bar.** You can search for items on the Mac by typing text or numbers into the Search bar. As you type, items that match your search term appear in the Finder window. By default, OS X searches both file names and file contents. But if you wait a moment before pressing Return to begin the search, a menu appears to let you limit the search to, for example, filenames or types of files, as Figure 1.4 shows.

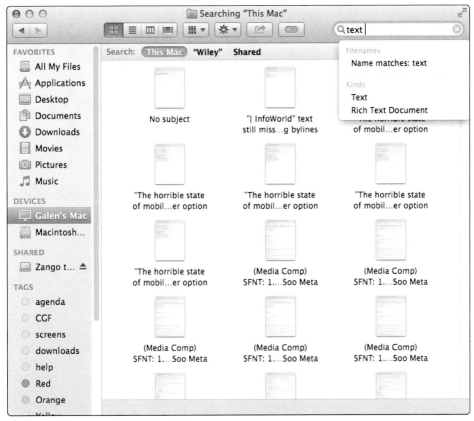

1.4 When you search files, you can narrow the search by pausing in the Search bar briefly to open a menu.

You can change what appears in the toolbar. Follow these steps:

1. **Open a Finder window.**

2. **Choose View ⇨ Customize Toolbar.** The Toolbar Customization sheet appears, as shown in Figure 1.5.

3. **To remove a button from the toolbar, drag its icon from the toolbar outside the Finder window.** When you release the trackpad, the selected button disappears. (You can always add it back later.)

4. **To add a button to the toolbar, drag it from the sheet and drop it on the toolbar where you want it to appear.** When you release the trackpad, the selected button is added to the toolbar.

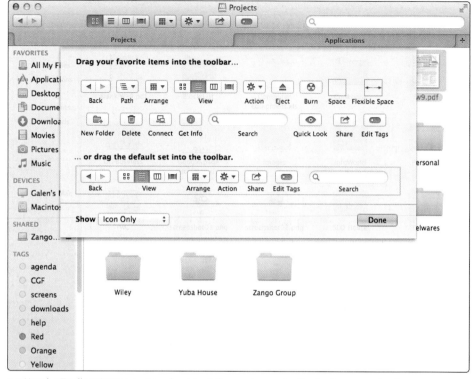

1.5 Use the Toolbar Customization sheet to define and organize the tools on your toolbar.

5. **Using the Show menu, choose how you want the buttons on the toolbar to appear.** Your options are Icon and Text, Icon Only, and Text Only.

6. **When you finish customizing the toolbar, click Done.** The Toolbar Customization sheet closes, and you see your customized toolbar in any Finder windows.

Note

To return the toolbar to its default state, open the Toolbar Customization sheet and drag the default set of buttons onto the toolbar.

Working with the Dock

The Dock is an important part of your Desktop space. By default, it appears at the bottom of the Desktop, but you can control many aspects of its appearance, including where it is located and, to a great degree, how it works. The Dock is organized into two general sections. The area to the left of the application/document separation line (the faint, dark line a few icons to the left of the Trash icon) contains application icons. The area to the right of this line contains icons for documents, folders, minimized Finder or application windows, and the Trash/Eject icon.

When folders appear on the Dock, they become stacks by default. When you click a stack, it pops up into a fan or appears as a grid (depending on how many items are in the folder), as shown in Figure 1.6, so you can work with the items it contains. You can disable this feature for any folder so it behaves more like a normal folder (more on that shortly).

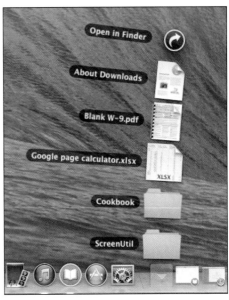

1.6 Clicking a folder's icon on the Dock causes its contents to either appear in a grid or fan out (as shown here), depending on how many items it contains and your preferences.

You can perform all the following functions from the Dock:

- **See running applications.** Whenever an application is running, you see its icon on the Dock. If the related preference is set (more details on this a bit later), a small, glowing blue light is located at the bottom of every running application's icon. Application icons also provide information about what is happening with those applications. For example, when you receive e-mail, a badge on the Mail application's icon changes to indicate the number of messages you have received since you last read messages.

- **Open applications, folders, minimized windows, and documents quickly by clicking the related icon.** You can drag applications from the Desktop or a Finder window to the Dock's left side and can drag folders, files, and drives to the Dock's right side to put an alias to the items on the Dock for one-click access later. Or right-click a running application's icon, and choose Options ⇨ Add to Dock to keep it in the Dock. Drag an icon out of the Dock to remove it from the Dock (the item is not deleted from your Mac). You can rearrange the application icons on the Dock by dragging them to the Dock location where you want them to reside.

- **Quickly switch among open applications and windows by clicking the icon for the item you want to bring to the front.**

- **Be alerted about issues.** When an application needs your attention, its icon bounces on the Dock until you move into that application and handle the issues.

- **Control applications and switch to any of their open windows.** When you right-click the icon of an application, a contextual menu appears. When the application is running, this menu lists commands, as well as all the open windows related to that application. When the application isn't running, you see a different set of commands (such as the Open command).

- **Customize its appearance and function.** You can control how the Dock looks, including its size, whether it is always visible, and where it is located using the Dock system preference, which I describe later in this chapter.

Note
To open a system preference—OS X's method for customizing much of the Mac's behavior—choose System Preferences to open the System Preferences application, and click the icon for the specific system preference you want to adjust, such as Dock or Security & Privacy.

Understanding how applications and folders work in the Dock

Two icons on the Dock are unique and always there: the Finder and the Trash.

- When you click the Finder icon (anchored on the left end of a horizontal Dock or at the top of a vertical one), a Finder window opens (if one isn't already open). If at least one Finder window is open, clicking the Finder icon brings the Finder window you used most recently to the front.

- The Trash icon is where all folders and files go when their time is done. When the Trash contains files or folders, its icon includes crumpled paper so you know something is in there. When you select an ejectable item (such as a DVD), the Trash icon changes to the Eject symbol. You can drag a disc, drive, volume, or any other ejectable item onto that icon to eject it.

Genius
To move between applications quickly, hold down ⌘+Tab. The Application Switcher appears. Click an icon to switch to its application, or while holding down ⌘ repeatedly press Tab to cycle forward through the list, or repeatedly press Shift+Tab to cycle backward through the list. When you release the keys, you switch to the selected application. You can also type Q to quit the selected application in the Application Switcher.

Unless an application is permanently added to the Dock (in which case, its icon remains in the same position), the icon for each application you open appears on the right (or bottom) edge of the application area of the Dock while running and then disappears when you quit the application.

Unlike open applications, open documents don't automatically appear on the Dock. Document icons appear on the Dock only when you minimize a document's window from the application using it or when you manually add them by dragging their icon from a Finder window.

In what Apple calls App Exposé, you can see a list of all open windows in a running application by right-clicking the application's Dock icon and choosing Show All Windows from the contextual menu that appears. Or just press the default shortcut (usually Fn+F10 or Control+down arrow); the same shortcut restores the regular view.

When you minimize an application window, it is pulled by default into the Dock using the Genie Effect. You can change this so the Scale Effect is used instead, via the Dock system preference. You can also change where the minimized application's document windows go: into the application's icon or into the document section of the Dock. When in the document section of the Dock, minimized windows are marked with the related application's icon in the lower-right corner of the Dock icon so you can easily tell from which application the windows came. Minimized windows disappear from the Dock when you maximize them or when you close the application from which they came.

Genius

When you hide an application, OS X also hides its open windows in the Dock, though you can quickly open one of its windows by right-clicking the application icon or pressing the default shortcut (usually Fn+F10 or Control+down arrow) and choosing the window you want. (The application's icon remains in the Dock, so you know it's still running.)

When you place a folder's icon on the Dock, it displays as a stack. A stack has some special characteristics, which is why it isn't just called a folder (however, you can configure a stack to behave like a folder). Two stacks are installed on your Dock by default: Downloads and Documents.

Stack icons sometimes take on the icon of the most recent file that has been placed into them. For example, if you last downloaded a disk image file, the Downloads stack icon is the one for a disk image. When you place an image into your Pictures folder and have that folder installed on your Dock, its icon is a thumbnail of the last image you placed in it.

When you click a stack icon, its contents fan onto the Desktop if there are only a few of them, or open into a grid if there are many. You can access an item on the fan or grid by clicking it. You can open the folder's contents in a Finder window by clicking Open in Finder.

To configure how an individual stack's icon behaves by using its contextual menu, right-click the stack icon to reveal its menu, as shown in Figure 1.7.

The following options are included in the menu:

- **Sort By.** Choose the attribute by which you want the items in the stack to be sorted. For example, choose Date Added to have the most recently added content appear at the bottom of the fan (if the stack is set to fan, of course).

- **Display As.** Choose Stack to have the icon look like a stack, or choose Folder to replace the stack icon with the folder's icon. The only difference is that when you select Folder, you always see the folder's icon on the Dock, as opposed to the icon of the most recently added item, which is what you see when Stack is selected.

1.7 Stacks have several configuration options.

Note

All Dock settings are specific to each user account; see Chapter 2 for more information. One user's Dock settings do not affect another's.

- **View Content As.** Choose Fan to see the default fan layout for the stack (until it contains too many items, at which point it uses the grid instead). Select Grid to have the folder's contents always appear in a grid. Select List to always display the contents in a columnar list; this is useful for folders that contain subfolders because you can select a subfolder to open its contents. Select Automatic to have OS X select the most appropriate view based on the folder's contents.

- **Options.** Choose Remove from Dock to remove the icon from the Dock. Choose Show in Finder to open a Finder window showing the folder's contents.

- **Open.** Choose this command to open the folder on the Desktop.

Changing the Dock's appearance and behavior

The Dock offers several behaviors that you can change to suit your preferences. These steps walk you through how to change various aspects of the Dock's appearance:

1. **Open the Dock system preference.**

2. **Drag the Size slider to the right to make the default Dock larger, or drag it to the left to make it smaller.** Note that the Dock doesn't grow any larger when it's completely full of icons, even if the slider isn't all the way to the right.

Note When your MacBook Pro is connected to one or more external displays, the Dock in OS X Mavericks automatically appears on the active display, meaning the one where the pointer is. In previous OS X versions, the Dock appeared only on the primary display, which you could change in the Displays system preference's Displays pane.

3. **Select the Magnification check box if you want to magnify an area of the Dock when you point to it.** Drag the Magnification slider to the right to increase the level of magnification or to the left to decrease it. This can make identifying items easier, especially if many items are on the Dock or when it is small.

4. **Select the position of the Dock on the Desktop by clicking Left, Bottom (the default), or Right.**

5. **From the Minimize Windows Using pop-up menu, choose Genie Effect to pull windows down to the Dock in a swoop when you minimize them, or choose Scale Effect to shrink them straight down into the Dock.**

6. **If you want to be able to minimize a window by double-clicking its title bar, select the Double-Click a Window's Title Bar to Minimize check box.**

7. **If you prefer windows that you minimize to move onto the related application's icon instead of to a separate icon on the right side of the dividing line, select the Minimize Windows into Application Icon check box.** With this setting enabled, you

must open the application icon's menu and select a minimized window to reopen it from the Dock, or switch back to the application and use its Window menu to choose the minimized window (unless the minimized window is also the application's active window, in which case you move into it directly).

8. **By default, application icons bounce as the application opens.** If you don't want this to happen, deselect the Animate Opening Applications check box.

9. **If you want the Dock to be hidden automatically when you aren't pointing to it, select the Automatically Hide and Show the Dock check box.** If you set the Dock so that it is hidden except when you hover the pointer at the bottom of the screen, you can use more of your display.

10. **To show the glowing dot icon under running applications, select the Show Indicator Lights for Open Applications check box.** These lights are useful because they help you more easily identify open applications when you glance at the Dock, even hidden ones.

You can turn Dock Hiding on or off at any time by pressing Option+⌘+D.

Note

Using the Launchpad

If you've used an iPhone, iPod touch, or iPad, you already know how to use the Launchpad on the Mac because it works in exactly the same manner as the Home pages on those devices. If you like the iOS style of accessing apps, the Launchpad provides one-click access to all your applications and utilities, and you can organize the Launchpad to make it work efficiently for you.

One difference between the Home pages on Apple mobile devices and the Launchpad is that only application icons can be stored on the Launchpad, whereas on an iPhone, iPod touch, or iPad, you can also store web page icons.

Note

Click the Launchpad icon on the Dock (it is located just to the right of the Finder icon by default) or perform a three-finger pinch (three fingers pinched against your thumb) on the trackpad. This preference is enabled by default in the Trackpad system preference. The Launchpad then fills the Desktop, and you see icons on the current page, as shown in Figure 1.8. To move to a different page, drag two fingers on the trackpad to the left or to the right. As you drag, the page flips to the next or previous page. You can also search for an app by entering all or part of its name in the Search field at the top of the Launchpad.

1.8 The Launchpad provides easy access to all your applications.

Note You'll notice that the Dock remains visible if it isn't hidden, or it becomes visible if it is hidden when the Launchpad is open. You can also use the Application Switcher while the Launchpad is displayed.

To open an application, click its icon. The Launchpad closes and switches to that application. Click a folder in the Launchpad to access the applications stored in it. The folder then expands, and you see the icons it contains, as shown in Figure 1.9.

To close the Launchpad without opening an application, click it (but not an application's icon), perform a three-finger expand gesture on the trackpad, or press Esc.

Note The Launchpad is actually an application. Therefore, you can add its icon to the Sidebar, open it by double-clicking its icon in the Application folder, and so on.

1.9 To access an app stored in a folder, click the folder's icon and then click the application's icon.

You can organize the icons on your Launchpad to make accessing them easier and faster. To change the location of icons on the Launchpad, open it and drag the icon you want to move to the desired location. You can change its location on the current page, or you can drag it off the screen to the left or right to move it to another page (you have to linger at the edge of the screen until the page changes). As you move one icon between others, they shift to make room for the one you are moving. When the icon is over the location you want, release it.

To create a new folder, drag one icon on top of another. Launchpad creates a new folder and tries to name it according to the type of applications you place together. The folder opens, and you see the icons stored there. To change the folder name, select it. When it is highlighted, type its new name.

You can place icons into existing folders by dragging them on top of the folder in which you want to place them. You can also reorganize icons within folders by dragging them around when the folder is open. To remove an icon from a folder, drag it outside of the folder window until the folder closes. To delete a folder, drag all its icons outside of it; when you remove the second to last icon, the folder disappears (folders can't contain just one icon).

You can remove applications purchased from the Mac App Store by clicking and holding an icon. After a moment, the icons begin to jiggle and the Remove button (X) appears. Click the Remove button, and then click Delete at the prompt. Removing an application from the Launchpad also deletes it from your MacBook Pro, so make sure you really don't want it before completing this action. To return the Launchpad to normal without deleting an application, click outside of any application icon.

Note
To remove applications that you didn't download from the App Store, run the application's uninstaller or drag it to the Trash, and then empty it.

Managing Your Desktop's Windows

OS X gives you a few ways to manage your Desktop's windows. As explained earlier, you can use the App Exposé feature in the Dock to display the windows for a running application, and you can use the Application Switcher to move among open applications. But those are methods to move among running applications and their windows, not to manage the Desktop itself.

OS X provides two basic methods for managing Desktop windows: the Show/Hide feature available to each application and the Mission Control application.

You can make all applications except the one you're running disappear from the Desktop by choosing Hide Others from their application menu or pressing Option+⌘+H. For example, in Mail, choose Mail ⇨ Hide Others. (They're still running, as you can see in the Dock or the Application Switcher.) You can also hide the current application by choosing Hide in the application menu (such as Word ⇨ Hide) or pressing ⌘+H. To restore all hidden applications, choose Show All in the application menu (such as iTunes ⇨ Show All).

Mission Control offers more complex controls, such as letting you create multiple Desktops (also called *spaces*) that you then run applications in. That way, you could have all the applications for a specific project running in one Desktop and your basic applications like Safari and Mail running in another. You then switch Desktops to see just those application groups. (You can access any application at any time via the Dock or Application Switcher, no matter what Desktop they are assigned to.)

To open the Mission Control view, click its icon on the Dock or swipe four fingers up the trackpad (the default gesture; see Chapter 5 for more information) or press Control+up arrow (the default shortcut, which you can change in the Mission Control system preference). You then see the thumbnails for the following items at the top of the screen, as shown in Figure 1.10:

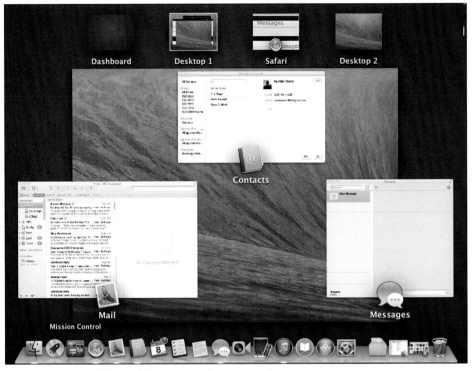

1.10 Mission Control shows all the open windows on your Desktops.

- Dashboard, the little-used application that lets you run widgets.

- Your spaces, named as Desktop X (where X is a sequential number).

- Applications that are open in full-screen mode (here, Safari).

In the center part of the window, you see all the applications running in the current Desktop, as well as their open windows. The application's icon and name accompany its windows. The Dock appears in its default location, and you can use it just as you would when working outside of Mission Control. At top are the Desktops, or spaces, you've created, as well as any applications running in full-screen mode (here, Safari).

Managing windows on the Desktop

As you work on documents, move to websites, check your e-mail, choose tunes to listen to, and all the other things you do on your MacBook Pro, you can accumulate lots of open windows on your Desktop. This makes it easy to multitask so you don't have to stop one activity to start another. The downside, though, is that it's easy to lose track of where the specific window you want is located, or you might have a hard time getting back to the Desktop.

Mission Control helps you manage screen clutter from open windows with these three modes:

- Show Desktop
- Show the active application's windows
- Show all windows on the current Desktop, all Desktops, the Dashboard, and full-screen apps

Each mode has a specific use, and you access them in slightly different ways. The Mission Control application doesn't need to be running for the first two modes, just the third.

Showing the Desktop

Showing the Desktop is useful when the Desktop on which you are working is so cluttered with application windows that you have a hard time finding anything. To clear away all your windows in one sweep, press the keyboard shortcut Fn+F11 (you can change this default in the Mission Control system preference). Now you can access the icons of folders, files, and drives on the Desktop without distraction. Your applications are still running, and you will see the edges of their windows pushed to the four sides of the Desktop. Press the shortcut again to see the normal Desktop with all open windows.

Showing the active application window

When you are working with multiple windows in the same application, it can be tough to get back to a specific window if you can't see all them at the same time. Press the keyboard shortcut (Control+down arrow, by default) or swipe down with four fingers (the default gesture) to see all open windows for the current application, as shown in Figure 1.11. Yes, this is the App Exposé view covered earlier that is also available from the Dock.

At the top of the screen, you see the windows that are currently open on the Desktop. Below these, you see any windows that are hidden or those that you worked with previously that are now closed (such as documents you have edited).

To switch to a window, click it; it is highlighted in blue when you hover the pointer over it. The window becomes active (if it is for a closed document, the document opens) and moves to the front so that you can use it. The rest of the open application windows then move to their previous positions.

Genius

When you have all the windows for an application showing, press Tab to quickly move through them. You can also use ⌘+Tab to open the Application Switcher bar, which shows all open applications, and then keeping holding ⌘ as you press Tab to move to the application on which you want to focus. When you release the ⌘ key, the windows for the selected application appear.

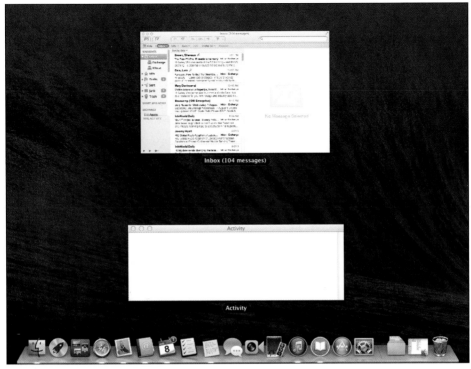

1.11 When you have many windows open in an application, Mission Control makes it easy to move into a specific one.

Showing all windows

In this mode, you see Mission Control, as previously shown in Figure 1.10, which shows your Desktops, applications running in full-screen mode, and the windows open in the active Desktop. Click a window to switch to it, or click a Desktop to switch to it, if you have multiple Desktops.

Using multiple Desktops

As you use your MacBook Pro, it's likely that you'll develop sets of tasks that you work on at the same time. For example, you might use Word to create text and Photoshop to create the images for a book. These kinds of activities invariably involve lots of windows. Although you can use Mission Control to manage all the open windows for an application, it's not very efficient because you can focus only on one window at a time, so it can still take some work to get to the windows you want to use.

But you can use Mission Control to create collections of applications and their windows on separate Desktops, also called *spaces*. This way, you can jump between sets easily and quickly. For example, if you use several Internet applications, you can create an Internet Desktop specifically for those, such as an e-mail application and web browser. To use your Internet applications, just open that Desktop and the windows are all in the positions you last left them. You might have another Desktop that contains Contacts and Calendar. You can then use these applications by switching to their Desktop. Multiple Desktops make moving to and using different sets of windows fast and easy. They also improve the efficiency with which you work.

To create a Desktop, hover the pointer over the upper right of the Mission Control view. When a large + icon (the Add Space button) appears, click it. Now drag any desired applications in the main Mission Control view to that Desktop to move them there. When not in Mission Control view, you can assign applications to the currently open Desktop by right-clicking the application icon in the Dock and choosing Options ⇨ This Desktop, as Figure 1.12 shows. To assign an application to all Desktops (that is, for applications you want easily available no matter what Desktop is open), choose Options ⇨ All Desktops instead.

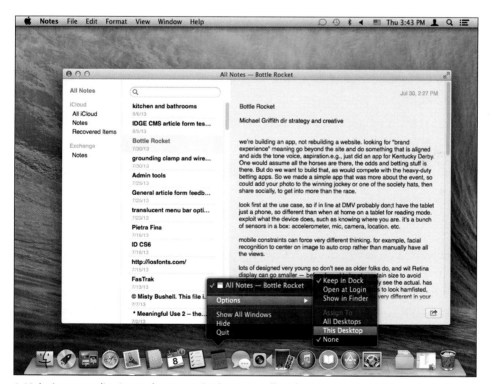

1.12 Assign an application to the current Desktop or to all Desktops using the Dock's contextual menu.

To unassign an application from a Desktop, display that Desktop, right-click the application icon in the Dock, and choose Options ⇨ This Desktop so the check mark beside that option disappears. To unassign an application from all Desktops, choose Options ⇨ None. Note that unassigning does not quit the application; it prevents the application and its windows from automatically opening in a specific Desktop the next time you run it.

A quick way to change Desktops—without needing to be in Mission Control view—is to swipe three or four fingers (depending on your trackpad's settings) to the left on the trackpad to move to a later space, or swipe to the right to move into a previous space. When you stop on a space, it becomes active and the windows open in it appear the same as they were the last time you used that Desktop.

Note The gestures or keyboard combinations you use to work with Mission Control depend on the preferences you set using the Trackpad and Mission Control system preferences.

When there are too many Desktops and full-screen applications for the names of each to be displayed, point to a Desktop or application; it is magnified and its name appears.

Note You can reorganize your Desktops by dragging their icons at the top of the Mission Control view.

To close Mission Control without changing spaces or windows, swipe four fingers down the trackpad or press Esc.

Configuring Mission Control

Now that you have a good understanding of Mission Control, you can configure it by setting your Mission Control preferences:

1. **Open the Mission Control system preference, shown in Figure 1.13.**

2. **Deselect the Show Dashboard as a Space check box if you don't want the Dashboard to be accessible in Mission Control view.**

3. **If you don't want Mission Control to automatically rearrange spaces based on the ones you've used most recently, deselect the Automatically Rearrange Spaces Based on Most Recent Use check box.**

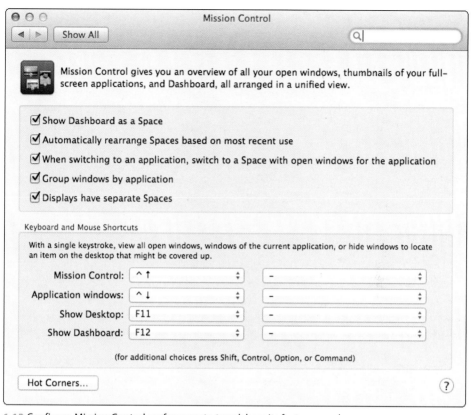

1.13 Configure Mission Control preferences to tweak how its features work.

4. **Deselect the When Switching to an Application, Switch to a Space with Open Windows for the Application check box if you don't prefer that.** If you select this option, when you switch applications, you also move into the Desktop in which the switched-to application has windows open.

5. **Deselect the Group Windows by Application check box if you don't want windows to appear on the Desktop clustered based on their application.** Deselecting this option makes it harder to tell what application will open when you click a window.

6. **If you don't want each monitor attached to your MacBook Pro to display as its own Desktop, deselect the Displays Have Separate Spaces option.** OS X Mavericks introduced this option. If selected, each monitor is automatically its own Desktop, so you can't have Desktops that go across multiple monitors. Deselecting this option makes Desktops display across all monitors, as if they formed one very large monitor. (I explain how to set up multiple monitors later in this chapter.)

7. **In the Keyboard and Mouse Shortcuts section, configure the keyboard shortcuts and mouse clicks to activate Mission Control, activate application windows (App Exposé), and show the Desktop and Dashboard.** Use the menus on the left to set key combinations and the menus on the right to set mouse-clicks. If you use function keys such as F10, you must hold down Fn for them to work; without holding Fn, these function keys control aspects of the MacBook Pro's hardware, such as sound volume and screen brightness, as the labels on the MacBook Pro's keys show. To use modifier keys with a function key, such as Option, hold down the modifier keys while selecting from the menu. Using modifier keys with function keys usually means you don't have to hold Fn. For example, if you hold down Option, the menus show ⌥ F1 through ⌥ F16; if you hold down Control and ⌘, the menus show ⌃⌘F1 through ⌃⌘F16.

8. **Click the Hot Corners button to open the Hot Corners sheet.** Use this sheet to set an action to occur when you point to that corner of the screen. For example, if you want the Launchpad to open when you move the pointer to the upper-right corner of the screen, select Launchpad on the menu in that location.

Using Applications in Full-Screen Mode

Many applications, such as Safari, Mail, iMovie, Aperture, and even the Finder, really benefit from all the Desktop room they can get to work more efficiently. That's why OS X lets applications appear in full-screen mode. In this mode, the application takes over the entire screen and its menu bars are hidden, as shown in Figure 1.14.

Note Developers must enable full-screen mode in their applications, so it's not available for all software. You can tell if an application supports full-screen mode because it has an icon of two opposing arrows in the upper right of its window.

Explore full-screen mode in applications that you use frequently to see if it helps you use them more efficiently. These pointers may help you:

- **Activate full-screen mode.** Choose View ⇨ Enter Full Screen, or press Control+⌘+F. The application's current window fills the screen and the menu bars are hidden.

- **Reveal the menu bars.** Hover the pointer at the top of the screen. After a few seconds, the menu bars appear and you can access them just as you do when you aren't working in full-screen mode.

- As covered earlier in this chapter, applications running in full-screen mode appear as spaces in Mission Control view.

- **Exit full-screen mode.** Choose View ⇨ Exit Full Screen, or press Control+⌘+F.

1.14 Using an application in full-screen mode gives it the most screen real estate possible.

Configuring Notifications

Many applications use notifications to communicate information to you. For example, Mail notifies you when you receive new messages, Calendar alerts you to upcoming events, Reminders reminds you about various things, and so on. The OS X Notification Center provides a central point of control for, and configuration of, the notifications with which you work.

Working with the Notification Center

To view the collection of notifications you have received, click the Notification Center menu located on the right end of the menu bar. The Notification Center pane appears, as shown in Figure 1.15. Notifications are grouped by the application from which they come. You can scroll the list to see all the notifications you have received. The order in which the groups are shown is determined by a preference setting (covered later in this chapter). When this is set to Manually, you can drag sections up or down the list.

1.15 The Notification Center provides a one-stop shop for the information that various applications are managing for you.

To see the details of a notification, click it. You then move into the related application and can work with the information. For example, if you click an e-mail notification, you are switched to Mail and can read the full message.

Of course, you don't have to open the Notification Center to see notifications. OS X provides several other ways to see notifications:

- **Badges.** These are counters that appear on an application's icon to let you know how many of something you have, such as e-mail messages, texts, updates for applications, and so on.

- **Banners.** These are small messages that appear in the upper-right corner of the screen, as shown in Figure 1.16, when something happens, such as when you receive a message.

Banners contain the icon of the app from which they come, and they can also show you a preview. They are nice because they don't interfere with what you are doing. If you ignore a banner, it disappears after a few seconds. If you

1.16 Banners are good because they don't require any action on your part.

click it, you move into the application that produced the banner. If you receive a new banner while a previous one is still visible on the screen, the second one displaces the first so that the latest one is displayed.

- **Alerts.** This is another means that applications use to communicate with you. There are alerts for many types of events, such as texts, reminders, missed call notifications, and so on. The main

1.17 Alerts require action to get rid of them.

difference between a banner and an alert is that alerts remain on the screen until you take some action, such as clicking Close or Snooze to dismiss an alert for an event, as shown in Figure 1.17.

- **Sounds.** These are audible indicators that something has happened. For example, when something happens in the Game Center, you can be notified via a sound.

OS X Mavericks lets you respond to some notifications without opening their applications, as Figure 1.18 shows. If you hover on the right side of their banners, you'll see buttons for actions such as Reply that you can take immediately from the notification itself. Examples include Mail and Messages.

1.18 Some banners let you reply to notifications without opening their associated application. In these cases, a window opens, such as the one for Messages here, to let you enter your reply.

You can also initiate social media posts to your Twitter, Facebook, and/or LinkedIn accounts from the Notification Center. Open it, scroll up to the top, and click the button for the desired service. (They must be configured in the Internet Accounts system preference, which was called Mail, Contacts, & Calendars before OS X Mavericks.)

You can also turn off notifications at the top of the Notification Center, such as when giving a presentation or simply when you want to work undisturbed. Use the Do Not Disturb switch (refer to Figure 1.19) to control whether notifications appear (it was called Show Alerts & Banners before OS X Mavericks).

As covered later in this chapter, you can enable or disable notifications, and configure them for specific applications. Applications also send individual notifications to the Desktop, such as when Calendar sends an alert about an event. The following sections explain several options you can configure for these notifications.

Configuring Notifications's display

You can configure your notifications on the Notifications system preference, shown in Figure 1.19. The applications for which you can configure notifications are shown in the list on the left side of the window. When you select an application, its notification options are shown in the right side of the window. You can configure each application's options individually.

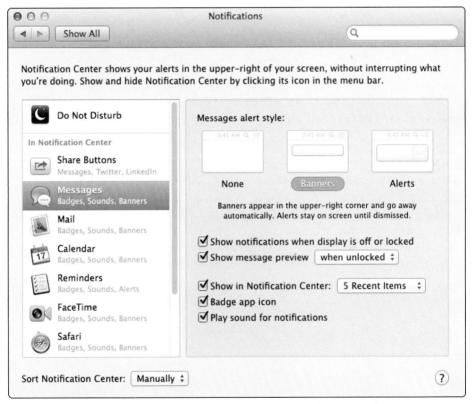

1.19 The Notifications system preference lets you configure how applications notify you.

These are some highlights and suggestions about configuring notifications:

- **Use the alert style buttons to configure the type of notifications the application uses.** The options are None, Banners, and Alerts.

- **Use the Show in Notification Center check box and menu to determine if the application's notifications are shown in the Notification Center, and if so, how many are shown.** If this is not selected, notifications from the application do not appear in the Notification Center.

- **If you want the notifications to display on the login screen, such as when the MacBook Pro has locked the screen due to non-use (as set in the Security & Privacy system preference) or when you've logged out of an account, select the Show Notifications When Display Is Off or Locked check box.** This feature is new to OS X Mavericks. A related feature available for some applications, such as Mail and Messages, is the Show Message Preview check box. Select it to display part of the message in the banner. Use its adjacent menu to determine whether those previews display always or only when the MacBook Pro's screen is not locked.

- **If you want the application's icon on the Dock (or elsewhere) to display a badge when you have new information, such as new messages, select the Badge App Icon check box.**

- **To disable the sound associated with an application's notifications, deselect the Play Sound for Notifications check box.**

- **Use the Sort Notification Center menu to determine how applications are listed in the Notification Center pane.** Choose By Time if you want the most recent information to appear toward the top of the pane, or Manually if you want to manually configure the order by dragging application sections up or down the pane.

To disable alerts and banners, scroll to the top of the Notification Center and set the Do Not Disturb switch to the On position. All alerts and banners are suppressed until you set the switch to the Off position again.

As Figure 1.20 shows, you can also set a regular time for when Do Not Disturb is automatically engaged, such as overnight, and control whether Do Not Disturb activates automatically when the MacBook Pro is asleep (so messages aren't visible on a MacBook in a public location when you've stepped away) or when you are connected to an Apple TV (so you don't disturb your movie or presentation). These controls are new in OS X Mavericks.

Additional controls over Do Not Disturb new to OS X Mavericks are the two When Do Not Disturb Is Turned On options: Allow FaceTime Calls From and Allow Repeated Calls. If selected, Allow FaceTime Calls From tells the MacBook Pro to ring through FaceTime calls from either everyone or

just the people you've marked as Favorites in FaceTime, based on what option you choose in the adjacent menu. If selected, Allow Repeated Calls lets a person try to call you multiple times via FaceTime; otherwise, only the first call rings through, and the others are ignored under the assumption you would have picked up the first time if you were available. It is meant to reduce the annoyance of those who keep calling and calling when they don't get a response.

Finally, the Share Buttons option in the list at the left of the Notifications system preference is how you control whether the buttons to initiate social posts appear at the top of the Notification Center. Click Share Buttons, and then select or deselect, as desired, the Show Share Buttons in Notification Center check box in the right side of the Notifications system preference.

1.20 You can schedule when the MacBook Pro enters Do Not Disturb mode in the Notifications system preference.

Working with Monitors

Current MacBook Pros have 13- or 15-inch LCD screens. No matter which display size you have, more is always better. Fortunately, you can maximize the amount of information you see on your MacBook Pro's screen by configuring its display. For even more working room, you can attach and use an external monitor, or you can broadcast your MacBook's output to an Apple TV using AirPlay. For the ultimate in Desktop space, you can connect your MacBook Pro to a projector. When you use an external monitor or projector, you can display the same image on the MacBook Pro and the external device, or you can expand your Desktop over both monitors. You can also configure the Desktop picture on your monitors to make your MacBook Pro's appearance more interesting.

Configuring the MacBook Pro's LCD screen

Although the physical size of the MacBook Pro's LCD screen is fixed, the amount of information that can be displayed on it (its *resolution*) is not. Setting the appropriate resolution is a matter of choosing the largest that you can view comfortably with no eyestrain. There are standard resolutions you can use, but which of these is available to you depends on the specific MacBook Pro you are using. For example, the 13-inch model has a different set of resolutions than the 15-inch model. Likewise, models with Retina screens support yet a different set of options. Follow these steps to find your maximum resolution:

1. **Open the Displays system preference.** As shown in Figure 1.21, the name shown at the top of the pane matches the monitor it configures.

2. **Go to the Display pane if it's not already visible.**

3. **To use the resolution that is optimal for the built-in LCD screen, select Best for Display and skip to Step 6.** The screen's resolution is set to what Apple considers optimal for its size.

4. **To manually select a resolution, select Scaled.** In the Resolutions section, you see all the resolutions supported by your MacBook Pro's screen. Resolutions are shown as the number of horizontal pixels by the number of vertical pixels, such as 1280 × 800. Larger values have a higher resolution. Some resolutions are stretched so they fill the screen; the MacBook Pro has a widescreen format display.

5. **Select a resolution.** The screen updates to the resolution you selected.

6. **Drag the Brightness slider to the right to make the screen brighter, or drag it to the left to make it dimmer.** Or select the Automatically Adjust Brightness check box to let OS X adjust the screen for you based on the surrounding lighting; it uses the MacBook Pro's camera to determine that lighting.

7. **Hide the System Preferences application by pressing ⌘+H.**

8. **Open several windows on the Desktop.**

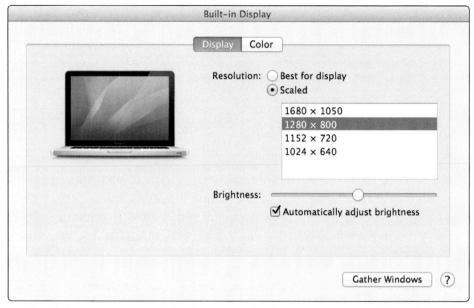

1.21 Use the Displays pane to maximize the amount of room you have on your Desktop, while still being comfortable for you to view.

Note

MacBook Pros with Retina screens don't support resolutions in the same way as those without them. On MacBook Pro with Retina screens, you can choose the Scaled option, but instead of selecting an actual resolution, you choose different scales. They look like different resolutions because the text and images change relative size the same as they do when you change the resolution.

9. **If you can see the information on the screen comfortably, switch to the System Preferences application (such as from the Dock) and select a higher resolution.**

10. **Repeat Steps 7 through 9 until you reach the maximum resolution or until the text is too small to comfortably read. Set the resolution to the highest that was comfortable to read.**

11. **Close the Displays system preference when done.**

Connecting and configuring an external monitor with a cable

Another way to add more screen space to your MacBook Pro is to connect an external monitor. This lets you add more screen real estate without shrinking the display, so you don't risk text getting too small to read. Plus, when you use multiple monitors, you can treat each one as a separate Desktop, making it easy to put, for example, photo-editing applications on a large external monitor where the extra size really matters while keeping your e-mail on the MacBook Pro's smaller screen.

You can use an external monitor in two ways: as an extension of your Desktop so you can open additional windows on it, or as *video mirroring*, which means the same information appears on all monitors.

When choosing an external monitor, the two most important considerations are size and cost. Larger monitors are better because they give you more working space. However, they tend to be more expensive, depending on the brand you choose. In most cases, if you choose the largest display you can afford from a reputable manufacturer, such as Apple, ViewSonic, or Samsung, you'll be in good shape.

To add an external monitor, connect it to the MacBook Pro's Thunderbolt port. To do this, you need a MiniDisplayPort-to-DVI adapter that converts the Thunderbolt connection to the standard DVI connector used on most modern displays. You can also use a MiniDisplayPort-to-VGA adapter to use your MacBook Pro with older displays or a MiniDisplayPort-to-HDMI adapter to connect to a TV or monitor that uses that TV-standard connector. Also, some MacBook Pro models, such as those with Retina displays, come with an HDMI port, so no adapter is needed.

Follow these steps to attach an external monitor to a MacBook Pro:

1. **Connect one end of the display's video cable to the MiniDisplayPort adapter and the other end to the DVI, VGA, or HDMI port on the monitor, depending on the kind of adapter you have.**
2. **Plug the MiniDisplayPort adapter into the Thunderbolt port.**
3. **Connect the display to a power source.**
4. **Power up the display.**

After an external display is connected to your MacBook Pro, follow these steps to configure it:

1. **Open the Displays system preference.** The Displays system preference opens on both the MacBook Pro's screen and the external monitor. The name of the pane on the MacBook Pro's screen is Built-in Display (it was named Color LCD before OS X Mavericks). The name of the pane on the external monitor is the name of that monitor. Also, notice that the Displays system preference on the primary display (by default, the MacBook Pro's screen) contains the Arrangement pane.

2. **Go to the Arrangement pane, shown in Figure 1.22, on the Displays system preference on the MacBook Pro's screen.** You see an icon representation of each display. The display marked with the menu bar at the top is the primary display, meaning where the menu bar and Dock appear by default.

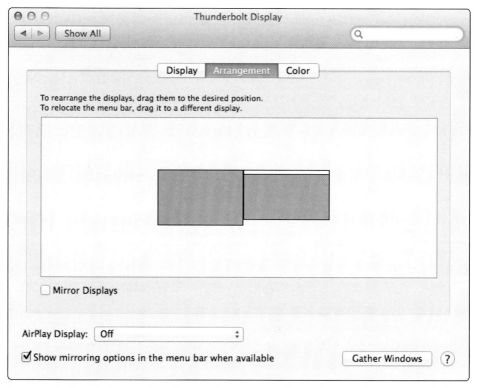

1.22 The MacBook Pro's screen is on the right (with the menu bar at the top, indicating that it is the primary display), while the external monitor is on the left.

3. **Drag the external monitor's thumbnail to where you want it relative to the MacBook Pro's screen.** Typically, this should match the physical location of the monitor compared to the MacBook Pro, such as to its side. But you can arrange the external monitor above, below, and to the side of the MacBook Pro. To move the pointer from one monitor, you must go through where they touch in the Arrangement pane. For example, if the external monitor is to the left of the MacBook Pro's screen in the Arrangements pane, you must move the pointer past the left edge of the MacBook's screen for it to move on to the external monitor's screen, and you must reverse that motion to get back to the MacBook's screen.

4. **If you want the external display to be the primary one, drag the menu bar from the MacBook Pro's screen thumbnail onto that of the external monitor.** When you release the trackpad button, the menu bar jumps to the external display.

5. **Go to the Displays system preference for the external monitor.** You can move the mouse to its monitor to get to it, or you can click Gather Windows to move the Displays system preference to the current monitor.

6. **To change the resolution, click Scaled and then select the desired resolution for the external monitor from the list of those available.** If the resolutions are significantly different between the two displays, you see a big change in appearance when you move a window between them. You may have to resize a window on one display that was the right size on the other.

7. **If the Refresh rate menu appears, choose the highest rate available.**

8. **Quit the System Preferences application.**

You can now use the space on the external display like you use the internal display. To place a window on the external display, drag it from the MacBook Pro display onto the external one. You can move windows, the pointer, and other items from one display to the other just as you can move them around the MacBook Pro internal display. You can configure windows on each display so you can see many at the same time. For example, you may want your primary documents open on the external display and your e-mail application open on the MacBook Pro display. The menu bar remains on the primary display, so if you do most of your work on the external one, you may want to make it the primary display to make menu access easier.

To stop using the external display, disconnect it from the MacBook Pro. If it was the primary display, the MacBook Pro's screen automatically becomes the primary one, and any open windows on the external monitors move onto the MacBook Pro's screen.

Note OS X Mavericks changes how the menu bar and Dock work with multiple monitors. In the past, they were fixed to the primary display, which made using applications on other monitors difficult. Now, the menu bar and Dock move to whatever monitor is active—that is, wherever your pointer is. Just give the MacBook Pro a few seconds to move the Dock to the new monitor when you first try to use it. Likewise, full-screen applications can now appear on non-primary displays, leaving the other monitors unaffected.

Connecting and configuring an external display with AirPlay

AirPlay enables a MacBook Pro to wirelessly broadcast its video to an Apple TV. This is a great way to display your MacBook Pro's output on a larger display, such as an HDTV. In OS X Mavericks, you can even use an Apple TV as a working Desktop for your MacBook Pro, not just as a way to deliver video or presentations.

To use AirPlay, your MacBook Pro must be on the same network as the Apple TV, and of course your Apple TV must be on and connected to a TV or other display. When this is the case, using AirPlay is a snap.

Follow these steps to set up external display via AirPlay:

1. **Be sure AirPlay is enabled on the Apple TV.** In the Apple TV's Settings screen, select AirPlay, and then select AirPlay On. Your MacBook Pro and Apple TV should find each other automatically.

2. **In the Displays system preference on the MacBook Pro, choose Apple TV in the AirPlay Mirroring menu.** Your MacBook Pro Desktop appears on the Apple TV display. If the Displays icon is in your menu bar, its icon should change to that of the AirPlay symbol; if so, you can click that icon and choose AirPlay rather than use the Displays system preference.

3. **In the Displays system preference, be sure to select the Overscan Correction and Show Mirroring Options in Menu Bar When Available check boxes.** The first option ensures the MacBook Pro's display fits fully on the screen connected to the Apple TV, and the second option ensures that the AirPlay controls are available from the MacBook Pro's menu bar. Figure 1.23 shows the system preference.

4. **Using the menu bar's Apple TV menu, choose the resolution to display, as Figure 1.24 shows.** To fit the resolution to the display's size, choose Apple TV; this makes your MacBook's resolution larger, fitting less on the screen. To fit the resolution to the MacBook Pro's screen, choose Color LCD or, if you're using an external monitor, the name of that monitor.

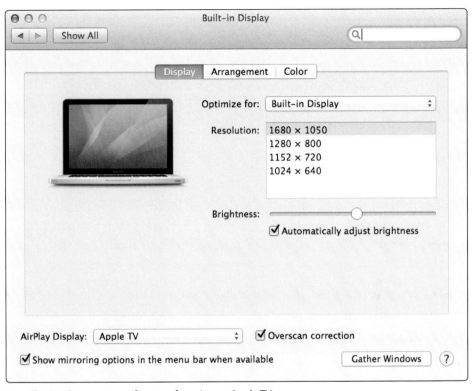

1.23 The Display system preferences for using an Apple TV.

When you use AirPlay, anything that appears on your Desktop also appears on the Apple TV display. To stop using AirPlay, choose Turn Off AirPlay Mirroring from the AirPlay menu in the menu bar.

Using a projector

If you make presentations, conduct training, or just want a really big display, a projector is the way to go. With one of these, you can broadcast your MacBook Pro display to very large sizes for easy viewing by an audience. Using a projector is similar to using an external display, so if you can work with those, you can work with a projector.

Genius

If you are using an unfamiliar projector, set the MacBook Pro resolution to a relatively low value, such as 1024 × 768. If the projector doesn't display, reduce the resolution to see whether it starts displaying. When it displays, increase the resolution until the projector is no longer capable of displaying the image.

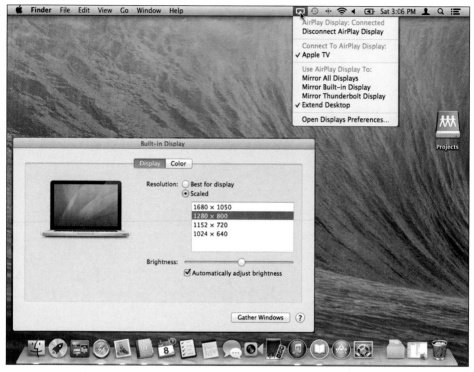

1.24 Use this Apple TV menu to configure how your MacBook Pro's output appears on an Apple TV.

Purchasing a projector is a bit more complicated and, usually, more expensive than purchasing a display. This list includes a few of the many things to consider when buying a projector:

- **Size.** A smaller projector is easier to carry, and as you move through airports and such, this is very important. Smaller projectors of the same quality are more expensive than larger ones, so find a balance between portability and price.

- **Resolution.** There is more variability in the resolution of projectors than displays. At the lower end of the price range, you'll find projectors that are capable of only 800 × 600 resolution. Many Mac applications can't even run at a resolution this low. The lowest resolution you should consider for a projector is 1024 × 768 (also called XGA). Higher resolutions are better but also more expensive.

- **Brightness.** The brightness of projectors is specified in lumens. Projectors with higher lumen ratings are generally able to throw larger and brighter images farther. How many lumens you need depends on many factors, most of which are probably beyond your control (such as the brightness levels of the location in which you'll be using the projector).

- **Throw range.** This measures the closest and farthest distances at which the projector can be used.

- **Video interface.** Like displays, the options for projectors include DVI, VGA, and HDMI. However, most projectors provide other input options, such as component, composite, and S-video. These are important if you use the projector with other sources, such as a DVD player.

- **Bulb life.** Like all other bulbs, the one in a projector eventually fails and must be replaced. Unlike bulbs for lights, you can expect to pay hundreds of dollars for a replacement projector bulb, so try to get one with a long life.

- **Cost.** Expect to pay several hundred dollars for a good-quality projector that has at least 1024 × 768 resolution.

Note Some projectors automatically select the appropriate input source, and some don't. If the projector isn't projecting an image, use its source menu to select the source to which your MacBook Pro is connected. You can also use the Detect Displays command on the Displays menu in the menu bar or on the Displays system preference's Display pane to see if that restores an image on the projector.

Using a projector is very similar to using an external display. You connect a projector to the MacBook Pro using the appropriate MiniDisplay adapter, depending on what type of connector the projector uses. You can also connect a projector to an Apple TV, either directly through the Apple TV's HDMI port or using an adapter such as Kanex's ATV Pro HDMI-to-VGA adapter.

Using mirroring versus showing separate screens

When you've plugged in an external monitor to the MiniDisplayPort or are using an Apple TV, you can mirror the contents of your MacBook Pro's screen to that other display or you can treat the other display as an additional space to place applications and Finder windows.

In the Displays system preference's Arrangement pane, select Mirror Displays to enable mirroring; deselect it to make the monitors separate. If the monitors are separate, drag their positions to what makes sense for you—side by side, one atop the other, and so on. The display thumbnail with the bar at the top is the primary display; double-click a monitor's thumbnail to make it the primary display.

In OS X Mavericks, you can use the Apple TV as a separate monitor, as Figure 1.25 shows—not just mirror to it as in previous versions.

1.25 Using the Apple TV as a separate monitor, in addition to a Thunderbolt display attached to the MacBook Pro and the MacBook Pro's LCD screen.

Genius

When you enable mirroring, all monitors are mirrored from the primary display. If you want some monitors to be mirrored and others to be separate, first connect only those you want mirrored to the primary display and then enable screen mirroring. Then connect the other monitors; they won't be mirrored.

Setting the Desktop Background

I confess that this section has nothing to do with efficiency. However, there's more to life than being efficient. Because you stare at your Desktop so much, you may as well have something interesting to look at, which is where Desktop pictures come in. You can set any image to be your Desktop picture. You can use the default images included with OS X, image files you create or download from the Internet, or (best of all) photos from your iPhoto or Aperture libraries. You can also configure your MacBook Pro so the Desktop background changes over time, to keep it even more interesting.

Perform these steps to configure your Desktop background:

1. **Open the Desktop & Screen Saver system preference.**

2. **Go to the Desktop pane.** On the center-left side of the pane are the sources of images from which you can select pictures for your Desktop, including Apple (default images), iPhoto (images from your iPhoto library, if iPhoto is installed), Aperture (images from your Aperture library, if Aperture is installed), and Folders (your Pictures folder plus any others you add).

Note When your MacBook Pro is connected to an external monitor, the Secondary Desktop pane appears on its display. You can use that pane to set the Desktop background on the external monitor separately from what you set for the MacBook Pro's LCD screen.

3. **Expand the source of images you want to work with by clicking the disclosure triangle to its left.** The contents of that source appear. For example, if you expand the Apple source, you see its folders. If you expand the iPhoto source, you see Events, Photos, photo albums, and so on.

4. **Select a source of images in the left side of the pane.** Thumbnails of the images in that source appear in the right side of the pane.

5. **Click the image that you want to apply to the Desktop, or choose a folder and select the Change Picture check box.** If you select a specific image, it fills the Desktop and you see it in the image well at the top of the Desktop pane, as shown in Figure 1.26. If you select a folder and the Change Pictures check box, you see an icon representing rotating images at the top of the pane, as shown in Figure 1.27. Use the adjacent menu to control how often the pictures change, and use the Random Order check box to have them change at random rather than in the order they appear in the folder.

Note You can use any folder as a source of Desktop pictures by clicking the Add button (the + icon) located at the bottom of the source list. Use the resulting settings sheet to move to and select the folder containing the images you want to use. After you click the Choose button, that folder appears as a source on the list and you can work with it just like the default sources.

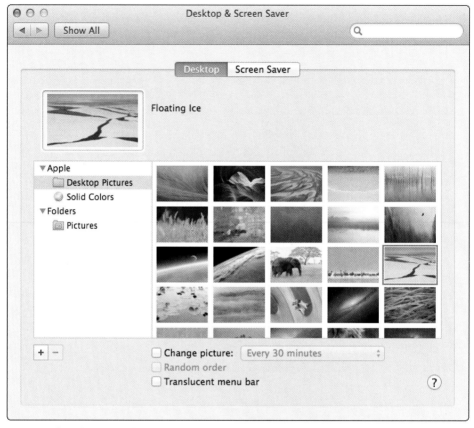

1.26 I've selected an image from the Apple library as my Desktop background.

Genius

You can set a different Desktop picture for each of your Desktops. Use Mission Control to move to the Desktop for which you want to set a picture, set it, and then switch to the next Desktop.

6. **If the image you selected isn't the same proportion as your current screen resolution, use the pop-up menu that appears just above the thumbnail pane to choose how you want the image to be scaled to the screen.** For example, choose Fit to Screen to have photos scaled so that they fit the screen (there may be blank margins on the sides in this case), Fill Screen to have photos scaled to fill the screen (some of the image may be cropped out to avoid having blank margins), Tile to have images that are smaller than the Desktop fill the Desktop space as a series of tiles, and so on.

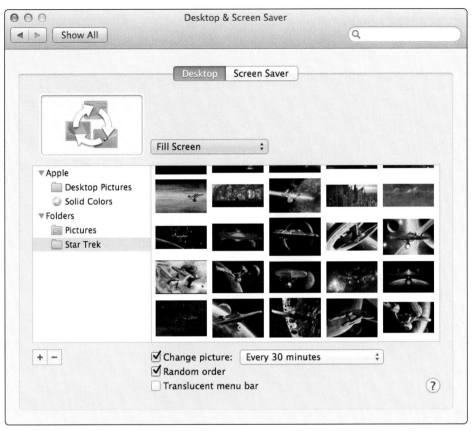

1.27 I've selected a folder of images and the Change Picture option so the background picture changes automatically.

7. **If the image doesn't fill the screen, click the Color button that appears to the right of the menu when it can be used.** The Color Picker opens. Use it to choose the background color that appears behind photos when they don't fill the Desktop.

8. **To make the menu bar translucent so you can see the Desktop background behind it, select the Translucent Menu Bar check box.** When this option is not selected, the menu bar becomes a solid color.

9. **Quit the System Preferences application.** Enjoy your Desktop's new look!

How Do I Manage User Accounts?

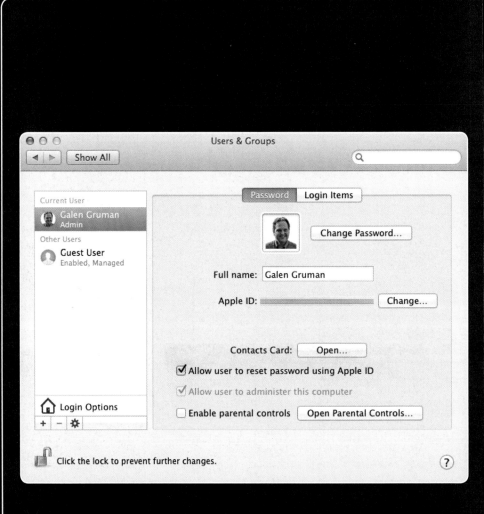

The MacBook Pro's OS X is a multiuser operating system, meaning that your MacBook Pro is designed to be used by multiple people. Each person has his or her own user account that includes a Home folder for storing files; system preferences for options such as Dock configuration, the Desktop picture, and screen resolution; application preferences; and security settings. When a user logs in, OS X configures itself based on that user's specific preferences and, in effect, becomes personalized. Understanding how to create and manage user accounts is an important part of getting the most out of your MacBook Pro.

Working with User Accounts

User accounts are a key part of OS X: Each user account is a separate instance of OS X, so multiple users can use the MacBook Pro in their own section, with their own apps and documents—as if each had his or her own MacBook. Even if just one person uses a MacBook, he or she has a user account that includes a password and sets the basic permissions for how others can access the Mac. It's critical to set up your user account properly to protect yourself.

You use several system preferences—Users & Groups, Parental Controls, Sharing, and Security & Privacy—to create and manage most user accounts on your MacBook Pro. But before jumping in, make sure you understand the following types of user accounts:

- **Root.** OS X is built on the Unix operating system, so it has an extensive security architecture that specifically controls what each user account can do and the resources it can access. The Root user account is unique because it bypasses all the limitations inherent to the other types of accounts (even Administrator accounts, described next). When you log in under the Root user account, the system doesn't limit anything you try to do. So the Root user account is the most powerful and, also, the most dangerous because you can do things that might damage the system or files that it contains. You typically use the Root user account only during troubleshooting tasks. Unlike the other accounts, you don't administer the Root user account using the Users & Groups system preference. I cover how to use the Root account later in this chapter.

- **Administrator.** This is the most powerful type of user account. When logged in under an Administrator account, you have complete access to the System Preferences application and can make changes to the operating system, including creating and managing user accounts or changing network settings. Administrators can also install software at the system level, where it can be accessed by all users. The user account that you create the first time you start your MacBook Pro is an Administrator account.

- **Standard.** When logged in under a Standard user account, a user can make changes related only to that specific account. For example, someone using a Standard user account can change his or her Desktop picture and application preferences, but not install applications to make them available to all users or create other user accounts. Standard user accounts can install applications in the Applications folder within their Home folders, for just that user's use.

Note By default, your MacBook Pro uses the Automatic Login feature. This automatically logs in the default user account (the one you created when you first started your MacBook Pro, unless you've changed it) as soon as you start your computer, which can disguise that you are accessing a specific user account.

- **Managed with Parental Controls.** The Parental Controls system preference lets you limit the access that a user has to various kinds of content, such as e-mail and websites. When you manage this kind of account, you determine specific types of content, applications, and other areas that the user can access. People using a managed account are prevented from doing all actions not specifically allowed by the Parental Control settings.

- **Sharing Only.** This type of account can only access your MacBook Pro to share files across a network. It has no access to the operating system or any files that aren't being shared.

- **Group.** Access to folders and files on your MacBook Pro is determined by each item's Sharing and Permissions settings, accessed in the Sharing system preference. One of the ways you can assign privileges to an item is by configuring a group's access to it. A group account is a collection of user accounts that is used only to set access privileges. You create a group, assign people to it, and use the group to set access permissions for files and folders.

Authentication

Some tasks require you to confirm that you have access to an Administrator user account. This is called authentication. When you work with an OS X capability that requires authentication, the Authentication status Lock icon is visible in the lower-left corner of the window. If the Lock is closed and some buttons or commands are grayed out (inactive), you need to authenticate before you can perform an administrator action. If the Lock is open, you are authenticated and can proceed with the action you want to perform.

To authenticate, click the Lock icon. The Unlock dialog appears, and if you are logged in using an account with Administrator rights, the full name associated with the current account appears in the Name field. If the Name field is empty, you are logged in under an account without Administrator rights. If the full name isn't for the Administrator account you want to use or the Name field is empty, type the full name for the account you want to authenticate with (for example, Galen Gruman) or the name of an Administrator account (such as ggruman).

Type the account password, and click Unlock. You are authenticated as an Administrator and returned to the system preference with which you were working. The Lock icon is now open and you can perform administrative tasks.

Creating Administrator or Standard user accounts

Follow these steps to create a new Administrator or Standard user account:

1. **Open the Users & Groups system preference shown in Figure 2.1.** In the list on the left side of the pane, you see the current user accounts. The user account under which you are logged in appears at the top of the list, and its details appear in the right pane of the window along with the tools you use to configure that account. At the bottom of the user list are the Login Options button, and the Add button (the + icon), Remove button (the – icon), and Action pop-up menu (the gear icon).

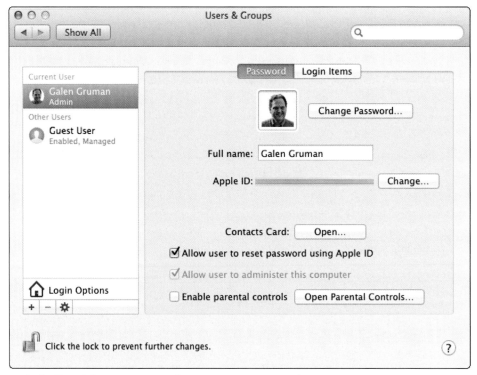

2.1 In the Users & Groups system preference, you can create and manage user accounts on your MacBook Pro.

2. **Authenticate yourself if needed (make sure the Lock icon is open).**

3. **Click the Add (+) button.** The New Account sheet appears.

4. **From the New Account pop-up menu, choose Standard to create a Standard user account or choose Administrator to create an Administrator account.** After it is created, you can change a Standard user account into an Administrator account or vice versa.

5. **Type a name for the account in the Full Name field.** This can be just about anything you want, but usually a person's actual name works best. The full name is one of the names that a user types to log in to or authenticate the account (if it is an Administrator account). OS X creates an account name based on the full name you type. For example, my full name is Galen Gruman.

6. **Edit the account name if you want to change it.** This name appears in a number of places, such as the path to the user's Home folder. Keep the account name short. Also, it can't include any spaces or some special characters. For example, my account name is ggruman.

7. **If you want to create a password yourself, type it into the Password box and skip to Step 8; if you want to use the Password Assistant to help you create a password, click the Password Assistant button (the key icon).** The Password Assistant appears, as shown in Figure 2.2. Choose the password type from the Type pop-up menu. There are a number of options, such as Memorable and Letters & Numbers. After you choose a type, the Assistant automatically generates a password of that type for you and enters it in the Password field on the New Account sheet. Optionally, drag the slider to the right to increase the length of the password, or drag to the left to decrease its length. The longer a password is, the more secure it becomes. A good password should include numbers or special characters to make it harder to crack. As you make changes to a password, the Quality gauge shows you how secure the password is. When the password shown on the Password Assistant is what you want to use, leave the Password Assistant open and click back in the New Account sheet.

Note

Although it isn't a good practice from a security standpoint, a user account isn't required to have a password. If you leave the Password and Verify fields empty, the user will have a blank or empty password. He or she leaves the Password field empty and clicks the Login or other button to complete the action. This is more convenient, faster, and easier than typing a password, but it is also much less secure.

8. **Retype the password in the Verify field, and type a hint about the password in the Password Hint text box.** This hint helps a user log in to the account when he or she can't remember the correct password.

9. **Click Create User.** The user account is created and appears on the list of accounts. You are ready to customize it by adding an image and configuring other elements.

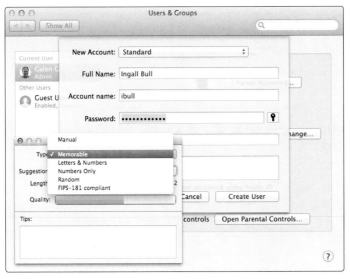

2.2 The Password Assistant helps you create secure passwords.

Note

The OS X FileVault feature is a way to protect the information stored under a user account so it can't be used without the appropriate password. I go into more detail about this feature in Chapter 14.

An image, such as a photo or other graphic, can be associated with a user account. User account images appear in various locations, such as the Login window. OS X automatically chooses an image for each user account from the default images it has. You can leave this as is, or you can use the following steps to customize the user account with an image of your choice:

1. **Open the Users & Groups system preference, and authenticate yourself, if necessary.**

2. **In the Accounts list, select the user account with which you want to associate an image (this can be your own account, too).**

3. **If you want to use an image already stored on your MacBook as the user's image, drag the file onto the image well, which is the box located to the left of the Change or Reset Password button; if you don't want to use a file for the image, click the image well.** (When you select the account currently logged in, the button is Change Password; when you select a different account, the button is Reset Password.) The image sheet appears; if you dragged an image file onto the well, you see the image you placed there ready to be edited, as shown in Figure 2.3, or you see the image that previously appeared in the well.

4. **If you want to use a different image, click the image well and get it from one of the panes in the settings sheet that appears.** The image sheet has at least three panes: Defaults, which shows you OS X's default images; Photo Stream, which displays images taken from iOS devices that are signed in to the same iCloud account as the MacBook Pro and have Photo Stream enabled (see Chapter 6); and Camera, which lets you use the MacBook Pro's camera to create a new image. Click the desired image, or take a photo by clicking Camera to open the Camera pane and taking a picture from it with the MacBook Pro's built-in camera. Other panes may appear, depending on what you have available: Recents, for recently selected images; Faces, for people's faces stored in the iPhoto and Aperture applications; and Linked, for people's faces stored in Contacts and linked social media accounts, such as Facebook.

2.3 An image you associate with the user account appears in several locations, including the OS X Login window.

5. **To change the image's crop, click Edit.** Then set the size of the image that is displayed by dragging the slider to the right to include less of the image or to the left to include more of it. The portion of the image that will be displayed is shown in the preview window. If the image is larger than the preview window, you can reposition the image within the preview window to change which part is visible by dragging the image inside the box until the part you want to be displayed is visible in the box.

6. **Click Done.** The sheet closes, and you see the image you configured in the image well in the Users & Groups system preference.

Genius

To apply special effects to a user account image, edit it and click the Effects button located just above the Done button. You see various effects that can be applied. Click the arrow buttons to scroll through all the effects. Click the effect you want to apply, and you return to the sheet where you see the image with the effect applied. Resize and place the image as needed, and click Done.

If the user has an Apple ID, click Set, type the user's Apple ID in that field on the resulting sheet, and click OK. This associates the user's Apple ID account with the OS X user account. An Apple ID is used for many purposes, including shopping in the iTunes Store, iBookstore, and App Stores. In most cases, the Apple ID is also used when working with iCloud. This is optional, and the user can add this information after he or she logs in to the OS X user account.

To allow the user to reset the OS X user account password by using his or her Apple ID, select the Allow User to Reset Password using Apple ID check box. This gives the user another way (in addition to using the hint you configure) to regain access to the OS X user account if he or she forgets the password.

If you selected the Standard account type but change your mind and want to make the user an Administrator, select the Allow User to Administer This Computer check box. This changes the account type to Administrator.

The user account you created now appears on the list of accounts, as shown in Figure 2.4, and is ready to use.

2.4 A user with a Standard account.

Setting Login Items for a user account

Any application or file added to the Login Items list for a user is automatically opened when a user logs in to his or her account. For example, if a user opens Safari and Mail every time she uses the MacBook Pro, you can add these applications to the user's Login Items so they open when she logs in. Here's how you can make life easier for users (including yourself):

1. **From the Login window, log in under the user's account.** Log in to your own account to set the Login Items for your own account. To log in as a different user, choose ⇨ Log Out and select the new user in the Log In window to log in as.

2. **Open the Users & Groups system preference.**

3. **Select the current user, and go to the Login Options pane, as shown in Figure 2.5.**

4. **Add items to the list by clicking the Add (+) button at the bottom of the pane.**

5. **Use the resulting settings sheet to move to and select the files you want to add to the list.** Hold the ⌘ key down to select multiple files at the same time.

6. **Click Add.**

7. **Select check boxes for any items on the list that you want to be hidden by default.** For example, if you want Mail to open but be hidden, select its check box.

The next time the user logs in, the files on the Login Items list open. Those you elected to hide do open, but are hidden.

2.5 Any files you add to a user account's Login Items pane open automatically when a user logs in.

Creating Group user accounts

Creating a Group user account is much simpler than the other types of accounts. Follow these steps to create one:

1. **Open the System Preferences application.**

2. **Click the Users & Groups icon.**

3. **Click the Add (+) button.**

4. **In the settings sheet that appears, choose Group from the New Account pop-up menu.**

5. **Type the group name in the Name field.**

6. **Click Create Group.** You move to the group's screen, on which you see all the user accounts on your MacBook Pro, as shown in Figure 2.6.

7. **Select the check box for each user whom you want to be a member of the group.** The group is ready to be used to assign access permissions to each member of the group.

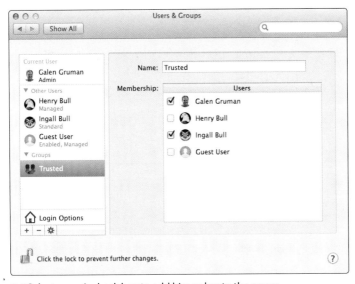

2.6 Select a user's check box to add him or her to the group.

Creating Sharing Only user accounts and enabling sharing

Typically, you create Sharing Only user accounts for groups of people who need to get to files on your MacBook Pro. Creating a Sharing Only user account is similar to creating other types of accounts. To create a new account in the Users & Groups system preference, choose Sharing Only in the New Account (+) pop-up menu and complete the New Account sheet, choosing Sharing Only in the New Account pop-up menu. When you finish with the creation process, you see that the only options available for the Sharing Only account are for the full name, image, password reset, and Apple ID.

You don't use a Sharing Only user account from your MacBook Pro; its purpose is to enable people to log in to your MacBook Pro from other computers. Provide the username and password to each person you want to allow to access your MacBook Pro. Those users can then log in to access files you share, when connected to the same network. However, make sure the files have sharing permissions set for the sharing user account.

First, you must enable sharing for that Sharing Only account. Follow these steps:

1. **Open the Sharing system preference, and click the File Sharing option in the left pane.** This both enables file sharing and shows the file-sharing settings at the right.

2. **Under the list of users at the far right of the window, click the Add (+) button.** As Figure 2.7 shows, this opens a settings sheet where you choose the Sharing Only and other accounts for which you want to enable sharing. Select the desired accounts, and click Select.

3. **Set the default permissions for each account by clicking its adjacent pop-up menu.** Choose from the following options: Read & Write, Read Only, and Write Only (Drop Box). The last option lets people place files only in a folder on your MacBook Pro called Drop Box.

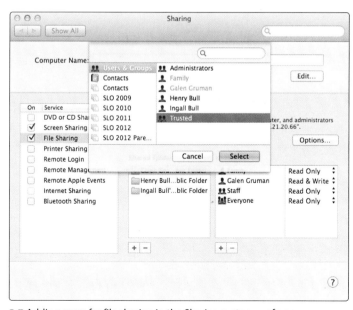

2.7 Adding users for file sharing in the Sharing system preference.

Note You get to the Drop Box folder by going to your Home folder (choose Go ⟳ Home in the Finder), opening the Public folder, and then opening the Drop Box folder in it.

4. **Close the Sharing system preference when you're finished.**

5. **To set different permissions for specific folders and/or files, select them in the Finder and choose File ⟳ Get Info.** This opens the Info window. Scroll to the bottom, and click the disclosure triangle next to Sharing & Permissions to reveal its options. This section works like the Sharing system preference's File Sharing controls: Click the Add (+) button to add users accounts, and select the permissions from the account's adjacent pop-up menu. Close the Info window when you're finished.

Changing user accounts

You change existing user accounts using the same set of tools that you use to create accounts. To make changes, follow these steps:

1. **Open the System Preferences application.**

2. **Click the Users & Groups icon.**

3. **Select the user whose account you want to change.**

4. **Use the tools in the right part of the pane to make changes to the user account, such as resetting a user's password or changing her Apple ID.**

Note The safest way to change an account's username is to delete the account and re-create it with a different username. However, when you delete a user account, you might delete all its files, so be careful about doing this.

Deleting accounts

If you no longer need a user account, you can delete it. Follow these steps:

1. **Open the System Preferences application, and click the Users & Groups icon.**

2. **Select the account you want to delete.**

3. **Click the Remove (−) button at the bottom of the user list.** A sheet appears with three options for handling the user's Home folder:

- **Save the Home folder in a disk image.** All the files in the user's Home folder are saved into a disk image located in the Deleted Users folder under the Users folder. You can access the files in the disk image by opening it.

- **Don't change the Home folder.** If you choose this option, the Home folder remains in its current location in the Users folder, but its permissions are changed so you can access it from an Administrator user account.

- **Delete the Home folder.** If you choose this option, all traces of the user are removed from your MacBook Pro. (To make the deletion even more permanent, select the Erase home folder securely check box.)

4. **Click OK.** The user account is deleted, and the user's Home folder is handled according to the option you selected.

Configuring e-mail, contacts, calendar, and social service accounts

Many services require a user account to access, such as e-mail, calendars, and contacts. You can configure such accounts in the Internet Accounts system preference (called the Mail, Contacts & Calendars system preference prior to OS X Mavericks). Any accounts you configure there are immediately available in the applications that can use them, including Mail, Calendar, Messages, and Contacts. Social accounts such as Facebook and Flickr become available to the Share button in applications such as Safari. Managing these accounts from one place is much easier than doing so in each individual application.

Follow these steps to add a services account:

1. **Log in to the user account for which you are adding or configuring service accounts.**

2. **Open the Internet Accounts system preference.** The accounts currently configured are shown on the Account list on the left side of the pane.

3. **To add an account, click the Add (+) button at the bottom of the Account list.**

4. **From the services list at the right, select the type of account you want to add from the following options: iCloud, Microsoft Exchange, Google, Twitter, Facebook, LinkedIn, Yahoo, AOL, Vimeo, and Flickr.** Select Add Other Account from the bottom of the list if the account is not provided by one of the named services, such as the POP or IMAP e-mail service provided by many Internet service providers or a chat account such as AIM or Jabber. The configuration sheet for the type of account you selected appears.

Note

Accounts you create from within an application, such as Mail, automatically appear in the Account list in the Internet Accounts system preference.

5. **Follow the on-screen prompts to complete the creation of the account.** For most of the named services, this requires typing the full name, account name, and password, and then clicking Set Up or Sign In. After typing this information, you select the compatible applications you want to be able to use the account with (such as Mail, Contacts, Notes, Reminders, Messages, and/or Calendar), as Figure 2.8 shows. If you select Add Other Account, you first choose the type of account you are creating, such as a Mail account, and then follow the on-screen prompts to complete the account configuration. After you complete the process, the account appears on the Account list on the left side of the system preference.

2.8 The details of a service account in the Internet Accounts system preference.

You can change a service account by selecting it on the list at left. Information about it then appears in the right part of the Internet Accounts system preference. You can select or deselect an application's check box to allow or prevent the application from using the account. You can click Details to change the service account's configuration. To delete a service account, select it and click the Remove (–) button at the bottom of the Account list.

Limiting access with parental controls

The OS X Parental Controls feature lets you limit a user's access to the following functionality and content:

- **Simple Finder.** When you limit users to the Simple Finder, they can access only their own documents and specific applications that you choose.

- **Limited applications.** You can use Parental Controls to create a list of applications to which the user has access.

- **System functions.** You can prevent users from administering printers, burning CDs or DVDs, changing their passwords, or changing the icons on the Dock.

- **Hide Profanity.** You can hide profanity in the OS X Dictionary application.

- **Websites.** You can prevent users from visiting specific websites.

- **People.** You can specify the people with whom the user can exchange e-mail or messages or connect with the Game Center.

- **Time Limits.** You can determine when the user can access his or her user account.

Using parental controls is a two-step process. First, create the user account that you want to limit in the Users & Groups system preference, as described earlier, except that you use the Managed with Parental Controls option in the New Account pop-up menu. You can convert an existing Standard account to a Managed one by selecting the Enable Parental Controls check box for it. Then configure the controls you want to use with the account.

You are now ready to use the Parental Controls system preference to configure restrictions for the user account. If you're in the Users & Groups system preference, select the Managed account you want to configure and click the Open Parental Controls button to open the Parental Controls system preference. Otherwise, just open that system preference from the System Preferences application.

Genius

You can manage Parental Controls from a different computer on the same network. To do this, first enable remote management on the computer with the Managed account by opening the Action menu (the gear icon) in that computer's Parental Controls system preference and choosing Allow Remote Setup. After that, you can manage this computer from another one on the same network, so a parent can manage a child's computer remotely. On the other Mac (such as the parent's), open the Parental Controls system preference and choose the Managed account's computer in the Other Computers section. After you log in with an Administrator account for that computer, you can remotely configure parental controls.

After you open the Parental Controls system preference, select the desired user (if not already selected) and begin choosing the desired options from the various panes.

Restricting system resources

With this setting, you can determine the Finder's behavior, the applications that a Managed user can access, and whether the user can change the Dock using the options in the Apps pane:

1. **Go to the Apps pane.** The Apps controls appear, as shown in Figure 2.9.

2.9 Use the Apps pane to configure a user's access to applications installed on the Mac.

2. **To enable the Simple Finder for the user, select the Use Simple Finder check box.** When the user logs in, he or she sees a very simple Desktop. Its Dock contains only three folders; when the user clicks one, it opens on the Desktop and provides access to only the applications that you enable and the documents that the user creates. Within Finder windows, everything opens with a single click.

3. **To limit the user's access to specific applications, select the Limit Applications check box.** Deselect the check boxes for the categories or individual applications that the user is not allowed to use. Select the check boxes for those the user is permitted to use. To limit the rating of applications that have been downloaded via the Mac App Store that the user can access, choose a level from the Allow App Store Apps pop-up menu. The options are Don't Allow, which prevents the user from opening any App

Store applications; Up to *age* (where *age* is 4+, 9+, 12+, or 17+), which limits the applications to those rated by the age category you select; or All, which allows all App Store apps to be used.

4. **If you don't want the user to be able to change the Dock, select the Prevent the Dock from Being Modified check box.** If you selected the Simple Finder option in Step 2, this option is disabled.

Restricting content

You can limit the user's access to various kinds of content using the options in the Web pane. There are two ways you can limit the user's access to websites.

The first is to select the Try to Limit Access to Adult Websites Automatically radio button and click Customize. On the resulting sheet, add the URLs you want the user to be able to visit to the top pane by clicking the upper Add (+) button and typing the URL, or block access to specific sites by clicking the lower Add (+) button and typing the URLs you want to block. Click OK. The user can visit the sites you added to the allow list and can't visit sites you typed on the prevent list. Access to other sites (such as adult websites) may be blocked, too.

The second way to limit a user's access to websites is by selecting the Allow Access to Only These Websites radio button. When you choose this option, the list of allowed websites (bookmarks) at the bottom of the pane determines the sites the user can visit. To add a site to the list (so the user can visit it), click the Add (+) button at the bottom of the list, choose Add bookmark, create the bookmark you want to add, and click OK. To organize the bookmarks on the list, click the Add (+) button at the bottom of the list and choose Add Folder. Name the folder, and add bookmarks to it. To remove a bookmark from the list so a user can't access the related website, select the bookmark and click the Remove (–) button.

Limiting people

In the People pane, shown in Figure 2.10, you can limit the people with whom the user of the Managed user account can interact via e-mail, messages, and the Game Center. You can define specific e-mail addresses and chat accounts with which the user can communicate. To provide more flexibility, you can also set the system to notify you when someone who is not on the approved list tries to communicate with the user. On the notification, you can choose to allow the contact, and the person is added to the approved list. If you choose to reject it, the communication is blocked.

To prevent the user from joining multiplayer games in the Game Center application, deselect the Allow Joining Game Center Multiplayer Games check box. To allow the user to add friends in the Game Center, select the Allow Adding Game Center Friends check box. To limit the user to e-mailing only specific people, select the Limit Mail check box. To limit the user to messaging only with specific people, select the Limit Messages check box. To define the people with whom the user can e-mail or message, click the Add (+) button. The Contact sheet appears, as shown in Figure 2.11.

Type the first and last name and the e-mail or chat address. Next, choose Email or AIM from the pop-up menu to identify the type of address you entered, and click Add.

2.10 Use the People pane to control with whom a user can e-mail, chat, or play games.

Note Adding an iCloud e-mail address allows both email and instant messages to be received from that person, if that person has set their iCloud account as a way to send iMessages (Apple's chat service) to the Messages application.

Or you add a contact from the Contacts application by clicking the triangle to the right of the Last Name box. Choose the person from the list that appears, and click Add. Their e-mail and AIM chat addresses are added.

If you want to receive e-mail requiring your permission when someone who is not on the list is involved in an e-mail exchange with the Managed user, select the Send Requests To check box (refer to Figure 2.10) and type your e-mail address.

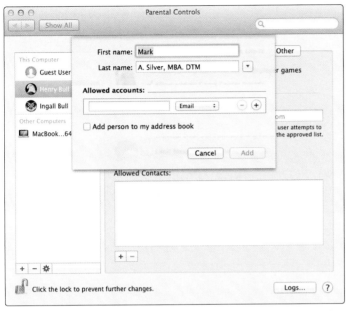

2.11 Configure the Contact sheet to allow the user to communicate with someone via e-mail or messaging.

Caution

The e-mail and chat controls work only with Mail and Messages. If the user can access other applications for these functions, the controls won't limit the user's access. Use the Apps pane's controls to set limits to ensure that the user can access only Mail for e-mail and Messages for messaging.

Setting time limits

You can use the Time Limits pane to limit the amount of time for which the user can use the MacBook Pro. When a time limit is reached or when the time is outside of an allowed window, the user can't log in to his or her user account. If the user is already logged in when the time limit is reached, he or she is logged out after a brief warning that allows time to save any open documents. Follow these steps to set time limits:

1. **Go to the Time Limits pane, shown in Figure 2.12.**

Note

When a user has been logged out because of time limits, a red circle with a hyphen in it appears next to the user's name in the Login window. The time at which the user can log in again is also shown.

2. **To set the amount of time for which the user can be logged in on weekdays and/or weekends, select the Limit Computer Use To check box in the corresponding section.** Set the time limit using the related slider.

3. **To prevent the user from being logged in to the user account for specific periods of time Sunday through Thursday, select the School Nights check box.** Type the time period during which user activity should be prevented, or use the stepper controls to increment or decrement the times.

4. **To prevent the user from being logged in to the user account for specific periods of time on Friday and Saturday, select the Weekend check box.** Type the time period during which user activity should be prevented, or use the stepper controls to adjust them.

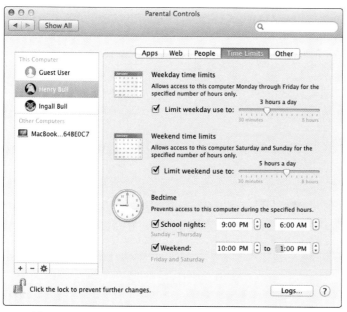

2.12 Although using a MacBook Pro can be lots of fun, use Time Limits to make sure it doesn't replace other important activities.

Note Time limits apply only to the Managed user account. If the user can log in under another user account, he or she can continue using the MacBook Pro regardless of the limits set on the Managed account.

Checking Up on Managed Users

Using the Logs button (which appears at the bottom of the Parental Controls system preference, no matter what pane is visible), you can view a Managed user's activities, such as websites visited, websites blocked, messaging sessions, and applications used. To see user activity, click Logs. Use the Show Activity For pop-up menu to set the timeframe of the logs you want to view. In the settings sheet that appears, use the Group By pop-up menu to determine how the events are grouped: Application or Date.

In the Log Collections list, select the kind of activity you want to see, such as Applications. In the right area of the pane, you see the activity related to that category. For example, when you choose Applications, you see a list of all the applications the user has accessed. To see each instance of application use, click the expansion triangle next to the application name. Under its icon, you see each date and time that the application was used and the amount of time it was used. When you select an application or activity, click Block to change the permissions for that application or activity, or click Open to open the application or website.

Setting other limits

You can limit the following actions by selecting or deselecting the related check boxes on the Other pane:

- The use of the camera (in OS X Mavericks only)
- The use of dictation
- Access to profanity in the Dictionary application
- Administering printers
- Burning DVDs and CDs
- Changing the user account's password

Using Automatic Login

The OS X Automatic Login feature does just what it says. You can choose to log in to a specific user account each time your MacBook Pro restarts. Follow these steps to enable Automatic Login:

1. **Open the Users & Groups system preference.**
2. **Click Login Options.** The Login Options pane appears, as shown in Figure 2.13.

3. **From the Automatic Login pop-up menu, choose the name of the user that you want to be automatically logged in at startup.** Choose Off to disable automatic login and always show the Login window at startup.

4. **Type the user's password. and click OK.** Each time your MacBook Pro starts or restarts, the user you chose is logged in automatically.

Caution

Enabling Automatic Login makes your MacBook Pro less secure. Anyone who has access to it can use it because no additional information is needed to log in. Although this feature is convenient, you should enable Automatic Login only if your MacBook Pro is in an area where you can control it and people won't be able to use it without your knowledge.

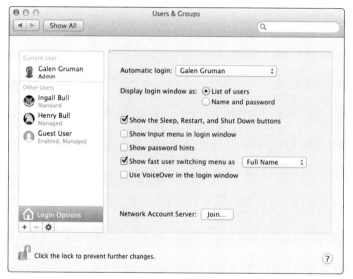

2.13 Use the Automatic Login pop-up menu to select which user account automatically logs in to your MacBook Pro at startup.

Configuring the Login Window

The Login window, shown in Figure 2.14, appears to prompt a user to log in. If Automatic Login is disabled, it appears when your MacBook Pro starts up. If a user logs out of his or her user account, the Login window also appears. You can also make it appear by choosing Login Window in the Fast User Switching menu (this is covered in the next section). Follow these steps to configure options for the Login window:

1. **Open the Users & Groups system preference.**

2. **Click Login Options.** The Login Options pane appears (refer to Figure 2.13).

3. **Select a Login window option by clicking one of these radio buttons:**

   - **List of Users.** When this option is selected, each user account's name and picture is shown on the Login window. The person logging in can click the appropriate user account to be prompted to type the password for that account. This option is more convenient because the user only has to recognize his or her user account and remember the password to be able to log in.

   - **Name and Password.** When this option is selected, the Login window contains empty Name and Password fields. The user must type the account's name (full name or account name) and password to be able to log in. This is more secure but less convenient because it requires a user to know both the user account name and password.

4. **If you want to be able to restart your MacBook Pro, put it to sleep, or shut it down from the Login window, select the Show the Sleep, Restart, and Shut Down Buttons check box.**

2.14 The Login window.

Caution If you've enabled Automatic Login, don't select the Show the Sleep, Restart, and Shut Down Buttons check box. If you do, someone can gain access to your MacBook Pro when the Login window is displayed without having a user account by clicking the Shut Down button and then restarting the MacBook Pro.

5. **If you want to be able to be able to choose the language layout from the Login window, select the Show Input Menu in Login Window check box.** This is useful if people who use different languages share your MacBook Pro.

6. **To show a hint when a user forgets his or her password, select the Show Password Hints check box.** The user can click the Forgot Password button to see the hint for his or her account.

7. **To have your MacBook Pro read the text in the Login window, select the Use VoiceOver in the Login Window check box.** This option is meant for visually impaired users.

Requiring a Password to Awaken the MacBook Pro

Requiring a password at startup is a key way to keep someone from accessing your applications and files. After all, applications like Safari can save passwords and even credit card information, so not having a password required can be dangerous. But after you've logged in to your MacBook Pro, anyone can access it when you're not around, making that initial password requirement ineffective after the Mac is on.

That's why you can tell the Mac to require a password to reawaken it after it's gone to sleep or the screen saver has engaged, both of which occur after the Mac has been idle for a while. (Set the idle time for the screen saver in the Desktop & Screen Saver system preference's Screen Saver pane, and set the sleep time in the Energy Saver system preference.) To force the use of a password when the Mac is awakened or the screen saver is running:

1. **Open the Security & Privacy system preference.** Go to the General pane if it's not already visible.

2. **Select the Require Password check box, and set the delay time in the adjacent pop-up menu.** You can choose Immediately to have no delay or choose one of the six delay options between 5 seconds and 4 hours.

3. **If you want to have a message display on the lock screen, select the Show a message When the Screen Is Locked check box and click Set Lock Message to enter the desired message.** The message could let people know that you are in a meeting until 4 p.m. or went to the grocery store, for example. (The Lock screen is what appears when someone tries to reawaken the MacBook or turn off the screen saver by typing on the keyboard or moving the trackpad; it's essentially the Login window.)

Note   To do more than require a password in the Security & Privacy system preference, you have to authenticate yourself first by clicking the Lock icon and entering your password.

4. **Close the system preference**.

In the Security & Privacy system preference, you can also disable automatic login by selecting the Disable Automatic Login check box.

Working with Fast User Switching

The Fast User Switching feature is great because it allows multiple users to be logged in at the same time. Instead of having to log out of your account for someone else to log in, the other user can log in by using the commands on the Fast User Switching menu. This is good because when you log out of an account, all processes may be shut down, meaning that all open documents and applications are closed. If you have lots of ongoing work, this can be a nuisance. But with Fast User Switching, other users can log in while your account remains active in the background. When you log back in to your account, it is in the same state as when the other user logged in, and you can get back to what you were doing immediately.

Fast User Switching is disabled by default; follow these steps to enable it:

1. **Open the Users & Groups system preference.**
2. **Click Login Options.**
3. **Select the Show Fast User Switching Menu check box.**
4. **On the menu, choose how you want the Fast User Switching menu to be identified.**
   You are given the following options:
   - Full Name (of the current user account)
   - Account Name (of the current user account)
   - Icon

To use Fast User Switching, open the Fast User Switching menu on the menu bar by clicking the name of the current user, the account name, or the icon. The Fast User Switching menu appears, as shown in Figure 2.15.

On this menu, you see these options:

- **List of user accounts.** Each user account configured on your MacBook Pro appears on the list.

- **Login Window.** Choose this command to cause the Login window to appear.

- **Users & Groups Preferences.** Choose this command to move to the Users & Groups system preference.

To switch to a different user account, choose it from the menu. The password prompt appears, if the account requires a password. If the password is entered correctly, that user account becomes active. The current account remains logged in but is moved to the background.

2.15 The Fast User Switching menu makes it easier to share your MacBook Pro with others.

You can have as many user accounts logged in simultaneously as you want. Remember, however, that each account that is logged in can have active processes, all using the MacBook Pro's resources. You don't want to get too carried away.

Genius

To quickly secure your MacBook Pro without logging out, choose Login Window from the Fast User Switching menu. The Login window appears, but you remain logged in (you see a check mark next to your username). For someone else to use your MacBook Pro, he or she must know the password to be able to log in (unless you've configured a user account to not require a password, which is not a good idea).

Working with the Root User Account

Because OS X is based on Unix, it includes the Root user account. In a nutshell, the Root user account is not limited by any security permissions. If something is possible, the Root user account can do it. This is both good and bad. It's good because you can often solve problems using the Root user account that you can't solve any other way. It's bad because you can also cause problems from which it can be difficult, if not impossible, to recover. By contrast, when you use an Administrator account, you have limited access to certain system files, so you cannot delete them; however, under the Root user account, anything goes, and it's possible for you to do things that cause your MacBook Pro to be unusable.

You should use the Root user account only for troubleshooting. Although you shouldn't use the Root user account often, when you need to use the Root user account, you'll really need it.

By default, the Root user account is disabled. You must enable it before you can log in to use it. Follow these steps to enable the Root user account with the Directory Utility application:

1. **Open the Users & Groups system preference.**

2. **Click Login Options, and click Join in the pane at right.**

3. **At the resulting prompt, click Open Directory Utility.** The Directory Utility application opens in its own window.

Genius

If you're comfortable using Unix commands, you can also enable and use the Root user account by opening the Terminal application and entering the appropriate commands to enable the Root user account, set its password, and log in.

4. **Authenticate yourself by clicking the Lock icon, entering your password, and clicking Modify Configuration.**

5. **In Directory Utility, choose Edit ⇨ Enable Root User.** You're prompted to create a password for the Root user account.

6. **Type a password in the Password and Verify fields, as shown in Figure 2.16.** I recommend using a different password from the one you use for your normal user account so it's more secure.

7. **Click OK.** The sheet closes, but nothing else appears to happen. Don't worry: The Root user account is now enabled, and you can use it.

8. **Quit the Directory Utility application.**

Because it has unlimited permissions, you can add or remove files to any directory on your MacBook Pro while you are logged in under the Root user account, including those for other user accounts. You can also make changes to any system file, which is where the Root user account's power and danger come from.

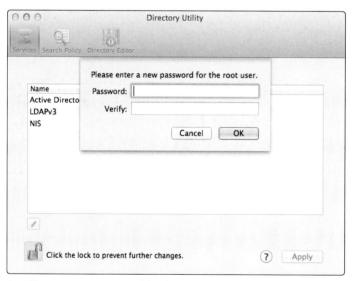

2.16 Create a secure password for the root account to prevent unintended access to it.

Note

The full name of the Root user account is System Administrator. Therefore, you see that term instead of Root wherever the full account name appears.

To log in to the Root user account, start from the Login window by choosing Login Window from the Fast User Switching menu, logging out of the current account, or restarting your MacBook Pro (if Automatic Login is disabled). If the Login window is configured to show a list of users, scroll down and select the Other username; the Name and Password fields appear. If the Login Window is configured to show name and password, you don't need to scroll because these appear immediately. Type *root* as the name, type the password you created for the Root user account, and click Login. You log in as the Root user account (or under root, as Unix aficionados would say). The Root user account's Desktop appears, and you can get to work.

Genius

To disable the root account, open the Directory Utility application and choose Edit ⇨ Disable Root User. You can change the Root user account's password by choosing Edit ⇨ Change Root Password.

When you are logged in to the Root user account, you can use your MacBook Pro the same way you do with other user accounts, except—and this is a big exception—you have no security limitations. You can place files into any folder, delete any files, or complete any other action you try, regardless of the potential outcome. Additionally, if you use the System Preferences application, you see that you no longer have to authenticate because all possible actions are always enabled for the root account.

Caution

Be careful when you work under the root account. You can cause serious damage to OS X, as well as to data you have stored on your MacBook Pro. You should be logged in under the root account only for the minimum time necessary to accomplish specific tasks. Log in, do what you need to do, and log out of the root. This minimizes the chance of doing something you didn't intend.

What Are My Internet Connection Options?

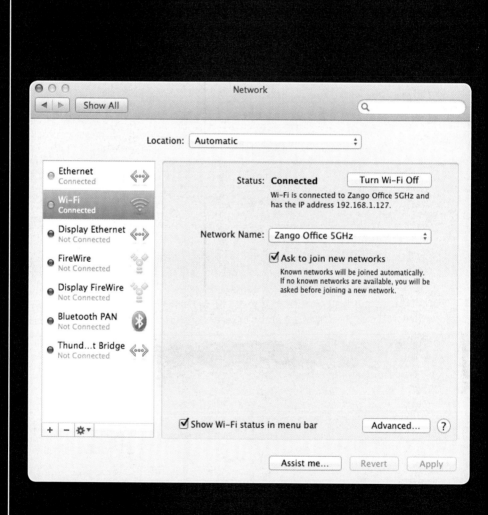

Being able to take advantage of the Internet is a skill that's almost as important as being able to read (of course, you have to be able to read to use the Internet, so reading still wins on the importance scale). Fortunately, your MacBook Pro is a perfect tool for getting the most out of the Internet. To use the Internet, you must be able to connect to it, which is where this chapter comes in handy. It covers how to connect in a variety of ways, and you likely will use several of them.

Setting Up a Local Network

You can connect your MacBook Pro to the Internet in many ways. Fortunately, one of the great things about using a MacBook Pro and related Apple technology is that you don't have to worry about all the technical details involved. It's quite easy to create and manage a local network that provides Internet access and other services, such as file sharing, to multiple computers.

You create a local network with two general steps. First, install and configure your router. Second, connect devices (such as computers and printers) to the wireless or wired network provided by the router.

Building a local network

Routers are commodity products: Many companies make them, and they're all similar. A router essentially lets multiple devices connect to the same network, so they can exchange files, connect to the same Internet service provider, and send other information among each other and between themselves and the Internet.

A router typically offers both wired Ethernet ports and wireless Wi-Fi capability that lets devices connect via radio waves. Some routers offer only wired ports, and some offer only Wi-Fi. One that offers both provides the most flexibility: Wired ports are faster, so if you can connect your MacBook Pro, printer, or other device via an Ethernet cable, you can get better performance. Wi-Fi connections are more convenient, because you don't need to run a wire, but the signal reach fades over distance, and performance can suffer as a result, as well as from interference with other devices.

Many network routers today are also broadband routers, meaning that they also have a wire that connects to your DSL, cable, or other Internet service. Thus, the router connects your local network to the Internet. If your router doesn't offer such an Internet port, you connect the router to an Internet modem, such as a DSL modem or cable modem over a wired connection.

Most routers require just a basic setup, which you typically do through a control panel accessed via your web browser (initially over a wired Ethernet connection between the router and your MacBook Pro). Your router provides its specific setup instructions. If you use Apple's AirPort Extreme Base Station or Time Capsule, you use the AirPort Utility in your MacBook Pro's Utilities folder (in the Finder, choose Go ⇨ Utilities) to set it up.

Note

Some routers come with a USB port to which you can connect a printer, hard drive, or thumb drive (a.k.a. USB stick). By doing so, that device is available to the other devices on your network. Generally speaking, your MacBook Pro sees such a printer when you click the Add menu (the + icon) in the Printers & Scanners system preference. But a USB storage device may not be visible as a drive on your MacBook Pro, and instead must be accessed through your browser or a utility program that comes with your router; see its instructions for details.

When setting up a router, make sure that:

- The router has a static IP address (that is, a permanent, unchanging Internet Protocol address that you can use to access it from your browser if needed, such as 192.168.1.1 or 192.168.2.254, as instructed in the router's setup manual).

- The router has a password so strangers can't reconfigure your network behind your back, such as to monitor your network traffic or to make your Wi-Fi network available without a password so they can tap into your network rather than use their own.

- DHCP is enabled. The Dynamic Host Configuration Protocol capability lets other devices connect to the router automatically over wired Ethernet and Wi-Fi connections. Specify the allowable range of addresses that DHCP can assign to devices; for example, if your router address is 192.168.1.1, you might set aside the range 192.168.1.10 through 192.168.1.200 for DHCP's use. That leaves the address ranges of 192.168.1.2 through 192.1681.9 and 192.168.1.201 through 192.168.1.254 for other uses.

- The Wi-Fi network is enabled, the network is given a unique name (also called an SSID), and optionally it has a password requirement for others to connect. (The Wi-Fi password is not the same as the router password described earlier.) The best password standard is called WPA-2, so use that if available. Some older network devices don't support WPA-2, so use WEP if you have such devices that you can't replace with more-secure modern versions. If you want to hide the network so people have to know its name and manually enter it to connect, disable the broadcast SSID feature (note that the control's name varies from router to router).

In addition, I recommend that you provide static IP addresses to devices that are always on, such as your Apple TV, TiVo, printer, and network hard drives. Doing so helps assure that they're always found by devices using them. To do so, you need to specify their IP address using whatever interface they have for their network setup (such as through a configuration panel on a printer, through the Settings app on an Apple TV, or through a Web browser). Be sure to use static IP addresses outside the range you set for DHCP; if the static IP address falls within the DHCP range, the device may not remain available on the network because DHCP tries to use them for something else.

Note   Routers typically support multiple versions of the Wi-Fi standard, known as 802.11. Recent devices should work over the fast 802.11g and 802.11n connections, and the newest MacBook Pros support the even faster 802.11ac connections. If you have a choice of Wi-Fi standards to enable, pick those with g, n, and (if available) ac. The older 802.11a and 802.11b standards run slowly and can slow down the whole network, so enable these only if you have older devices that require them and that you can't replace. Of course, if you enable these older Wi-Fi standards—some routers may not give you a choice about doing so—but have no devices that use them, you won't experience any slowdown.

If possible, set up a Wi-Fi-capable router in a central area so it provides the maximum amount of wireless coverage where you install it. You can expect the signal to reach about 50 to 100 feet, depending on your home's construction. It can reach 300 feet if there are no obstructions. For a larger space, you can buy wireless repeaters to extend the signal range or connect via Ethernet cable an additional router to function as a repeater (turn off DHCP on them, and give them a static IP address, as their manuals explain).

Apple's Network Gear

Apple offers its own routers: the Apple AirPort Extreme Base Station and Time Capsule.

The AirPort Extreme Base Station is a relatively simple device that contains a Wi-Fi radio and has four Ethernet ports. One of those wired ports connects to your broadband Internet modem, so you have three Ethernet ports for use in your local network. The base station offers a USB port to which you can connect a USB printer or to a USB hard drive, making either device available over the network to all computers to use.

The Time Capsule is an AirPort Extreme Base Station with the addition of an internal hard drive. You can use this drive to store any kind of data, but it is ideal for backing up your MacBook Pro using OS X's Time Machine application (backing up with a Time Capsule and Time Machine is covered in Chapter 14).

Both of Apple's routers use the AirPort Utility, found in the Utilities folder on your MacBook Pro, for setup.

Unless your router also functions as your cable or DSL router, you need to use an Ethernet cable to connect the cable or DSL modem to the router's wide-area Ethernet port, which is usually marked WAN, WWAN, or with a different color.

Connecting your MacBook Pro and other devices

After the router is set up, connect your MacBook Pro and other devices to it.

I explain the intricacies of MacBook Pro network connections later in this section, but for a wired Ethernet connection, basically you connect one end of an Ethernet cable to the Ethernet port on the router and the other to your MacBook Pro or other device.

For a wireless connection, basically you need to turn on Wi-Fi on your MacBook Pro, which you can do in the Network system preference, select the Wi-Fi network set up in the router, and enter the password (if it has one). You can also use the Wi-Fi icon in the menu bar (the triangular icon of four arcs) to select a network to connect. Your MacBook Pro remembers the Wi-Fi networks you've connected to, so if you're later in range of one, it automatically reconnects. This is a major convenience for laptop users who are likely to use multiple networks.

Other devices, such as printers, have their own interface for connecting to Wi-Fi; refer to their manuals for instructions.

Connecting via Wi-Fi

To be able to connect to a Wi-Fi network, you first enable Wi-Fi on your MacBook Pro. After Wi-Fi is enabled, you can find and connect to a wireless network. Follow these steps to configure your MacBook Pro to use Wi-Fi:

1. **Open the Network system preference.**

2. **Click the Wi-Fi option in the list of available network options in the left part of the pane.** The Wi-Fi tools appear in the right part of the pane, as Figure 3.1 shows.

3. **If Wi-Fi is currently off, turn it on by clicking the Turn Wi-Fi On button.** Wi-Fi services start, and your MacBook Pro begins scanning for available networks. Select the desired one from the Network names pop-up menu. If you've previously connected to an available network, your MacBook Pro joins that network automatically and its name appears as the selected network in the Network Name pop-up menu.

4. **If you want to be prompted to join new networks as you come in range of them, select the Ask to Join New Networks check box.** When your MacBook Pro is in an area with networks you've not previously connected to, you're prompted to connect to them.

5. **Select the Show Wi-Fi Status in Menu Bar check box to put the Wi-Fi menu on your menu bar.** You can use this menu to quickly select and control your Wi-Fi connection. When Wi-Fi is turned off, the menu bar icon looks like an empty slice of pie; when you're connected, the slice contains several black arcs; when the MacBook is seeking a Wi-Fi connection, those arcs appear to radiate.

3.1 The Network system preference showing a Wi-Fi connection.

6. **Click Advanced.** You see the Advanced settings sheet, which you can use to configure additional aspects of your Wi-Fi connection. In the Advanced settings sheet, go to the Wi-Fi pane shown in Figure 3.2. Now adjust the settings as desired, and click OK when you're finished to apply them:

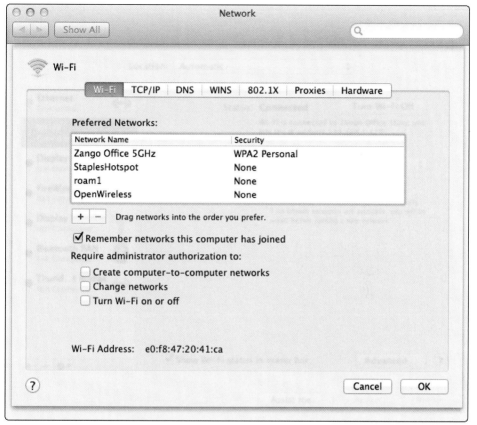

3.2 This sheet provides several useful options that you should configure to make working with Wi-Fi networks even faster and easier.

- To get rid of a Wi-Fi network for automatic joining, select it and click the Remove button (– the symbol). To add a new one, click the Add button (the + icon).

- To edit a Wi-Fi network's settings, you have to remove it and add it back. If the reason to edit a Wi-Fi setting is to change the password, don't bother: When your MacBook Pro tries to connect, it displays an alert asking for the correct password. After it's correctly entered, that new password is saved in the Wi-Fi setting for you.

- If you don't want your MacBook Pro to automatically remember previously used networks, deselect the Remember Networks This Computer Has Joined check box. Networks that the MacBook Pro remembers become your preferred networks, and you automatically join these by default.

- If multiple networks are remembered, you can drag them up or down in the list of Preferred Networks on the Wi-Fi pane to determine the order in which they are joined. Put the network you want to use first at the top of the list, and your MacBook Pro connects to that one first when it is available. If not, it looks for the second network on the list and continues this process until it finds an available network.

- In the Require Administrator Authorization To section, select or deselect the check boxes to prevent or allow changes without administrator authorizations. For example, if you don't want non-administrator users to be able to turn Wi-Fi on or off, select the Turn Wi-Fi On or Off check box.

To manage your wireless network connections, use the Wi-Fi menu in the menu bar, as shown in Figure 3.3. The following information can be accessed from the Wi-Fi menu:

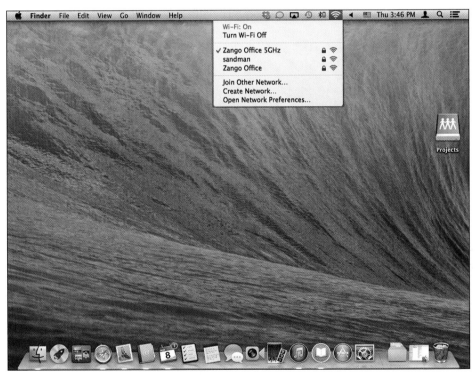

3.3 The Wi-Fi menu is a fast and easy way to identify wireless networks in range of your MacBook Pro.

- **Signal strength of the current network.** When you are connected to a wireless network, the number of dark arcs at the top of the menu indicates the strength of the signal.

- **Wi-Fi status.** The first two items relate to Wi-Fi status. If it is turned on, you see Wi-Fi: On at the top of the menu with the command Turn Wi-Fi Off below it. If your MacBook Pro is searching for a network to connect to, the status is Scanning. If Wi-Fi is not enabled, the status is Wi-Fi: Off and the command is Turn Wi-Fi On.

- **Available networks.** The second section of the menu shows you all the networks within range of your MacBook Pro. If you are currently connected to a network, you see a check mark beside it. If a network is marked with the Lock icon, it is secure, and you need a password to join it. To join a (different) network, select it from the menu, enter its password if requested, and click Join. (If you deselected the Remember Networks This Computer Has Joined check box in the Network system preference, you can select the Remember This Network check box when connecting to a network via the Wi-Fi menu if you don't want to have to manually connect to the selected network in the future.)

- **Join Other Network.** You use this command to join a hidden network for which you must know the network name and password. A settings sheet appears, where you enter this information and click Join.

- **Create Network.** This option lets you create a network with the MacBook Pro as the "router" to which other devices can connect. For example, if you are working in a group that doesn't have access to a network, you can create one to allow the group to share files through your MacBook Pro.

- **Open Network Preferences.** This command opens the Network system preference.

Connecting via Ethernet

Ethernet connections are fast; in fact, your MacBook Pro may perform better with an Ethernet connection than it does with a Wi-Fi one. This speed difference may not be very noticeable for Internet activity, but transferring files via Ethernet in a local network is much, much faster. Ethernet connections are also more secure because their signals travel over a cable. Because you must be physically connected to the network with a wire, it's much harder for someone to intercept or interfere with the signal.

When you travel, Ethernet ports into a network are generally available in businesses, schools, and some hotels. In hotels, the ports are enabled, but in businesses or schools, most open ports are disabled for security. If a port isn't enabled, you need to contact someone in the IT department to have it enabled for you.

Note

It's a good idea to carry an Ethernet cable with you as part of your MacBook Pro tool-kit, because some locations, such as hotels, that offer a wired connection don't always provide a cable. If you have a Retina model, your MacBook doesn't have an Ethernet port, so you need a Thunderbolt-to-Ethernet adapter as well.

Of course, keeping your MacBook Pro physically connected to the network can be limiting; you can't work just anywhere you want. And some MacBook Pro models don't have an Ethernet port, so you must have an Ethernet adapter to be able to connect the computer to an Ethernet network.

Connecting a MacBook Pro to a router is very straightforward over Ethernet: Simply plug one end of the Ethernet cable into your MacBook Pro's Ethernet port and the other into an unused Ethernet port on the router. If the router is set up to use DCHP, the connection should just work.

Caution

You can connect a cable or DSL modem directly to the Ethernet port on your MacBook Pro to provide it with an Internet connection, rather than go through a router. However, this exposes the MacBook Pro to attacks from the Internet. If you do connect it directly, make sure that you enable the OS X firewall by opening the Security & Privacy system preferences, as explained in Chapter 13. If you connect via a router, chances are good that it has its own firewall already enabled, but you may still want to turn on the OS X firewall on your MacBook Pro to be doubly sure.

If connecting your MacBook Pro to an Ethernet network doesn't quickly get the Mac on the network, do some troubleshooting in the Network system preference. First, select Ethernet from the list of available connections. (If your Ethernet connection comes through an Apple Thunderbolt Display, select Display Ethernet instead. And if you're using a USB-to-Ethernet or Thunderbolt-to-Ethernet adapter, select USB/Thunderbolt Ethernet Adapter.) Status information appears at the right, as shown in Figure 3.4. If you see Connected, your MacBook Pro is connected to an active network. If the status is something else, such as Not Connected, check the connections to make sure the cable is plugged in correctly. If the status continues to be something other than Connected, the Ethernet port may not be active.

If the Network system preference shows a connection but the MacBook Pro is not connecting to the network, try these steps:

- If the router is set to use DHCP, make sure that the Configure IPv4 pop-up menu in the Network system preference is set to Using DHCP. If the IP address begins with 169 (called a *self-assigned IP address*), the router and MacBook Pro are not communicating properly; the same could be true if the subnet mask is not 255.255.255.0). Try choosing Manual from the Configure IPv4 pop-up menu and entering a static IP address and the subnet mask 255.255.255.0. In the IP address, the first three segments should be the same as the router's ID (the Router information in the Network system preference), and the final segment should be a number outside the DHCP range you set for the router. So, if the router's IP address is 192.168.2.254 and the DHCP range is 192.168.2.1 through 192.168.2.150, use a static address such as 192.168.2.200.

- If the router is not set to use DHCP, choose Manual from the Configure IPv4 pop-up menu and enter a static IP address as just described.

- Try one of the steps listed later in this chapter's section on troubleshooting.

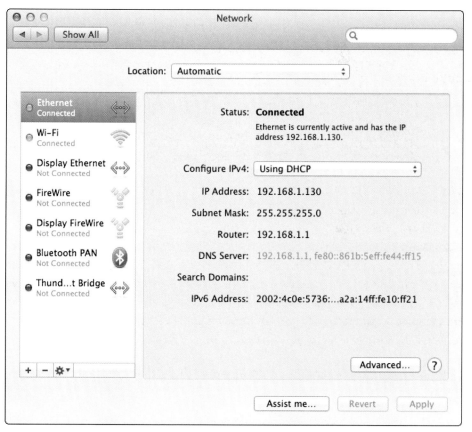

3.4 Select Ethernet on the list of available connections to see the connection status.

Connecting via cellular modem

Using a cellular modem—also called a hotspot and, after the name of a popular device, a MiFi—you can get an Internet connection from anywhere within the service area covered by the device and cellular service plan you are using. If you travel regularly, a cellular modem can be a much more convenient way to connect to the Internet while you are on the move. Because the connection is the same for you no matter where you are, you don't have to find and sign onto networks in various locations, making a cellular modem much easier to use. A cellular modem can also be less expensive to use than purchasing temporary Wi-Fi hotspot service multiple times in the same time period at hotels, cafés, airport lounges, and the like.

The primary downside of cellular modems is that the networks they access aren't available in every location. Like cell phones, you need to be within a covered area to be able to access the service provided on the network. Another downside of a cellular modem is that its connection can be a bit slower than some wireless or wired connections that may be available to you. Then there's the cost issue: Most cellular modems require a service plan of one or two years, so if you don't use it regularly, it may cost more than paying for Wi-Fi hotspot usage when needed (and when available). And data rates can be sky-high.

Here's what to look for when considering a cellular modem, including cell phones that can act as one:

- **Mac compatibility.** Most USB cellular modems, such as Novatel's MiFi, are compatible with OS X. But you can assure Mac compatibility by using one that connects the Mac to the modem via Wi-Fi rather than requiring a physical connection. Plus, a Wi-Fi-connected cellular modem lets other devices use it too, such as your iPad or iPod touch.

- **Coverage areas.** Check that the network's coverage area matches the locations in which you use your MacBook Pro. Make sure you focus on the coverage area for cellular *data* connections (most maps also include cell phone network coverage).

- **Connection speed.** The download speed is the most important because when you use the Internet, you primarily download data. Of course, faster is better. In the United States, 3G connections are standard, but faster 4G (a.k.a. LTE) connections are becoming widely available. You should try to get a 4G device if your provider has a 4G network because a faster device can connect to a slower 3G network if it's all that's available to you.

- **Costs.** A number of costs should factor into your decision, including the cost of the device itself (in many cases, this is free for a new account), the monthly cost of the account (usually dependent on the amount of data allowed per month), contract requirements (such as an annual commitment or by month), and possible activation fees.

● **Return allowance.** Trying a cellular modem is a bit of a gamble in terms of the coverage area and performance that you'll actually experience. For example, even if you primarily use your MacBook Pro in covered areas, your location and objects in those areas can interfere with the performance of your connection. Ask for a trial period when you purchase a device so you can return it if it doesn't work for you. Some providers allow this, and some don't.

Genius Some smartphones and tablets provide a feature called *tethering*, where they act as a cellular modem, letting you connect your MacBook Pro to them via Wi-Fi, so the MacBook taps into their cellular connection. Tethering typically costs extra, and on smartphones it often requires a one- or two-year commitment, making it prohibitively expensive for occasional travelers. But tablet plans are usually available with pay-as-you-go options, without a tethering surcharge, so a tablet like a cellular-capable iPad is often your best cellular modem option. Even better, iPads let you change the SIM chip when you go overseas, so you can use a (usually cheaper) local cellular plan when abroad—something not always available when using smartphones for tethering and even less available when using a cellular modem.

After you obtain a cellular modem, you need to install and configure it. The details depend on the specific device and the service provider that you use. Refer to these general steps to set up your device:

1. **Install the cellular modem's software, if required.** This software includes the drivers and other software associated with the operating system and the application you use to connect to the network.

2. **Connect the device to your MacBook Pro.** For example, when you use a MiFi device, you connect it to your Mac using a USB cable. If the device uses Wi-Fi, connect to it as you would any Wi-Fi network—from the Wi-Fi menu in the menu bar.

3. **If prompted, restart your MacBook Pro.** Devices that require installation of drivers and so on often require you restart your MacBook after installing that software.

After the cellular modem is installed and configured, connecting to the Internet is usually pretty simple. Again, the details depend on the specific device and service you use.

A device that connects via USB typically requires that you use its own application to make the cellular connection. But even some Wi-Fi–capable devices require that you run their software to set them up. Although the steps vary from device to device, they're usually a variation of these steps:

1. **Launch the cellular modem's connection application.** In the application's window, you see the types of wireless connections that are available to you, including those available through Wi-Fi.

2. **Select the connection you want to use.**

3. **Click Connect.**

After you configure a device to connect via Wi-Fi network, you usually just need to power it on to use it in the future. And connect your MacBook Pro to it over Wi-Fi, of course.

Connecting via iPhone or iPad

If you have an iPhone or cellular iPad and a service provider that supports it, you can connect your MacBook Pro to the Internet via your device's cellular data network; the iPhone or iPad becomes the cellular modem.

The specific steps you follow to connect to the Internet via tethering depend on the particular network you use. However, these general steps should help you get set up:

1. **Add tethering capabilities to your iPhone's or iPad's service plan.** You can usually do this via your account's website. In most cases, adding this capability requires additional fees based on the amount of data allowed per month. In the U.S., iPads don't require a separate tethering plan or fee.

2. **Access the tethering settings on the iPhone or iPad by going to the Settings app.** Go to the Cellular pane to see the cellular settings.

3. **Tap Personal Hotspot.** The label changes to Set Up Personal Hotspot if you haven't set up tethering previously. Tap Set Up Personal Hotspot, and follow the on-screen instructions to complete the configuration.

After tethering is set up, go to the Settings app on your iPhone or iPad, tap Cellular, and then tap Personal Hotspot to enable the cellular modem function. As Figure 3.5 shows, you have three options:

- **Wi-Fi.** Connect your MacBook Pro to the iPhone's or iPad's Wi-Fi network, which provides the connection coming through the device's cellular connection.

- **Bluetooth.** Connect your MacBook Pro to the iPhone or iPad via Bluetooth, which provides the connection coming through the device's cellular connection. (See Chapter 4 for information about connecting your MacBook Pro to other devices via Bluetooth.)

● **USB.** Connect your MacBook Pro to your iPhone or iPad using the iOS device's Dock-to-USB or Lightning-to-USB cable, just like when you sync your device. If the tethered connection isn't detected and available on your MacBook Pro immediately, open the Network system preference to select it, choose Using DHCP from the Configure pop-up menu, and click Apply. The MacBook Pro should then be able to access the Internet via the device's network.

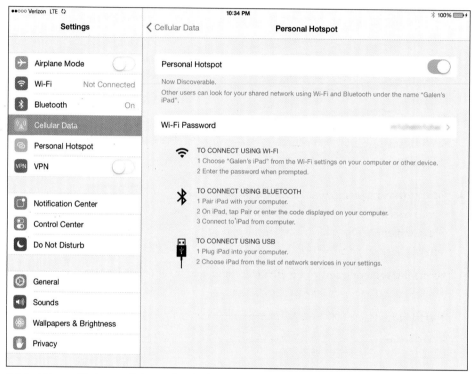

3.5 Enabling an iPad as a cellular modem in the Settings app, for use by a MacBook Pro; iPhones have a similar capability.

Managing Multiple Network Connections

With OS X, you can have multiple connections active at the same time. You can also determine which connection option your MacBook Pro uses first. In this section, I cover how to configure the connections you use. You can also use locations to create sets of connections so you can easily reconfigure your MacBook Pro for connectivity at specific locations, such as home or office.

Configuring network connections

You use the Network system preference to manage your MacBook Pro's connections. Follow these steps to configure network connections:

1. **Open the Network system preference.** Along the left side of the pane, you see all the connections configured on your MacBook Pro (refer to Figure 3.4). Connections marked with a green dot are active and connected, and those marked with a red dot are not. Connections marked with a yellow dot are active, but not connected to anything. The connection at the top of the list is the current one.

2. **Select a connection.** Detailed information about the connection and the controls you use to configure it appears in the right of the pane. You've used some of these controls already to configure Wi-Fi and Ethernet connections, as explained earlier in this chapter. Configuring other kinds of connections is similar.

3. **Remove a connection that you don't use by selecting it and clicking the Remove button (the – icon) at the bottom of the connection list.**

4. **Choose Set Service Order from the Action pop-up menu (the gear icon).** The Services settings sheet appears.

5. **Drag services up and down in the list until they are in the order that you want your MacBook Pro to use them, starting at the top of the list and moving toward the bottom.** Typically, you want the fastest and most reliable connections at the top of the list. Each connection is tried in turn until one works. If you order them by their speed and reliability, the best available connection is always used.

6. **Click OK.** Your changes in the Services sheet are saved, and the sheet closes.

7. **Click Apply.** The changes that you've made on the Network pane are saved and take effect.

Managing network connections with locations

In addition to having multiple connections active, you can use locations to define different sets of connections so you can easily switch between them. For example, you may use one Ethernet configuration to connect to the Internet at home and a different one to connect when you are at work. Creating a location for each set of connections makes switching between them simple because you only have to configure them once. After they are configured, you can switch between them by simply choosing a different location. Without locations, you may have to reconfigure the Ethernet connection each time you are in a different place with your MacBook Pro.

As covered earlier in this chapter, you can have multiple connections active at the same time. If you use only one configuration for each connection, you don't need to use locations. But you will want to use locations when you use different configurations of the same type of connection (such as an Ethernet) depending on where you are.

Your MacBook Pro includes one default location called Automatic. You can create new locations when you need them, or you can change and delete existing ones. Perform the following steps to configure a new network location:

1. **Open the Network system preference.** The current location is shown on the Location pop-up menu at the top of the window.

2. **From the Location pop-up menu, choose Edit Locations.** The Locations settings sheet appears. In the top pane of the sheet, you see the current locations that are configured on your MacBook Pro.

3. **Click the Add (+) button at the bottom of the sheet.** A new location called Untitled appears.

4. **Type a name for the new location, and press Return.**

5. **Click Done.** The new location is saved, and you return to the Network pane. The location you created is shown on the Location pop-up menu, as shown in Figure 3.6.

6. **Perform any of the following actions to configure the location:**
   - **Select a connection, and configure it.**
   - **Delete a connection that you don't want to include in the location.**
   - **Add a connection by clicking the Add (+) button at the bottom of the list of connections.** On the resulting sheet, choose the interface you want to use from the Interface pop-up menu, type a name, and click Create. The connection is added to the list, and you can configure it.
   - **Set the order in which you want the connections in the location to be used.**

7. **Click Apply.** Your changes are saved, and the location becomes active.

Note

If one of the current locations is similar to the one you want to create, choose Edit Locations in the Location pop-up menu, select it in the Locations settings sheet that appears, choose Duplicate Location from the Actions pop-up menu (the gear icon), and give the copy a different name. This is faster than re-creating a location from scratch.

3.6 The location called Office is currently selected in the Location pop-up menu and is enabled.

Perform one of the following actions to change the location you are using:

● **Open the Network system preference, and choose the location you want to use from the Location pop-up menu.** If the Apply button becomes active, click it to apply the location (some configuration changes require this, while others do not).

● **Choose ❖ ⇨ Location ⇨** *locationname* **(where** *locationname* **is the name of the location you want to use).** After you select a location, a check mark appears next to it on the menu to show you that it is active. Note that the Location menu doesn't appear unless you have at least two locations configured on your MacBook Pro.

Perform the following steps to edit or remove locations:

1. **Open the Network system preference.**

2. **Choose Edit Locations from the Location pop-up menu.** The Locations sheet appears.

Note

If you have created at least one location, you can quickly jump to the Network pane by choosing ⌘ ➪ Location ➪ Network Preferences.

3. **Perform any of the following tasks:**

   ⦾ To rename the location, select it, open the Action pop-up menu (the gear icon), choose Rename Location, type the new name, and press Return.

   ⦾ To delete a location that you no longer use, select it, and click the Remove (–) button at the bottom of the sheet.

   ⦾ To duplicate a location, select it, open the Action pop-up menu, choose Duplicate Location, type the new location's name, and press Return.

4. **Click Done.** You return to the Network system preference.

Troubleshooting an Internet Connection

The time will come when you try to connect to a website or send e-mail and you see error messages instead, like the one shown in Figure 3.7. This probably won't happen often, but you do need to know what to do when a good Internet connection goes bad. In general, the solutions to most connection problems are relatively straightforward.

One of the difficulties in solving an Internet or network problem is that there are typically a number of links in the chain, including your MacBook Pro, other computers, a router, and printers, to name a few. There are, however, three general sources of problems: Computers and other devices connected to the network (clients), the router, or the cable or DSL modem that you use to connect to the Internet.

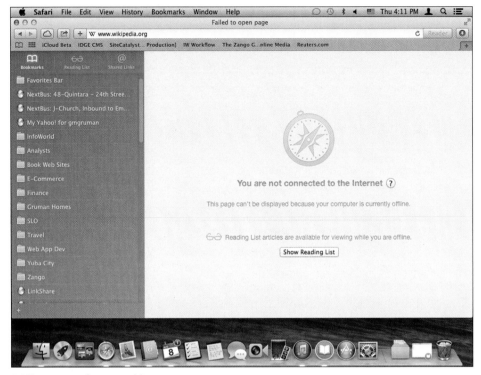

3.7 Houston, we have a problem.

Because there are multiple devices, the first step in solving an Internet or network issue is to determine the source of the problem. The three sources of problems can be classified into two areas: client devices or the network. To determine which area is the source of an issue, try the same action that resulted in an error on your MacBook Pro on a different computer that uses the same connection (such as a Wi-Fi connection) and is on the same network. If the problem also occurs with other computers, you know that it is network-related, which is covered in the next section. If the problem doesn't occur on a different computer, you know it's specific to your MacBook Pro, which is covered later in the chapter.

Solving a network connection problem

Solving a network connection problem can be tricky because there are multiple potential sources of the problem both within and outside the network, the latter of which are out of your control. Start with basic steps and try to determine which part of the network is causing the problems so you can begin to solve them. Perform the following steps, working from the first element in the chain:

1. **Check the status of the modem.** Most modems have activity lights that indicate whether they are powered up and have a working connection. If the modem appears to be working, move on to Step 2. If the modem doesn't appear to be working, move on to Step 6.

2. **Check the status of the router.** It also has a light that uses color and flashing to indicate its status. If the light indicates that the router is working, move on to Step 3. If not, move on to Step 4.

3. **Disconnect power from the router and the modem.** Wait at least 20 seconds, and then reconnect power to the modem and then to the router. This resets the network and often solves the problem. Try what you were doing when you first encountered the problem. If you're now successful, you're finished. If not, continue on to the next steps.

4. **If the modem's power light is on (which it probably is) but the Internet connection light is not, contact your Internet service provider to make sure service is available.** Periodically check the modem status lights until the normal status lights appear; when they do, you should be good to go. If service is available, the provider can run some diagnostics from the source to determine if your modem is connected, and whether the problem lies between your modem and the provider or is an issue with the modem and its configuration. If the source of the problem is the modem itself, the provider can help you troubleshoot and solve the issue.

Genius

If Internet connectivity is critical to you, consider adding a backup connection that you can use if your primary one goes down. One choice for this is a cellular modem, which is useful for other purposes as well. Another option is to be aware of available Wi-Fi hot spots in your area, such as a café, so that if your primary Internet connection goes down, you can take your MacBook Pro to a Wi-Fi hot spot to work until your connection is restored.

5. **Remove power from the router, wait 10 seconds, and reconnect it.** If the router's status light (it may have separate ones for Ethernet and Wi-Fi, so check both) shows an active connection, the problem is solved; if not, you need to further isolate the problem.

6. **Ensure that the firewall is set on your MacBook Pro (see Chapter 13), and then connect the MacBook Pro directly to the cable or DSL modem using an Ethernet cable.** Now try an Internet activity. If it works, you know the problem is with the base station, and you can continue with these steps. If you can't get an Internet connection directly from the modem, you know that the problem is with the modem or the Internet connection; contact your provider for assistance.

Caution Never connect a computer directly to a cable or DSL modem without some sort of firewall protection. To enable the OS X firewall, open the Security & Privacy system preference, go to the Firewall pane, and click Start. Even with this option enabled, it's not a good idea to leave the computer directly connected to the Internet for more than a minute or two.

7. **Troubleshoot the router until you solve its problem.** You might need to reset and reconfigure it. See the documentation that came with the router; if you use an Apple router, use your smartphone to go to the Apple support website at www.apple.com/support/airport for help.

Solving a MacBook Pro connection problem

When you know the network is performing and other devices have connectivity, you can focus on the MacBook Pro to solve the issue. Perform these steps to troubleshoot MacBook Pro connection issues:

1. **Try a different Internet application or website.** If one works but another does not, you know the problem is related to a specific application or website, and you can trouble-shoot that application. (Unless the website is your own, you can't troubleshoot it, so you'll just have to try again later.) If no Internet application or website works, continue with these steps.

2. **Open the Network system preference.**

3. **Check the status of the various connections.** If the status for a connection is Not Connected, as shown in Figure 3.8, you need to reconfigure it to get it working.

4. **If the status is Connected, choose ⌘ ⇨ Restart.**

5. **Click Restart at the prompt.**

6. **After the MacBook Pro restarts, try the activity again.** Restarting when you have a problem is always a good idea because it's easy to do and solves many issues.

Note When you can't access a web page because of a network issue, applications such as Safari (the Mac's default web browser) present the Network Diagnostics button. Click it to start the diagnostics application, and follow its instructions to try to solve the problem.

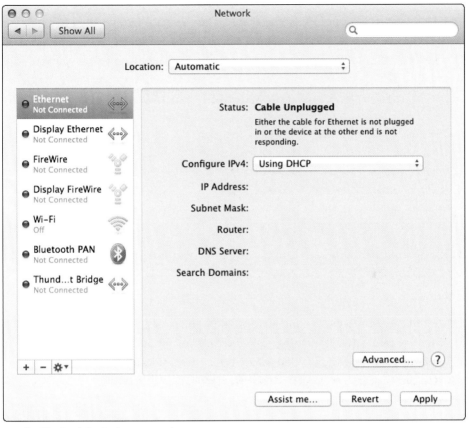

3.8 This MacBook Pro isn't connected.

Finding help for Internet connection problems

Although the steps in this section help with many Internet connection problems, they certainly won't solve them all. When they don't work, you have a couple of options.

First, find a computer that can connect to the Internet and go to http://www.apple.com/support or www.google.com. Search for the specific problem you are having, and use the results you find to solve it.

Second, disconnect everything from your network, make sure that the firewall is on, and connect your MacBook Pro directly to the modem. If the connection works, you know the problem is related to the network. Start with the router, and add other devices one by one until you find the source of the problem. If the connection still doesn't work, you need help from your Internet service provider, IT support person, or a network-savvy friend to solve the problem.

How Do I Share Files, Printers, Videos, and More?

At a very early age, we were all told the virtues of sharing. Well, the MacBook Pro is very virtuous. It's built to share: files, web pages, printers, scanners, calendars, contact information, and images. Sharing files has long been a Mac capability, but in recent years Apple has extended sharing to many more kinds of information, both through its own applications and through social media services like Facebook, Twitter, Flickr, and LinkedIn. Chances are good that if you want to share something from your MacBook Pro, you can. Of course, you can email the information or file to a person, but there are many other ways to share as well.

Using the Share Sheet

You've no doubt seen the button in various applications that looks like an arrow emerging from a tray. If you use an iPhone, iPad, or other iOS device, you know this is the Share button. It lets you share the content at hand with other people via social services like Facebook, Twitter, LinkedIn, Vimeo, and Flickr. It can also share that content via e-mail, opening it or a link to it, as appropriate, in the Mail application. It can likewise share via Apple's Messages chat application. It can also share files with other Mac users on the local Wi-Fi network via Apple's AirDrop services, described later in this chapter. And it sometimes offers other capabilities, such as the ability to bookmark a web page or save it in the Reading List in the Safari browser. Figure 4.1 shows Safari's Share sheet and the Twitter window that appears when sharing a URL in a tweet.

The Share sheet's list of services varies from application to application based on what it makes sense for that application to share with.

Telling your MacBook Pro about your social accounts is easy:

1. **Open the Internet Accounts system preference by choosing ➪ System Preferences and clicking the Internet Accounts icon.** Note that before OS X Mavericks, it was called Mail, Contacts & Calendars.

2. **Click the desired service from the list at the right.** If the list is not visible (for example, if you see the details for a specific existing service), click the Add button (the + icon) at the bottom of the left pane. The social services available are Facebook, Flickr, LinkedIn, Twitter, and Vimeo. (The other services listed handle e-mail, contacts, calendar, and/or chat connections.)

4.1 The Share button in applications like Safari lets you share content with others through social media sites, e-mail, and, when available, services like AirDrop. Top: The Share sheet for Safari. Bottom: The window that appears when tweeting from the Share sheet.

3. **In the settings sheet that appears, enter the sign-in information for that service, as Figure 4.2 shows.** Then click Next or Sign In, depending on the service.

4.2 Top: Adding a Facebook account in the Internet Accounts system preference. Bottom: Enabling contacts synchronization for a LinkedIn account.

4. **After you've set up the social account, you can link it to the Contacts application to sync the contact information for your friends in those services with those in the Contacts application.** Select the Contacts option to do so, and click the Update

Contacts button if available. Doing so ensures that people's photos, social accounts, and other contact information gets transferred to your MacBook.

5. **Close the System Preferences application when you're finished adding social accounts.**

What applications support Share sheets? Here's the list of those that come with OS X:

- AppleScript Editor shares scripts via AirDrop, Mail, and Messages from its Open dialog.

- Automator shares scripts via AirDrop, Mail, and Messages from its Open dialog.

- Contacts shares contact cards via AirDrop, Mail, and Messages.

- Finder shares files via AirDrop, Mail, Messages, Facebook, Flickr (images only), LinkedIn, Twitter, and Vimeo (videos only).

- iPhoto shares images via Mail, Messages, Facebook, Flickr, iCloud's Photo Stream, and Twitter.

- Maps shares files via AirDrop, Mail, Messages, Facebook, Flickr (images only), LinkedIn, Twitter, and Vimeo (videos only).

- Notes shares notes via Mail and Messages.

- Preview shares files via AirDrop, Mail, Messages, Facebook (images only), Flickr (images only), and Twitter (images only).

- QuickTime Player shares files via AirDrop, Mail, Messages, Facebook, Flickr, LinkedIn, YouTube, and Vimeo (videos only). Note that there is no option to set up YouTube in the Internet Accounts system preference, so you need to sign in after selecting it from this Share sheet.

- Safari shares URLs via AirDrop, Mail, Messages, Facebook, LinkedIn, and Twitter.

- TextEdit shares files via AirDrop, Mail, and Messages.

Sharing Photos, Music, and Movies

You can share media files from your MacBook Pro. The method differs based on what you're sharing.

iPhoto lets you create Photo Streams, which are shared image collections. (You can also create them in Photos or iPhoto in iOS devices.) Select an image in your library, click the Share button, choose iCloud (labeled Photo Stream in OS X versions prior to OS X Mavericks), and click the desired existing Photo Stream or, to create a new one, New Photo Stream in the pop-over. When you create the Photo Stream, you can invite other iCloud users to see and post to it, as well as make the Photo Stream public (but read-only) so anyone can see it on the web. Figure 4.3 shows the setup.

4.3 Adding a photo to an iCloud Photo Stream.

You can also display a slideshow from iPhoto on your MacBook Pro and use AirPlay mirroring (see Chapter 1) to send the slideshow to a TV or projector connected to an Apple TV.

iTunes lets you share music and videos to AirPlay devices, such as speakers and Apple TVs. Click the AirPlay icon, and select the devices to send the audio or video to in the pop-over that appears, as Figure 4.4 shows. (Click Multiple to send it to multiple AirPlay devices simultaneously, and then select the devices, such as speakers in each room.)

4.4 Use the AirPlay button to share music or videos with AirPlay devices such as an Apple TV.

And you can use Bluetooth to stream audio to a Bluetooth device, such as a wireless speaker or headset. To set up a device for access via Bluetooth, follow these steps:

1. **On the other device, enable Bluetooth and enable discovery or visibility.**

2. **On the MacBook Pro, open the Bluetooth system preference and wait for the other device to display in the Devices list, as Figure 4.5 shows.** Click Pair when it appears, and if requested, confirm the connection. You might be asked to enter the passcode requested or simply to confirm the other device is showing the same code on its screen as on the MacBook's. (If the device had been previously connected, it should reconnect automatically.)

Note

On a Mac, be sure Bluetooth is on by opening the Bluetooth system preference and clicking Turn Bluetooth On if it is off.

3. **The audio device should now be where sound is sent from your MacBook Pro; if not, open the Sound system preference, and select the Bluetooth device in the Output.**

4.5 Available and previously connected Bluetooth devices appear in the Bluetooth system preference.

Sharing Calendars

OS X's Calendar application lets you share your calendar with others, making them public but uneditable by others. For example, you click the Calendars button to open the Calendars pop-over, right-click an iCloud calendar, and choose Share Calendar from the contextual menu that appears. Enter the name or e-mail address of an iCloud user to have that person join the calendar; this is a great way for families to share common events. Or select the Public Calendar option to create a URL that anyone can use to view a calendar on the web—great for teams. Figure 4.6 shows the setup.

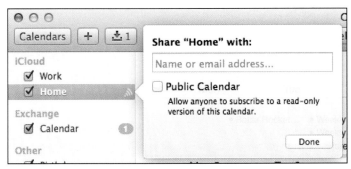

4.6 Sharing an iCloud calendar.

Sharing Maps with an iOS Device

OS X Mavericks introduces the Maps app to the MacBook Pro, letting you search locations and get driving and walking directions. After you've found the directions to a destination, you can send them to your iPhone, iPad, or iPod touch running iOS 7, so those directions are ready to use on the road. (Realistically, you'll use this feature only with an iPhone or a cellular iPad, so you can follow your location relative to the directions while driving or walking.)

Sharing the directions is very simple after you have found the directions:

1. **Enter or search an address in Maps's Search field on your MacBook Pro**. The results appear in a pop-over.

2. **Enter an address or person's name in the Start field if you don't want to start from the current location detected by your MacBook Pro.**

3. **Click the Driving button (car icon) or Walking button (person icon) to select the type of directions you want.**

4. **Click the Directions button in the pop-over, and then click the Directions button to get the directions to it.** (The Directions button in the toolbar shows and hides the directions on the map.) If multiple directions to your destination are shown, select the desired one on the map.

5. **Click the Share button above the map, and choose the device to send the directions to, as Figure 4.7 shows.**

6. **On your iOS device, tap the Show option in the alert that appears; the shared directions then display, as also shown in Figure 4.7.** (If the device is locked, you may see a notice on your lock screen; slide its icon to open the Maps app with the directions.) Tap Start to begin following them. You can also retrieve earlier directions by clicking the Directions button (the blue curved arrow) in Maps on your iOS device and selecting the desired directions.

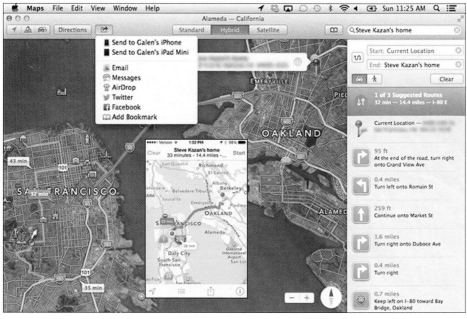

4.7 Use the Share button to send directions from the Maps application on the MacBook Pro to an iOS device. Inset: The directions in the iOS device's Maps app.

Sharing Files

If you have more than one computer on your local network, the ability to share files among them is really useful. Not only can you easily move files between them, but you can also store files on one computer and work on them using any other computer on the network. The MacBook Pro has several methods to share files.

Sharing files with AirDrop

AirDrop is the OS X file-sharing feature that lets you easily share files with other people. To do so, you simply drop the files you want to share on an icon representing the person with whom you want to share it. Unlike the other sharing techniques covered in this chapter, AirDrop requires little configuration and works automatically as long as the computers sharing files are 2011 models or newer, are all running OS X Lion or later, and have Wi-Fi turned on.

To use AirDrop, open a Finder window and select AirDrop on the sidebar, as shown in Figure 4.8. AirDrop automatically identifies all the other compatible Macs in range of your MacBook Pro that have Wi-Fi turned on (they appear at the bottom of the window) and that also have a Finder window with AirDrop selected. It's important to remember that everyone who wants to share files must have an open Finder window or tab with AirDrop selected.

Note The Macs don't have to be on the same Wi-Fi network to use AirDrop, but they must have Wi-Fi turned on.

4.8 When you select AirDrop on the sidebar, you see all the other Macs in range of your MacBook Pro that also have AirDrop selected.

To share a file with someone, simply drag it onto her AirDrop icon in your Finder window. At the prompt, click Send.

The person with whom you are sharing the file must accept it by clicking either Save or Save and Open. When the user clicks Save, the file is saved in the Downloads folder inside the Home folder. If the user clicks Save and Open, the file is saved in the same location and opens in the associated application. If the user clicks Decline, the file isn't copied, and you see a message stating that the user has declined your request; click OK to dismiss it.

Using AirDrop is a great way to easily move files between computers. Its limitation is that each computer must have AirDrop selected. This means that action is required on both sides to share files, unlike the other sharing techniques covered in this chapter. Also, someone must send you a file for you to get it; you can't access it otherwise. However, if you want to quickly get a file to someone else, it is a great option.

Genius

If you regularly use your MacBook Pro near other people with whom you want to share files, open AirDrop in a dedicated Finder window and minimize that window on the Dock. That way, your AirDrop is always available to others, and you don't take up valuable Desktop space with its window. (To keep AirDrop out of the way, you can also have AirDrop run in a tab in a Finder window you keep open.) If someone sends you a file, the AirDrop window pops up and a prompt appears on your Desktop automatically.

Sharing with file sharing

OS X has file-sharing features that provide more control and functionality for sharing files than AirDrop offers. Using file sharing lets you provide other users with access to any location on your MacBook Pro so they can use that location as if it were on their own computers. Likewise, you can use the files and folders other users share on the network.

Complete the first two (the third is optional) of the following tasks to enable other computers to access files stored on your MacBook Pro:

- Configure user accounts to access your MacBook Pro from other computers.
- Configure file-sharing services on your MacBook Pro.
- Set specific security privileges on the files and folders you share.

Configuring sharing user accounts

To access files on your MacBook Pro, a user must have a valid user account on it (see Chapter 2) that he or she uses to log in to access the files that you are sharing. Group is the only type of user account you can't use to share your files. Any Administrator, Standard, Managed with Parental Controls, or Sharing Only user accounts can access your MacBook Pro. The Sharing type of user account is especially intended to provide only sharing access to your MacBook Pro, while the access that the others have depends on the type. For example, an Administrator user account has administrator access to your MacBook Pro when logged in across the network.

If sharing files is all you want the user to be able to do while logged in to your MacBook Pro, create a Sharing user account. If you want to provide broader access to your computer, create a Standard or Administrator account instead. (See Chapter 2 for more help on creating and managing user accounts on your MacBook Pro.)

Note By default, a user account called Guest User exists on your MacBook Pro (and every Mac, for that matter). This is a Sharing Only account that doesn't require a password for use. Initially, it provides access only to the Public folders in each user's Home folder. However, when you provide permissions to Everyone (more on this later), those permissions also apply to the Guest User account and provide more access to files and folders.

Configuring file sharing

The second part of enabling file sharing is to configure your MacBook Pro to share its files, choose the folders you want to share, and determine the user accounts and permissions with which you want to share those folders. Perform these steps to get it set up:

1. **Open the Sharing system preference.**

2. **To set the name by which your computer is recognized on the network, type a name for the computer in the Computer Name field.** The default name is *yourname*'s MacBook Pro (where *yourname* is the name you entered when you configured your MacBook Pro for the first time during the startup process). You can leave this as is or create a different name.

Note The name you see in the Computer Name field is a nickname. Your computer's real name is shown in the text below Computer Name. It is created based on the name you typed, but it is translated into acceptable syntax, and the extension .local is added to it. For example, any spaces are replaced with hyphens, and prohibited special characters are transformed. If you click Edit, you can edit the *true* name of your computer on the network.

3. **Select the On check box next to the File Sharing service in the left pane of the window.** File sharing starts up, you see its status change to On, and you see your computer's address and name just below the status text, as shown in Figure 4.9. Below this, you see the Shared Folders section, which lists the folders currently being shared. By default, the Public folder (with each user account's Home folder) is shared. In the Users section, you see the user accounts with which the selected folder is shared and the permission each user account has to that folder.

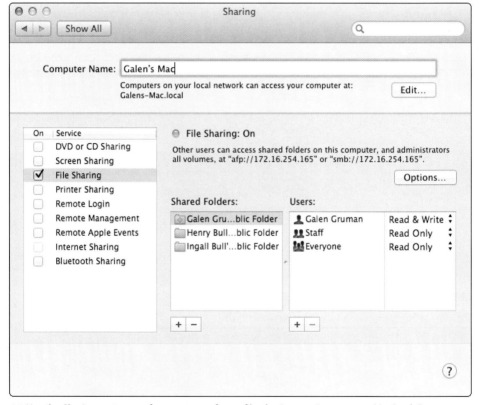

4.9 Use the Sharing system preference to configure file-sharing services on your MacBook Pro.

4. **To share a folder, click the Add button (the + icon) at the bottom of the Shared Folders list.** The Select sheet appears.

5. **Move to and choose the folder you want to share.** You can share only folders for which you have Read & Write access.

6. **Click Add.** You return to the File Sharing pane, and the folder you selected is added to the Shared Folders list. You see the default user accounts and associated permissions for

that folder in the Users section. Initially, you see that your user account has Read & Write permissions; the other users and permissions will differ depending on the user accounts you have on your MacBook Pro.

Note

One user is called Everyone. This *does* actually mean what it says. It represents absolutely everyone who uses your MacBook Pro or can access it over the network. When you set a permission for Everyone, it is applied to all user accounts except those for which you set specific access permissions, so be careful with this option.

7. **To allow a user account to access the folder, click the Add (+) button at the bottom of the Users list.** The User Account sheet appears, showing all the user accounts configured on your MacBook Pro and all your contacts, as shown in Figure 4.10.

8. **Select Users & Groups, and then select the user accounts with which you want to share the folder.**

4.10 Choose the users with whom you want to share the selected folder on this sheet.

9. **Click Select.** You return to the File Sharing pane and see the users on the Users list. After you add users to the list, you set the permissions that each user has to the folder you are sharing.

Note   If you click the Contacts option (or any of the groups in your contacts) in the User Account sheet, you can access any person in your Address Book. If you select a contact in your contacts you're prompted to create a password so that person can share files on your MacBook Pro. This creates a Sharing Only account for that person on your MacBook Pro.

10. **With the folder for which you want to allow access selected, select a user from the Users list on the File Sharing pane.**

11. **On the pop-up menu at the right edge of the Users list, shown in Figure 4.11, choose from the following list which permissions the selected user account should have for the folder:**

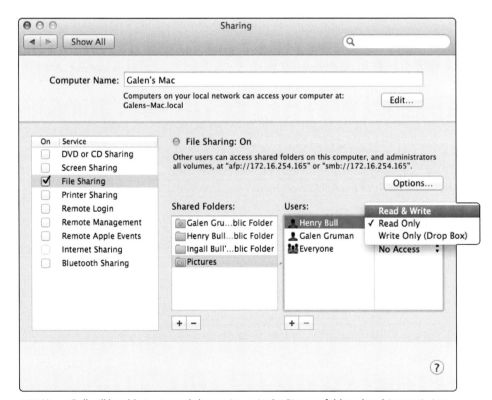

4.11 Henry Bull will be able to see and change items in the Pictures folder when his permission setting is Read & Write.

- **Read & Write.** The user can open and change the contents of the folder.

- **Read Only.** The user can see and open the items in the folder, but can't change them.

- **Write Only (Drop Box).** The user can't see the contents of the Drop Box folder or change them. All she can do is place files within the folder. Every Mac has the Drop Box folder already set up in its Public folder, but you can set other folders to be write-only as well.

- **No Access.** This option (available only for Everyone) prevents any access to the folder by anyone except the users shown on the Users list.

Genius

If you'll be accessing files on your MacBook Pro from other Macs, it's a good idea to create a user account with the same name and password on each computer. This makes it much easier for you to log in.

12. **Repeat Steps 10 and 11 for each user on the Users list.**

13. **To remove a user's access to the folder, choose the user, click the Remove button (the – icon) at the bottom of the Users list, and then click OK in the warning sheet.**

14. **To unshare a folder, choose it on the Shared Folders list, click the Remove (–) button at the bottom of the Shared Folders list, and then click OK in the warning sheet.**

After you complete these steps, all that remains is to provide the user account information to the people with whom you'll be sharing your folders.

Say Hello to Bonjour

Bonjour is the name of the Apple technology introduced way back in OS X 10.2 Jaguar that makes it possible for devices on a network to automatically find each other. This means you don't have to bother with addresses or browsing through various paths to find the device you want to work with. Bonjour lets you automatically find all the Macs on your network. Many other devices, such as printers, are also easily found with Bonjour as well. Even Windows computers can use Bonjour as long as they have the free Apple Bonjour for Windows software installed (you can get it easily by searching for it on the Apple website).

Setting sharing permissions from the Finder

As I mentioned earlier in this chapter, you can set up shared folders in the Sharing system preference. You can also view and set sharing information for files and folders from Finder windows. Follow these steps to check it out:

1. **Open a Finder window.** Move to the folder or file for which you want to get (or set) sharing information, and select it.

2. **Choose File ⇨ Get Info.** The Info window for that file or folder appears.

3. **Expand the Sharing & Permissions section at the bottom, as shown in Figure 4.12.** You see each user account and the permissions it has to the file or folder you selected in Step 1.

4. **To set permissions for the folder, authenticate yourself under an Administrator account by clicking the Lock icon and providing the required user account and password.**

5. **Use the Add (+) button to add users to the folder or select users.** Click the Remove (–) button at the bottom of the window to remove users from the folder.

6. **Use the Privilege pop-up menus to set the access permission for each user.**

4.12 In the Sharing & Permissions section of the Info window, you see and can set the access that users have to a folder or file.

Note To quickly apply a set of permissions to everything in a folder, select it and open the Info window, and then set the sharing permissions as explained earlier in this chapter. From the Action menu (the gear icon), choose Apply to Enclosed Items. Click OK at the prompt. All the files and folders in the selected folder now have the same sharing settings.

Accessing shared files

Although it is better to give than to receive, there's also the expression *share and share alike*. You can access files being shared with you in one of these ways:

- Browse using the sidebar
- Go directly to a shared source by its address

Both of these methods work, but the browsing option is the quickest and easiest. If you are accessing a device that supports Bonjour, browsing is definitely the way to go.

Using the Sidebar to access shared files

Thanks to Bonjour, as soon as your MacBook Pro is connected to a network, any computers that are sharing files are immediately recognized and mounted on your Desktop, making it easy to access the files they are sharing. Perform these steps when you want to access shared files:

1. **Open a Finder window.** I recommend using Columns view for consistency with these steps and easier access to the shared files.

2. **In the Shared section of the Sidebar, select the computer with the files that you want to access.** In the first pane, you see the computer's name, its icon, your current connected status (as Guest, which happens automatically), and the Public folders for each user account on that computer (along with the Public folders under other user accounts on your MacBook Pro).

3. **Click Connect As.** The Login dialog appears. The Registered User option is selected automatically.

Note You don't need to log in to access Public files and folders. This is because you are automatically logged in under the Guest User account as soon as your MacBook Pro detects another computer on the network that has file sharing enabled.

Note The other two options in the Login dialog are Guest (under which you are signed in automatically as soon as you select the computer) and Using an Apple ID. If you choose the latter, you can select your Apple ID to log in to the file-sharing computer. This is especially useful if you are accessing files on a computer that is already set up with your Apple ID.

4. **In the Name field, type the name of the user account you want to use to log in.** This should be the name of the user account created for you to access the files you are allowed to share.

5. **Type the account password in the Password field.**

6. **Select the Remember This Password in My Keychain check box.** This lets you log in automatically in the future.

7. **Click Connect.** Your MacBook Pro connects to the computer and mounts all the folders being shared with you in the Finder window, as shown in Figure 4.13. The resources you see are those for which the account you are using has Read, Write Only (Drop Box), or Read & Write permissions.

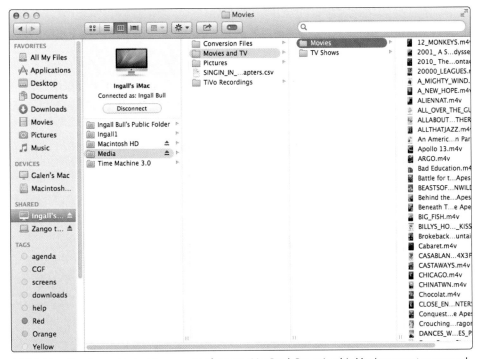

4.13 A friend has logged in to his computer from my MacBook Pro using his Mac's account name and password.

8. **Select the folder containing the files with which you want to work.** The files in that folder become available to you only if you meet one of the following conditions:

- **You have Read Only permission to a folder.** You can view the files it contains (you can't, however, save any changes you make to the files) or drag them to a different location to copy them. You can't move any files into the folder, delete files from it, or save any files there.

- **You have Read & Write permission to a folder.** You can do anything you want with the files it contains, including making changes, copying, or deleting them.

- **You have Write Only (Drop Box) permission to a folder.** You can't see its contents. All you can do is drag files into the folder to copy them there.

Genius If you copy a file from a folder for which you have Read Only permissions to a new location, it is copied in the locked state. If you try to make changes to it, you are warned that it is locked. If you click Overwrite in the warning box, a new version of the file is created that contains the changes you made. From that point, it behaves the same as a file you created on your MacBook Pro.

Accessing shared files using a URL

For computers that are not using Bonjour, you can access a computer that is sharing its files by using its address (its URL) on the network. Follow these steps to connect to a computer via its URL:

1. **If the computer you want to access is a Mac, open its Sharing system preference and select File Sharing.** You see the computer's address (starting with afp://) under the File Sharing status information. Use the address to log in to the computer.

2. **From the MacBook Pro's Desktop, choose Go ⇨ Connect to Server.** The Connect to Server dialog appears, as shown in Figure 4.14.

4.14 Using the Connect to Server command, you can log in to a file-sharing computer through its network address.

3. **Type the address of the computer you want to access in the Server Address field.**

4. **Click Connect.** The Login dialog appears.

Note

If your network uses Dynamic Host Control Protocol (DHCP), which most do, the address of the computer can change. If you can't connect to a computer to which you've successfully connected before, check its address to see if it has changed. If you use Bonjour to connect to a computer, you don't have to worry about this, because the address changes are managed automatically.

5. **In the Name field, type the name of the user account with which you want to log in.**

6. **Type that account's password in the Password field.**

7. **Select the Remember This Password in My Keychain check box.** This lets you log in automatically in the future.

Genius

If you regularly connect to a certain computer, add it as a favorite by clicking the Add (+) button in the Connect to Server dialog. It is added to the list of favorites shown under the Server Address field. You can move back to an address by selecting it and clicking Connect. You can also return to a recent server by opening the Recent pop-up menu (the clock icon) at the right edge of the Connect to Server dialog.

8. **Click Connect.** The Volume Selection dialog appears. In this dialog, you see the folders and volumes that are available to your user account on the computer to which you are logging in.

9. **Select the volumes you want to use.**

10. **Click OK.** Your MacBook Pro connects to the other computer, and each volume you selected is mounted on your Desktop. You can use the contents of the volume according to the permissions the user account has for each item.

Genius

If you have Finder preferences set so that connected servers appear on your Desktop, you see an icon for each volume you're accessing on the sharing computer. You can access a shared volume by simply opening its icon. You can also always access shared volumes in the Finder by choosing Go ⇨ Computer.

Sharing files with Windows PCs

If your network includes both Macs and Windows PCs, you can share files between them. The process is similar to sharing files between Macintosh computers, but (as you probably guessed) there are some differences.

Sharing files on a MacBook Pro with a Windows PC

The process of configuring files to share with Windows PCs is very similar to the one for sharing files with Macs.

First, you must follow these steps to enable Windows file sharing:

1. **In the Sharing system preferences, click Options.** The Options sheet appears, as shown in Figure 4.15.

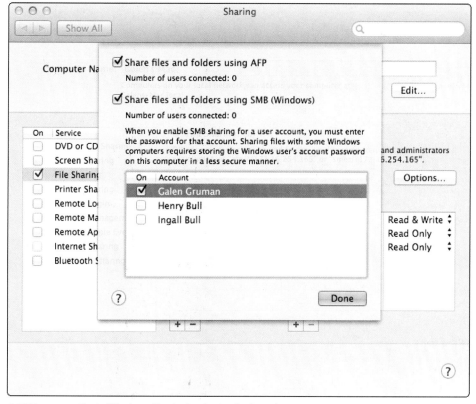

4.15 You can activate Windows file sharing in the Options sheet.

2. **Select the Share Files and Folders Using SMB (Windows) check box.**

3. **Select the On check box for a user account that you want to be able to access files on your MacBook Pro from a Windows PC.** The Password dialog appears.

4. **At the prompt, type the password for the user account in the Password field.** This is the same password you created when you set up the user account.

5. **Click OK.** The dialog closes, and you return to the Options sheet.

6. **Click Done.** Shared files are available from Windows PCs on the network.

Note You configure Windows sharing by user account, but you control the folders that are shared using the tools in the Sharing system preference. Thus, you can't share some folders with only Windows or only Macs. If you want to configure a folder to limit sharing only to Windows PCs, create a unique user account for Windows PC users.

Accessing files from a Windows PC

After you configure your MacBook Pro to share files with Windows computers, you can access them from a Windows PC. Windows has many versions out there, and many variations and details relate to networking for each. This section describes a fairly common configuration on a Windows computer. If you have a different configuration, the details may be a bit different, but the overall process should be similar. Also, these steps assume that the Windows PC is already connected to the same local network as the MacBook Pro, through a wireless or wired connection.

Something to consider first is that Windows networking relies on the concept of *workgroups*. The Macs you want to connect to from Windows machines must be in the same workgroup. By default, the workgroup on both the Macs and Windows machines is called Workgroup. If you haven't changed the workgroup on the Windows PC, you don't need to do anything on the Mac. If you have changed the Windows workgroup, go to the Network system preferences on the Mac, select the active network connection, click Advanced, go to the WINS pane, enter the new workgroup name in the Workgroup field, click OK, and then click Apply.

Perform these steps to access shared files from a Windows PC:

1. **On a Windows XP or 7 PC, choose Start ➪ All Programs ➪ Accessories ➪ Run.** The Run tool opens, as shown in Figure 4.16. On a Windows 8 PC, open the File Explorer and click the Network icon in the list at the left. In the URL bar, click the word *Network* in the URL bar to select it.

2. **Type the network address to the Mac on which file sharing permissions have been set up.** Include \\ before the address, as shown in Figure 4.16. Click OK (in Windows XP and 7), or press Enter (in all versions of Windows). (The network address for a Mac is shown in the File Sharing pane in its Sharing system preference.)

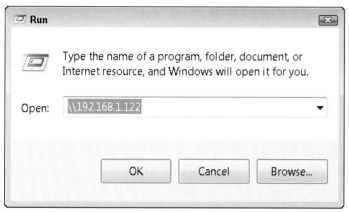

4.16 On a Windows XP or 7 PC, use the Run tool to enter the network address of the Mac with the files you want to share.

3. **In the Enter Network Password dialog that appears, enter the Mac's user name and password in the User Name and Password fields, respectively, and click OK to log in.** The Windows PC connects to the Mac, and you see all the volumes, folders, and files to which you have access based on the Mac's sharing configuration, as shown in Figure 4.17.

After the Mac's shared resources are mounted in the Windows Explorer (in Windows XP and 7) or File Explorer (in Windows 8), as shown in Figure 4.18, you can open them according to the permissions associated with the user account and resources you are using.

125

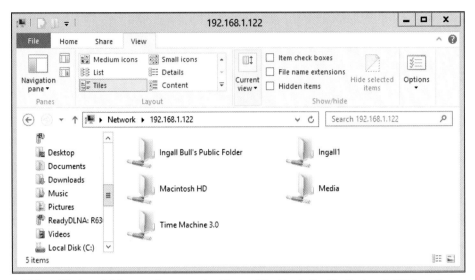

4.17 On a Windows 8 PC, enter the network address of the Mac in the File Explorer's URL bar after selecting the Network icon from the list at the left. You can then access the Mac's shared resources, as shown for Windows 8 here.

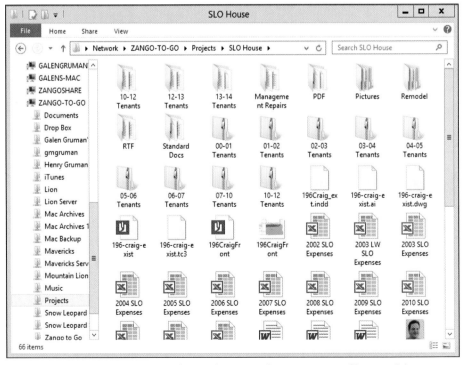

4.18 Here, I've connected to my MacBook Pro from a Windows PC to access files stored there.

Sharing files from a Windows PC

Perform these steps to share a folder and its files from a Windows PC:

1. **Right-click the folder you want to share**.

2. **Choose Share With.**

3. **Choose Specific People.** The File Sharing dialog opens.

4. **From the drop-down list, choose the person with whom you want to share the item you selected.** The options include all the user accounts on the Windows computer along with Everyone and Homegroup.

5. **Select which permission from the following list you want to provide for the item:**

    - **Read.** The user can only see the contents of the folder.

    - **Read/Write.** The user account can open and change the contents of the folder.

    - **Remove.** The user can delete items from the shared item.

6. **Click Share.** Windows begins sharing the file.

7. **Click Done.** You're ready to access the shared folder from another computer on the network.

Accessing shared files from a Windows PC using a Mac

To access shared files from a Windows PC, you need to know its address on the network (unless it is running Bonjour, in which case it should appear on the Sidebar, the same as a Mac that is sharing files). You also must have a username and password. Perform these steps to log in:

1. **From the Finder, choose Go ⇨ Connect to Server.** The Connect to Server dialog appears.

2. **Type the address of the computer you want to access in the Server Address field.** The address should start with *smb://*, followed by the computer's network address. For example, if the computer's network address is 192.168.1.125, you would type *smb://192.1688.1.125.*

3. **Click Connect.** The Login dialog appears.

4. **In the Name field, type the name of the user account you want to use to log in.** If your user account is part of a domain on the Windows PC, you must add the domain and \ as a prefix to the user account, as in *xyz\useraccount* (where *xyz* is the domain with which *useraccount* is associated).

5. **Type that account password in the Password field.**

6. **Select the Remember This Password in My Keychain check box.** This lets you log in automatically. A dialog appears showing you the folders being shared.

7. **Click the shared resource you want to use on the Mac.** The shared folder is mounted on your Desktop, and you can access it according to your permissions, as Figure 4.19 shows.

Sharing files via Bluetooth

The Bluetooth radio that connects mice, trackpads, and headsets to a MacBook Pro can also be used to send and receive files to and from other computers and mobile devices. The devices need to be close; Bluetooth's range is just 10 feet or so.

To connect via Bluetooth, you must have Bluetooth on your MacBook Pro and on the devices you want to connect. The devices also must be discoverable or visible, meaning they broadcast their availability. The Bluetooth settings for your device will have an option to make Bluetooth discoverable or visible; it usually is in that mode for just a minute or two, to save battery power. On a Mac, Bluetooth is on and discoverable by default.

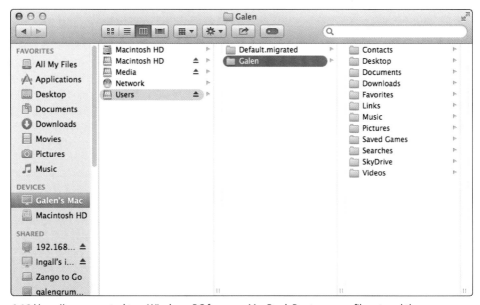

4.19 Here, I've connected to a Windows PC from my MacBook Pro to access files stored there.

Follow these steps to set up a device for access via Bluetooth:

1. **On the other device, enable Bluetooth and enable discovery or visibility.** On a Mac, be sure Bluetooth is on by opening the Bluetooth system preference and clicking Turn Bluetooth On if it is off.

2. **On the MacBook Pro, open the Bluetooth system preference and wait for the other device to display in the Devices list.** Click Pair when it appears and, if requested, confirm the connection. You may be asked to enter the passcode requested or simply to confirm that the other device is showing the same code on its screen as on the MacBook's.

3. **On the MacBook Pro, open the Sharing system preference and select the Bluetooth Sharing option if you want other devices to be connected to your Mac for Bluetooth file sharing.** In the Bluetooth Sharing pane, shown in Figure 4.20, you also set how to handle file-transfer requests in the When Receiving Items pop-up menu and the When Other Devices Browser pop-up menu. The receiving options are Accept and Save, Accept and Open, Ask What to Do, and Never Allow. The browse options are Always Allow, Ask What to Do, and Never Allow. In both cases, you can set the folder where files are received or may be browsed.

4.20 The Bluetooth Sharing pane of the Sharing system preference lets you establish sharing behavior.

To share files with your MacBook Pro, the other Bluetooth device must support file exchange. Many do not, including the iPhone, iPad, iPod touch, Google Nexus 7, and many other tablets and phones. But some do, such as the Samsung Galaxy S4 phone.

When you're ready to send a file from your Mac, follow these steps:

1. **Click the Bluetooth icon in the MacBook Pro's menu bar; from the menu that appears, select the device you want to share with, and then select Send File to Device from its submenu, as Figure 4.21 shows.** Devices in bold are detected, whereas those in regular font had connected in the past but aren't currently connected. For such non-connected devices, choose the device name from the Bluetooth icon's menu and then choose Connect to Network from the submenu.

Note You can also choose Send Files to Device and choose the desired device in the dialog that appears.

2. **Select the desired file in the Select File to Send dialog that appears.**
3. **Click Send after selecting the files.**
4. **A status box appears showing the progress of the transfer.** Note that the other device may ask you for permission to accept the file, so be sure to watch its screen as well.
5. **When the transfer is over, the status box disappears.** The file is stored in whatever location the device stores transferred files.

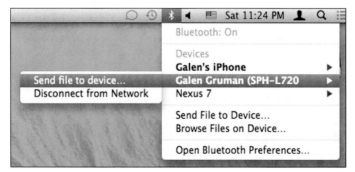

4.21 Initiating a file transfer from the MacBook Pro to a Bluetooth device (here, a smartphone).

If you want to take a file from the other device and bring it to your MacBook, click the Bluetooth icon in the menu bar, choose Browse Files on Device, and select the device from the list in the dialog that appears. If the device can be browsed, you see a list of available files to select from.

Sharing Screens

With screen sharing, you can control a Mac over the local network just as if you were sitting in front of it. This is very useful when helping other users on your network. Instead of physically moving to their locations, you can simply log in to their computers to provide help. Like file sharing, you can configure screen-sharing permissions on your MacBook Pro. You can also share the screens of other Macs that have screen-sharing permissions configured.

Sharing your MacBook Pro screen with other Macs

To share your MacBook Pro screen with other Macs on your network, follow these steps to configure screen-sharing permissions:

1. **Open the Sharing system preference.**

2. **Select Screen Sharing in the list at the left.** The controls for screen sharing appear. (If you select the On check box in this step, you don't need to perform Step 8. However, it's usually better to select and configure a service before you turn it on.)

3. **Click Computer Settings.** The Computer Settings sheet appears.

4. **Select the Anyone May Request Permission to Control Screen check box if you want to allow anyone who can access your MacBook Pro to request to share your screen.** If you leave this deselected, only user accounts for whom you provide screen-sharing permissions can control your MacBook Pro.

5. **Select the VNC Viewers May Control Screen with Password check box, and type a password if you want people using virtual network computing connections to be able to control your MacBook Pro.** For a local network, you really don't need to allow this, so in most cases you can leave this deselected. VNC is designed to work over the Internet, such as for when you want to help parents who live elsewhere with their computer.

6. **Click OK.** The sheet closes.

7. **Choose one of the following options in the Allow access for section:**

   - **All Users.** Select this to allow anyone who has an account on your MacBook Pro to share its screen.

- **Only These Users.** Select this to create a list of user accounts that can share your screen. To add to the list, click the Add (+) button at the bottom of the user list. The User Account sheet appears. It works just like the User Account sheet in the File Sharing pane covered earlier in this chapter: In the sheet that appears, select the user accounts with which you want to share your screen, and click Select. (You can also create a sharing account based on anyone in your contacts.) You return to the Screen Sharing pane, and the user accounts you selected are shown on the user list.

8. **Select the On check box for Screen Sharing.** (You may have already selected this in Step 2, so be careful to not deselect it and turn Screen Sharing off.) Screen-sharing services start, and your MacBook Pro is available to users on your local network according to the access permissions you set. The Screen Sharing status becomes On, and under that status you see the screen-sharing address of your MacBook Pro on the network, as shown in Figure 4.22.

4.22 This MacBook Pro can share its screen with all its user accounts.

When someone wants to share your MacBook Pro, you may see a permission dialog on your screen if the user requests permission to share your screen. To allow your screen to be shared, click Share Screen in that dialog. The other person will see and be able to control your MacBook Pro.

Sharing another Mac's screen on a local network

You can access other Macs being shared with you by browsing the network for available computers or by moving to a specific address. These steps allow you to connect to another Mac and share its screen:

1. **Open a Finder window.** I recommend using the Columns view because it is easier to follow the rest of these steps when using it.

2. **In the Shared section of the Sidebar, select the Mac with the screen you want to share.**

3. **Click Share Screen.** This button appears below the Finder window's toolbar only if the Mac you selected has granted screen-sharing permission. The Login dialog appears.

4. **Use one of the following options to share the other Mac's screen:**

   - To request permission to share the screen, select the By Asking for Permission radio button, and then click Connect and wait for the person using the other Mac to grant permission. On the Mac with the screen you are trying to share, a permission dialog appears. If the user allows you to share the screen, the other person's Desktop appears in the Screen Sharing window on your MacBook Pro, as Figure 4.23 shows. You can now work with the shared Mac as you would your own.

   - To log in using a user account with screen-sharing permissions, select the As a Registered User radio button, and type the username in the Name field and the password in the Password field. (To enable automatic login in the future, select the Remember this Password in My Keychain check box.) Then click Connect.

   - To share screens via an Apple ID, select Using an Apple ID, and then select the ID you want to use on the Apple ID pop-up menu. The Apple ID has to be one associated with that other Mac.

Note If you request screen sharing from an account that isn't currently logged in on the computer screen you want to share, you see a dialog that lets you either request to share the screen of the current user or to access the computer using the account under which you are logging in virtually. If you choose the latter option, you can use the account's folders and files even though it isn't active on the Mac sharing its screen.

When you share a Mac's screen, you use the Screen Sharing application. Its window (which has the name of the shared Mac screen as its title) contains the Desktop of the shared Mac screen, including open Finder windows, applications, and documents, as shown in Figure 4.23. When your pointer is inside the Screen Sharing application window, any action you take is also done on the shared Mac screen. When you move outside the window, the pointer affects only your MacBook Pro (you still see the other Mac's pointer on its screen).

Caution

When you use screen sharing, you have the permissions granted by the user account you use. Be careful that you don't accidentally do something you didn't intend to on a shared computer. For example, don't use the shortcut ⌘+Q to quit applications when using the Screen Sharing application because that quits the active application on the shared Mac, not the Screen Sharing application itself. To close the Screen Sharing application on your Mac, choose Screen Sharing ⇨ Quit.

To move information from the shared computer to your own, copy it from the shared computer by choosing Edit ⇨ Copy in its Finder, and then choose Edit ⇨ Get Clipboard on your MacBook Pro. This copies what you pasted to the other computer's Clipboard on your MacBook Pro where you can then paste it into your applications. To move information in the other direction, copy it on your MacBook Pro, and choose Edit ⇨ Send Clipboard. This moves the data from your Clipboard to the Clipboard on the shared Mac, where it can be pasted into open documents.

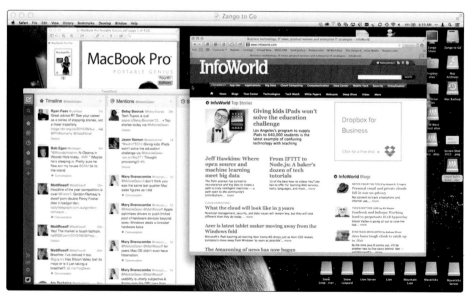

4.23 This Screen Sharing window shows a MacBook Pro being controlled from an IMac.

Note

The Mac whose screen is being shared to your MacBook Pro displays a new icon in the menu bar while sharing is occurring: the Screen Sharing icon, which looks like two overlapping displays. That Mac's user can disconnect the screen-sharing session from that icon's menu.

You can also access the following menus at the top of the Screen Sharing window:

- **View ⇨ Switch to Observer Mode.** By default, you can take control of the other Mac. Choose this option if you only want to watch what is happening on that computer. The menu option then becomes View ⇨ Switch to Control Mode so you can switch back to that mode if desired.

- **View ⇨ Turn Scaling Off.** By default, Screen Sharing resizes the other Mac's screen to fit in your MacBook Pro's screen, which can make it larger or smaller. Choose this option to have the screen appear at actual size; if that is larger than the size of the Screen Sharing window, you'll have to scroll to see the entire screen. The menu option then becomes View ⇨ Turn Scaling On so you can switch back to that view if desired.

- **Connection ⇨ Save Screen Capture As.** Choose this to capture a screenshot of the contents of the screen you are sharing.

- **Edit ⇨ Use Shared Clipboard.** This option must be checked to be able to copy and paste data between your MacBook Pro and the shared computer. (It is enabled by default.) After you have copied something, you can use the Edit ⇨ Get Clipboard and Edit ⇨ Send Clipboard commands.

- **View.** If the shared computer has more than one display, choose the display you want to see at the bottom of this menu. You can also choose Both Displays (if it has two screens) or All Displays (if it has more than two) to see windows for each; this is the default.

- **Window.** If you are sharing the screens of multiple Macs, you can choose which window to bring to the forefront in this menu; open screen-sharing sessions are listed at the bottom. You can close a screen-sharing session by closing its window using the Close box.

Sharing Printers and Scanners

Printers are a great resource to share on a network because you seldom need one printer for each computer. Typically, one or two printers per network are more than sufficient for everyone's printing needs. There are two basic ways to use printer sharing to make printers available on a network. You can connect a USB printer to your router, if it has a USB port, and share it from there, or you can connect a USB or Ethernet printer directly to your MacBook Pro and share it with others via the network.

The same techniques let you share scanners, including those in multifunction printers.

Note If a printer is networkable, you don't need to share it. Instead, connect the printer to the network through an Ethernet or Wi-Fi connection. This is better than printer sharing because no computer resources are required for the networked printers; they're simply available to all Macs and PCs on the network.

If your printer doesn't have Ethernet or Wi-Fi connectivity, you can make it into a network printer by connecting it to the USB port of your router, if it has one. Note that you may have to configure the router to make the printer available; see the router's setup instructions for details. Another option is the $100 Lantronix xPrintServer Home Edition box: You plug the printer into it and plug the xPrintServer into your router via an Ethernet cable. Now your printer is available as a network printer—plus it supports AirPrint, so iPads, iPhones, and iPod touches can also print to it over Wi-Fi. (Some network printers also support AirPrint, but for those that don't, the xPrintServer also fixes that omission for up to two network printers.)

If a Mac has a printer connected to it directly through Ethernet or USB, you can share that printer with the network. However, for other computers to use that printer, the Mac to which it is connected must be active (it can't be asleep) and connected to the network. Because you'll probably move your MacBook Pro around often, this isn't convenient. However, if your network includes a desktop Mac to which a printer is connected, these steps allow you to share it:

1. **Connect and configure the printer to the Mac from which it is being shared.**

2. **Open the Sharing system preference.**

3. **Select the On check box for the Printer Sharing service in the list at the left.** The service starts up.

4. **Select the check box for the printer you want to share.** Other computers can use the printer by adding it via the Printers & Scanners system preference. The printer's name is the current printer name with *@yourmacbookpro* (where *yourmacbookpro* is the name of the computer to which the printer is attached).

5. **Optionally, control who can print by specifying users in the Users pane; click the Add (+) button to add users.** (It works like the similar feature in the File Sharing pane covered earlier in this chapter.) To block specific people or groups from printing to the selected printer, add them as users and choose No Access as their permission level in the adjacent pop-up menu.

You can also share a printer or scanner in the Printers & Scanners system preference. Select the device in the pane at the left, and then select the Share This Printer on the Network or Share This Scanner on the Network, depending on the device selected.

Sharing an Internet Connection

Any Mac can share its Internet connection with other computers, making it sort of a router. I don't recommend this for a permanent network because, for one reason, the Mac must be active all the time for the network to be available. However, it can be very useful when you are traveling with your MacBook Pro. You can share an Internet connection that you get via Ethernet with other computers or devices (such as an iPad) using Wi-Fi. You can also share an Internet connection that you get through Wi-Fi over your MacBook Pro's Ethernet port.

Note You can't share an Internet connection using the same network connection from which the computer is getting its own Internet connection. For example, if your computer is using Wi-Fi to get its Internet connection, you can't use Wi-Fi for other devices to access that Internet connection; instead, they would need to use some other connection type, such as Ethernet, to share that Internet connection.

There's a quick way to share an Ethernet connection via Wi-Fi to other devices, if your MacBook Pro is connected via an Ethernet cable to an Internet-connected router:

1. **Click the Wi-Fi icon in the menu bar, and choose Create Network from its menu.**

2. **In the dialog that appears, type a name for the network you are creating in the Network Name field.** This is how others identify the network you provide.

3. **Optionally, choose the channel for the network on the Channel pop-up menu.** The default channel usually works, but you can choose a specific channel if your network has problems. If there are already other Wi-Fi networks in the same area, it is more likely that you will have to use a different channel.

4. **Optionally, choose WPA2 Personal from the Security pop-up menu.** I recommend that you always create a secure network. If you choose this option, type a password for the network in the Password and Confirm Password fields.

5. **Click Create.** The dialog closes. Note that the Wi-Fi icon in the menu bar changes to show a Mac, so you know your Internet connection is being shared via Wi-Fi.

To turn off the Internet sharing via Wi-Fi, choose Disconnect from the Wi-Fi icon's menu.

These steps let you share any Internet connection, such as sharing a Wi-Fi connection to others via Bluetooth or sharing a Wi-Fi connection to others via Ethernet:

1. **Connect and configure your MacBook Pro to access the Internet.**

2. **Open the Sharing system preference.**

3. **Select the Internet Sharing service from the list at the left.** Its controls appear in the right pane.

4. **From the Share Your Connection From pop-up menu, choose the service through which you are connecting to the Internet, such as Wi-Fi, Ethernet, Display Ethernet, FireWire, or a cellular modem.**

5. **In the To Computers Using list, select the On check box for the connection that other computers use to get their Internet connection from your MacBook Pro.** For example, to share an Internet connection via Bluetooth, select the On check box for Bluetooth. You can select multiple connection types. The only one you cannot select is the one already selected in the Share Your Connection From pop-up menu, because other devices cannot use the incoming Internet connection to your MacBook Pro. If you select Wi-Fi, click the Wi-Fi Options button to enter a network name and optionally to change the Wi-Fi channel and require a password to connect.

6. **Select the On check box for Internet Sharing in the list at the left.**

7. **Click Start in the confirmation sheet that appears.** Your MacBook Pro starts sharing its Internet connection.

8. **Quit the System Preferences application.**

Other computers and devices can now connect to the Internet using any of the options selected in the To Computers Using list. Turn off Internet sharing by deselecting Internet Sharing in the list to the left of the Sharing system preference.

How Can I Control My MacBook Pro and Maintain Battery Power?

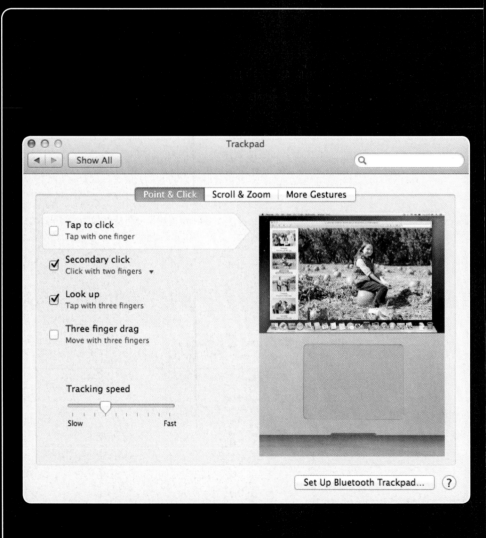

To get the most from your MacBook Pro, you can customize the keyboard and trackpad so they work according to your preferences. You might want to add a mouse, external trackpad, or external keyboard to your toolkit, especially for those times when you are using the computer at a desk. Bluetooth mice, trackpads, and keyboards let you do this without being tethered by cables. And, of course, you can't control your MacBook Pro if it's out of power, so you need to know how best to manage the MacBook Pro's battery.

Using the Trackpad Effectively

A trackpad is an ideal input device for a mobile computer because it provides as much control as a mouse, but it doesn't require anything external to be connected to the computer. The MacBook Pro's trackpad provides all the basic capabilities you need to point and click, but it doesn't stop there: It also supports gestures. Using combinations of your fingers and motion, you can manipulate objects in applications, scroll windows, zoom in and out, and so on. You can use the trackpad much more effectively by taking advantage of its gestures and tweaking all its options to suit your preferences.

You can configure the trackpad to work according to your preferences with the Trackpad system preference. The Trackpad system preference divides its controls among three panes, as shown in Figure 5.1: Point & Click, Scroll & Zoom, and More Gestures.

5.1 Use the Trackpad system preference to tweak the trackpad's behavior to your preferences.

Use these panes to configure the gestures you want to use for each of these general tasks. Go through each pane's options to enable and configure the gestures you want to use. Select a gesture's check box to enable it. If a gesture has a pop-up menu for further configuration, open the menu and choose an option for the gesture. For example, you can set the number of fingers (three or four) for the Mission Control control gesture.

Consider these notes as you configure and work with gestures:

- **There are three possible gestures for a right-click (called a secondary click in the Trackpad system preference) on a two-button mouse: Tap with two fingers, click the bottom-right corner of the trackpad, or click the bottom-left corner.** The difference between a click and a tap is that when you tap, you don't depress the trackpad button, whereas when you click, you do depress the button.

- **The three-finger drag lets you move objects on the screen by touching three fingers to the trackpad and moving your hand until the object is where you want it to be.** When you lift up your fingers, the object drops into its new location. If you used older versions of OS X, you may find this a big improvement over the somewhat difficult drag-and-lock feature.

- **Use the Tracking Speed slider on the Point & Click pane to set how far the pointer moves for the same movement of your finger on the trackpad.** The faster you set the tracking speed, the farther the pointer moves on the screen for the same motion of your fingers on the trackpad.

- **In the Scroll & Zoom pane, the Scroll Direction: Natural gesture may be a bit confusing at first.** In previous versions of OS X, when you drag your fingers, the scroll bars move in the same direction as your fingers. For example, when you drag your fingers toward you, you scroll down the screen. With the Scroll Direction: Natural option enabled, the movement is the opposite; dragging your fingers toward you results in the content moving down the screen (the scroll bar moves up the screen). This is the same movement that happens on an iPhone, iPod touch, or iPad. Although it seems perfectly natural when you use your fingers on a screen, it may be counterintuitive on a trackpad, especially if you've used previous versions of OS X. I recommend you try this option for a while to see if it does, indeed, seem natural to you.

● **Take extra time to explore the options in the More Gestures pane.** This is where you set gestures for the OS X features that really benefit from them, including navigation between pages, moving between applications in full screen, Mission Control, and so on. Most of these gestures have options that you should check out, too.

Augmenting the MacBook Pro's Built-in Hardware

Working on a laptop is great when you're on the road, but at a desk, it may not be ergonomic, because you typically have to bend your head down and crouch to see the screen. Also, the keyboard location for optimal typing can make the screen's position less than optimal. It makes sense to have an external keyboard, mouse or trackpad, and monitor available when your MacBook Pro is used extensively at your desk. Chapter 1 explains how to connect a monitor to your MacBook.

To connect a USB keyboard, mouse, or trackpad, just plug the device into your MacBook Pro's USB ports or into a USB hub connected to your MacBook Pro. (Some monitors include such hubs to save desk space.)

If you don't like cords, consider getting a Bluetooth mouse, trackpad, and/or keyboard (Apple makes very nice ones). Be sure Bluetooth is enabled on your MacBook Pro and that the peripherals are set to discovery mode, as Chapter 4 explains. (For Apple's devices, press and hold their power buttons for a couple seconds; you'll see their indicator lights flash briefly.)

Then go to the appropriate system preference—Keyboard, Mouse, or Trackpad—and click the Set Up Bluetooth Keyboard, Set Up Bluetooth Mouse, or Set Up Bluetooth Trackpad button. The MacBook searches for the peripheral and displays its name when found. Click Continue, and follow the pairing instructions to connect it. You can now configure the device in the relevant system preference.

Note that if a keyboard, mouse, or trackpad is connected to another computer or mobile device, it will not be found by your MacBook Pro; Bluetooth devices can be connected to only one computer or mobile device at a time.

Using the Keyboard Effectively

The MacBook Pro keyboard is used not only for typing but also for controlling your computer, particularly through keyboard shortcuts. In this section, I cover how to configure the basic functions of the keyboard and how to use it to efficiently control your MacBook Pro and how to control the language it uses.

Configuring the keyboard

Follow these steps to configure your keyboard:

1. **Open the Keyboard system preference, and go to the Keyboard pane.**

2. **Click and drag the sliders at the top of the pane to configure how keys repeat when you hold them down.** The Key Repeat slider controls how fast the corresponding character repeats while the key is held down, and the Delay Until Repeat slider controls how long you hold the key down before it starts repeating.

3. **If you want the function keys to behave as standard function keys instead of the default actions they are programmed to perform (such as F2 to brighten the display), select the Use All F1, F2, etc. Keys as Standard Function Keys check box.** If you select this option, you must hold down the Fn key and press the appropriate key to perform its default action (such as Fn+F10 to mute your MacBook Pro, rather than the standard F10). If you *don't* select this option, you must hold down the Fn key and press the appropriate key to perform the action that applications have assigned to it. For example, Adobe InDesign uses F7 to display the Alignment panel, but on a MacBook Pro pressing F7 rewinds music or video. To use InDesign's intended F7 function, press Fn+F7. Table 5.1 lists the current generation of MacBook Pro's default function keys (older models may have different key arrangements).

4. **To enable the keyboard's backlighting, select the Adjust Keyboard Brightness in Low Light Conditions check box and use the slider to set the amount of time backlighting remains on when the computer is not being used.** To conserve battery power, you want this time to be short, but not so short that the illumination turns off too fast for it to be of any use to you.

Genius

When backlighting is on, you can use the following function keys to manually control its brightness: F5 to decrease it and F6 to increase it.

5. **If you want the Keyboard and Character viewers to be available in the menu bar, select the Show Keyboard & Character Viewers in Menu Bar check box.**

6. **To change which modifier keys perform which function, click the Modifier Keys button.** The Modifier Keys sheet appears, as shown in Figure 5.2. For each of the four modifier keys, use the pop-up menu to select the action that you want to occur when you press that key. For example, if the Control key is more convenient for you, you might want to set it to be the ⌘ key, because you use it more frequently. You can select No Action to disable a key, in which case it is grayed out on the sheet. Click OK when you're finished.

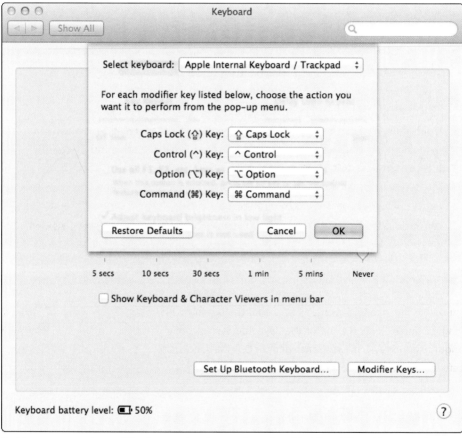

5.2 You can remap the modifier keys, such as having Control act like ⌘ and ⌘ act like Control.

Genius

I rarely use the Caps Lock key, but I have accidentally turned it on many times and found myself TYPING IN ALL CAPS, which is very annoying. You can disable this key by choosing No Action on its pop-up menu. Ah, now you don't have to yell as you type just because you accidentally press this key.

Table 5.1 The MacBook Pro's Default Function Keys

Function Key	What It Does
F1	Decreases display brightness
F2	Increases display brightness
F3	Opens Mission Control
F4	Opens or closes the Launchpad
F5	Decreases the brightness of keyboard backlighting
F6	Increases the brightness of keyboard backlighting
F7	Rewind/Previous in various applications, such as iTunes
F8	Play/Pause in various applications, such as iTunes
F9	Fast Forward/Next in various applications, such as iTunes
F10	Mutes sound
F11	Decreases volume
F12	Increases volume
Eject (non-Retina models)	Ejects the selected ejectable device or disc (if one is inserted)
Power (Retina models)	Turns the MacBook Pro on or off

Configuring language settings

You can configure the languages you use for the keyboard, along with other input preferences, using the Input Sources pane of the Keyboard system preference (this pane had been in the Language & Text system preference prior to OS X Mavericks) and the Language & Region system preference (prior to OS X Mavericks, this was the Language pane of the Language & Text system preference).

Selecting the keyboard layout

The Input Sources pane is where you make different languages' keyboard layouts available to your MacBook Pro. Different languages lay out the keys differently on a keyboard, and even though the keys on your MacBook Pro's keyboard are arranged for the country in which you bought it, you can have it act like the keyboard in another country. Just be sure you know that other country's keyboard arrangement, because the labels printed on the keyboard will still be for your country of purchase.

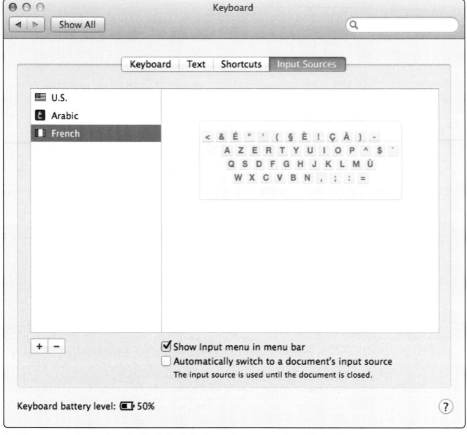

5.3 You can configure the MacBook Pro's keyboard to use any (or all) of 73 languages.

Follow these steps to add keyboard layouts:

1. **Open the Keyboard system preference, and go to the Input Sources pane, shown in Figure 5.2.**

2. **Click the Add (+) button.**

3. **On the resulting settings sheet, select a language whose keyboard layout you want to be available, and click Add.** Some languages have multiple keyboard layouts available; if so, they appear in the upper right of the settings sheet; select the ones you want to add before clicking Add.

4. **Repeat Steps 2 and 3 for each language keyboard layout you want to add.**

In the menu bar, you'll see a new icon of the flag for the current keyboard layout's language, such as an American flag for U.S. English. Click that icon to get the Input Sources menu of the other active keyboard layouts, and choose a different keyboard language to switch to that keyboard layout.

To see the keyboard layout, choose Show Keyboard Viewer from the Input Sources menu; a window appears with a miniature version of the keyboard that shows you the selected language's layout. You can even click the keys on that virtual keyboard to enter them. As you type on the physical keyboard, the keys you press are briefly highlighted in the Keyboard Viewer, as an aid to typing with an unfamiliar keyboard layout. If the Keyboard Viewer option doesn't appear in the Input Sources menu, go to the Keyboard system preference's Keyboard pane and select the Show Keyboard & Character Viewer in Menu Bar option. You also need to have the Show Input Menu in Menu Bar option selected in the Keyboard system preference's Input Sources pane.

Note

In the Input Sources pane is the Automatically Switch to a Document's Input Source option. If you select it, the keyboard layout automatically changes to that of the document's input source. That saves you the hassle of switching the keyboard layout yourself, but of course it can be confusing if you don't realize that a document used a different input source. Not all applications record the input source used, so not all documents switch if this option is selected.

Setting OS X's language and regional settings

The Language & Region system preference, shown in Figure 5.4, controls the languages used by OS X itself, for menus, alerts, and so on. Typically, you have just one language—the one for the country in which you bought your MacBook Pro. But you can add other languages, so a MacBook Pro used in a multilingual environment can switch from one language to another. There are 167 languages available, but OS X works in only 31 of them. The others are less-used languages and dialects—even the fictional Klingon from *Star Trek*—that OS X doesn't support in menus and alerts but that, if enabled, helps it properly work with applications and websites using those languages.

Follow these steps to add a language:

1. **Click the Add (+) button below the Preferred Languages list.**

2. **In the settings sheet that appears, select the languages you want to add and click Add.** The 31 fully supported languages are at the top of the list, and the other 136 are listed after a dividing line. To select multiple languages, ⌘+click each one.

3. **Drag the languages up or down the list to change their order, keeping the one you want to be the default (primary) at the top of the list.** Your MacBook Pro displays an alert box asking you to restart to change the primary language. You can delay the restart, but the new primary language isn't active until you do.

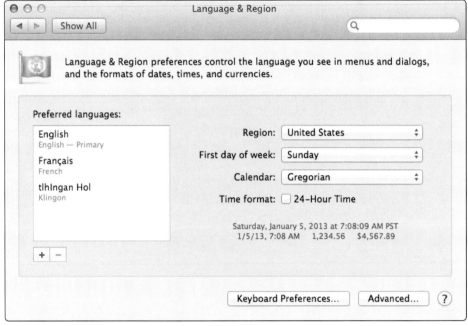

5.4 You can configure the MacBook Pro's user interface to use any (or all) of 31 languages, and enable application and website support for 136 others.

The rest of the Language & Region system preference lets you set up regional defaults such as the first day of the week, calendar, time format, and—via the Advanced button—currency display, default measurement units, date display, and time display. Choose the desired country or region from the Region pop-up menu, and customize its defaults as desired using the other controls in the system preference.

Controlling spelling, quotation marks, dashes, and text substitution

The Text pane of the Keyboard system preference, shown in Figure 5.5, controls how applications handle spelling, quotation marks, dashes, and text substitution as you type. (Prior to OS X Mavericks, the Text pane was in the Language & Text system preference.)

Note

These controls only affect applications designed to use Apple's text services, which includes Apple's various applications. Other applications, such as Microsoft Word, may use their own settings.

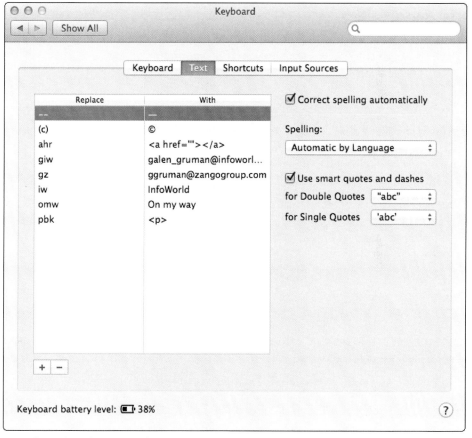

5.5 In the Keyboard system preference's Text pane, you can configure global substitutions and other text settings.

Follow these steps to configure global symbol and text substitution in the Text pane:

1. **Click the Add (+) button at the bottom of the substitution list.** A new, blank entry appears in the list.

2. **In the Replace side, type the characters to be replaced. In the With side, type what those characters will be replaced with.** For example, to have (c) replaced with the © symbol, enter (c) in the Replace side and © in the With side.

The substitution is added to the list and is immediately available. To remove a substitution, select it and click the Remove (–) button.

Note OS X Mavericks automatically syncs text substitutions with other Macs and iOS devices using the same iCloud account. Thus, you may see the substitutions you used to have missing in the Keyboard system preference's Text pane, replaced by those you set up in iOS's Settings app, in its Keyboard pane's Shortcut settings.

You can also control spell-checking in compatible applications. To enable spell-checking, select the Correct Spelling Automatically check box, which is enabled by default. Normally, OS X spell-checks based on the language used for the text, but if you want to force the same language on all text, choose that language in the Language pop-up menu; choose Automatically by Language to return to the default behavior.

The Set Up option in the Languages pop-up menu lets you select and deselect the languages that are spell-checked. There's little reason to disable other languages—you never know when you might use them—but there are two languages whose default options you may want to override: English and Portuguese. In the Setup sheet, you can enable or disable four variants of English (Australian, British, Canadian, and U.S.) and two variants of Portuguese (Brazilian and European) based on the variants you use.

Use the two Smart Quotes pop-up menus to determine what is substituted when you press either single or double quotes. One controls the style of quotation marks for double quotes and the other for single quotes. The option selected by default is the one for your MacBook Pro's primary language, so there's usually little reason to change these selections.

Controlling your MacBook Pro with keyboard shortcuts

OS X includes support for many keyboard shortcuts by default. For example, you've probably used ⌘+Q to quit applications. There are many more keyboard shortcuts available to you. The only challenge to using keyboard shortcuts is learning (and remembering) which ones are available to you. Fortunately, as described in the following list, you can discover keyboard shortcuts in many ways:

● **The Shortcuts pane of the Keyboard system preference.** If you go to this pane, you see a list of OS X keyboard shortcuts. Select the type of shortcuts in which you are interested on the left side of the window, and the current shortcuts appear in the right side, as shown in Figure 5.6. You can also use this pane to change the current shortcuts and create new ones.

5.6 You should become familiar with the keyboard shortcuts for the commands you use most frequently.

● **Menus.** When you open menus, keyboard shortcuts are shown next to the commands for which they are available.

● **Mac Help.** Open the Help menu, and search for shortcuts for the Finder and your favorite applications.

153

Configuring keyboard shortcuts

Using the Keyboard system preference's Shortcuts pane, you can configure keyboard shortcuts. You can enable or disable the default keyboard shortcuts, change them, or add your own. Perform the following steps to configure default keyboard shortcuts:

1. **Open the Keyboard system preference, and go to the Shortcuts pane.** At the left, you see a list of standard OS X keyboard shortcuts in various categories, such as Launchpad & Dock, Mission Control, Keyboard, and Screen Shots.

2. **Select the category containing the shortcuts you want to change.** The current commands and associated shortcuts display at the right.

3. **Disable or enable any listed shortcut by deselecting or selecting its check box.**

4. **To change the key combination for a shortcut, double-click that shortcut in the list, and when it is highlighted, press the new key combination you want to use for that command.**

Creating your own keyboard shortcuts

You can follow the steps below to create your own keyboard shortcut for any menu command in any application:

1. **Identify the specific command for which you want to create a keyboard shortcut.** If it is a command specific to an application, note the exact name of the command (including whether it includes an ellipsis). You can find commands on application menus or by accessing an application's Help system.

2. **Go to the Shortcuts pane of the Keyboard system preference.**

3. **Select App Shortcuts in the left side of the pane.**

4. **Click the Add (+) button at the bottom of the list of shortcuts.** The Add Shortcut sheet appears, as shown in Figure 5.7.

5. **From the Application pop-up menu, choose All Applications if you want the shortcut to be available for all applications, or choose a specific application to create the shortcut only for it.**

Note

The applications shown on the Application pop-up menu are only those in the Applications folder. To access an application not shown, choose Other and use the Open dialog that appears to select the application for which you want to create a shortcut.

5.7 You can use this sheet to create your own keyboard shortcuts in any application.

6. **In the Menu Title box, type the name of the command for which you want to create a shortcut exactly as it appears on its menu.** If the command contains an ellipsis, you must also include it. (Press Option+: to enter an ellipse character.)

Note

You can type the name of any command on any menu in an application, even if it is nested within other commands. For example, Word has a Page Break command that you use to manually insert a page break in a document. To choose the command, you open the Insert menu, choose Break, and then choose Page Break. To create a shortcut for this command, type Page Break in the Menu Title field.

7. **In the Keyboard Shortcut field, press the key combination for the shortcut that you want to use to access the command.**

8. **Click Add.** The sheet closes and you return to the Shortcuts pane. The shortcut you just added is shown either under the related application in the Application Shortcuts category or under All Applications if you configured it that way in Step 5.

9. **Open the application in which you created the shortcut.** The keyboard command you created now appears next to the command in the application's menu.

10. **Test the shortcut.** Sometimes, applications already have a shortcut mapped to the one you create, which can cause a conflict. You can resolve these either by disabling the application's shortcut or choosing a different keyboard shortcut.

Navigating with the keyboard

One of the least used (but most useful) aspects of keyboard shortcuts is keyboard navigation. You can use the keyboard to access almost any area on your MacBook Pro in any application, including the Finder. For example, you can open any menu item by using only keys, even if that item does not have a keyboard shortcut assigned to it.

To see what the default keyboard navigation tools are, open the Shortcuts pane of the Keyboard system preference. Next, select Keyboard. The commands and how they work are explained in Table 5.2. Remember that you normally need to hold down the Fn key to use the function keys, as explained earlier in this chapter.

Table 5.2 Keyboard Navigation

Default Shortcut (hold the Fn key down if the standard function key preference is not enabled)	Action	What It Does
Control+F7	Changes how Tab moves focus	By default, pressing the Tab key in windows, dialogs, and panes moves you only between text boxes and lists. This command toggles between that mode and having the Tab key take you to every element in a pane, dialog, or window.
Control+F1	Turns keyboard access on or off	This enables or disables the next five shortcuts.
Control+F2	Moves focus to the menu bar	This highlights the Apple menu; use the Tab or arrow keys to move to other menus and commands on the menu bar.
Control+F3	Moves focus to the Dock	This makes the Finder icon on the Dock active. Use the Tab or arrow keys to move to icons on the Dock.

Default Shortcut (hold the Fn key down if the standard function key preference is not enabled)	Action	What It Does
Control+F4	Moves focus to the active window or next window	This moves into the currently active window or takes you to the next if you are already in a window.
Control+F5	Moves focus to the window toolbar	If you are using an application with a toolbar, this makes the toolbar active. Use the Tab or arrow keys to select a button on the toolbar.
Control+F6	Moves focus to the floating window	If you are using an application that has a floating window, this takes you into that window.
⌘+'	Moves focus to the next window	This moves you among the open windows in the current application.
Option+⌘+'	Moves focus to the window drawer	Some applications use a drawer that appears on the side of the application's window. It contains tools, much like a toolbar. This shortcut moves you into the drawer of the current window.
Control+F8	Moves focus to the status menus	If you have enabled additional menus (such as the Displays menu) in the OS X menu bar, this command highlights the first one. Use the arrow or Pane keys to move to, or select, menus and their commands.
⌘+spacebar	Selects the previous input source	When you have multiple input sources configured, this returns you to the one you used most recently.
Option+⌘+spacebar	Selects next source in Input menu	When you have multiple input sources configured, this moves you to the next one on the menu.

Note

When something, such as a menu, is ready for your action (in other words, when it is selected), OS X calls that *being in focus*. After it is in focus, you can move to any menu or command by pressing the right and left arrow keys simultaneously until the menu you want to use is highlighted. Then use the down-arrow key to open the menu. After it's open, use the down-, up-, left-, and right-arrow keys to select the command you want. When that is selected, press Return to activate it. It takes a little effort to get the hang of this, but after you do, you can quickly move to any menu command.

Using the Character Viewer

The Character Viewer is a tool to help you find special characters in various languages and symbol fonts and quickly apply them to your documents. You can open the Character Viewer in the following ways:

- In the menu bar, click the Input Sources menu and choose Show Character Viewer.
- In the Finder, choose Edit ⇨ Special Characters.

Note

Be sure to select the Show Keyboard & Character Viewers in Menu Bar check box in the Keyboard system preference's Keyboard pane, to have the Input Sources menu appear on the menu bar. Its icon is an asterisk in a box, unless you have multiple keyboard layouts enabled, in which case it is a flag representing the current keyboard layout's country.

When the viewer opens, you see that it has three sections, as shown in Figure 5.8. The section at the left shows the categories of available characters. When you select a category, the characters within it appear in the center section. When you select a character, details about it appear in the right section.

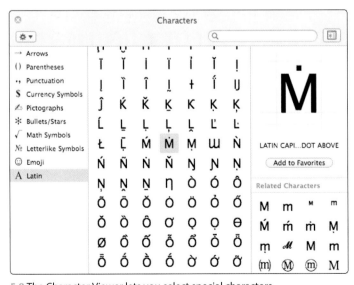

5.8 The Character Viewer lets you select special characters.

Perform these steps to find and use a special character:

1. **In a document, put the cursor where you want to insert a special character.**

2. **Open the Character Viewer.**

3. **Select the category of the character you want to view in the left section of the Character Viewer.** For example, select Math Symbols to view mathematical symbols. The characters in the category you select appear in the center pane.

Genius

To display additional categories of characters, open the Action pop-up menu (the gear icon) and choose Customize List. Select or deselect the check boxes for the categories of characters you want, or do not want, to see.

4. **Select the character you want to insert.** Details about it appear in the right section of the Character Viewer, with a large preview at the upper right.

5. **View the Related subsection and, if available, Font Variation subsection to see different versions of the character by font.** These appear in the lower right of the Character Viewer.

6. **To insert the character, double-click it.** It is inserted into the document using the font variation you selected, if any.

Here are some more pointers about using the Character Viewer:

- **Favorites.** If you click Add to Favorites, the current character is added to your character favorites category, which appears after you add at least one favorite. You see your favorites list by clicking the Favorites category.

- **Recents.** If you click the Recently Used item at the top of the category list, the characters you've used recently appear, and you can use them again. (This item appears only after you have inserted at least one character.)

- **Search.** You can search for characters by typing a description in the Search bar, such as *cedille* to get characters with that accent or *sum* to see mathematical symbols related to summing. Characters meeting your search criterion are shown in the right pane. The Search Results category also appears in the left pane for easy access to your last search.

- **Character size.** To change the size of the characters displayed in the Character Viewer, choose Small, Medium, or Large from the Action pop-up menu.

Using Voice Recognition Effectively

OS X uses voice recognition two ways: to take dictation and to control the MacBook Pro with commands. (Chapter 10 explains how to set up a microphone for your MacBook Pro.)

Using dictation

You set up dictation in the Dictation & Speech system preference, shown in Figure 5.9. Its options are simple:

1. **Select On to enable dictation.**

2. **Select Use Enhanced Dictation to allow for speech recognition when the MacBook Pro is not connected to the Internet.** When you first select this option, OS X downloads the language files needed to work offline.

3. **Choose the Audio source using the menu below the microphone icon.**

4. **Choose the language to be converted to text using the Language pop-up menu.**

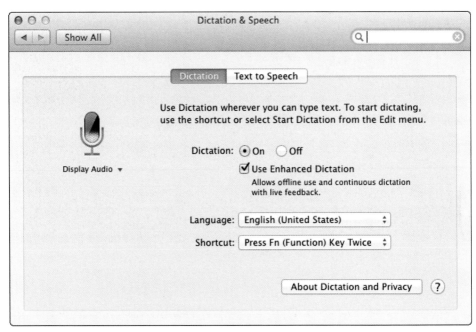

5.9 The Dictation & Speech system preference is where you enable dictation.

5. **Choose the keyboard shortcut to initiate dictation using the Shortcut pop-up menu. The default shortcut is to press Fn twice.**

6. **Quit the System Preferences application.**

To have the MacBook Pro convert your speech into text, have the text cursor active in a text field or other text area, press the dictation shortcut (or choose Edit ⇨ Start Dictation in the application you're dictating into), and begin speaking. The Dictation control appears, as shown in Figure 5.10. Click Done when you're finished speaking, and wait for the text to be inserted. You'll no doubt have to edit it for accuracy, but if you speak clearly and not too fast it does a pretty good job.

5.10 The Dictation control appears while dictation is enabled.

Using voice commands

Designed for people with disabilities, OS X's Speakable Items feature can be a handy way to control your Mac via voice, such as when giving a hands-free presentation. You set up voice control in the Accessibility system preference's Speakable Item pane, shown in Figure 5.11 (select Speakable Items from the bottom of the list at the left).

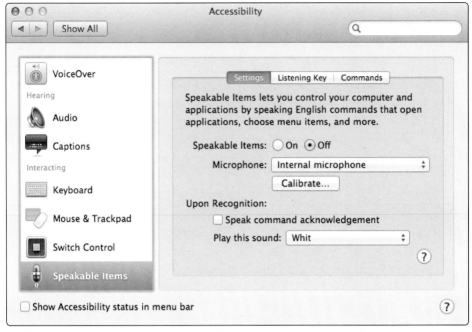

5.11 The Speakable Items pane of the Accessibility system preference.

Here's how to set it up:

1. **In the Settings subpane, select On.**

2. **Choose the audio source from the Microphone pop-up menu.** If you plan to use a Bluetooth headset or a USB microphone, be sure it is connected first, so it appears in the list.

3. **Click Calibrate to run through some speaking examples to help OS X learn your pronunciation and cadence, so it understands you better.**

4. **Choose a sound in the pop-up menu in the Upon Recognition section for the MacBook Pro to play when it understands your command, as an acknowledgment that it understood you.** You can also select the Speak Command Acknowledgment check box to have the MacBook say back to you the command it heard.

5. **In the Listening Key subpane, change the default from Esc by clicking Change Key and entering a new listening key.** The listening key is what you press while you're speaking a command.

6. **If you want OS X to listen always for commands, select the Listen Continuously with Keyword option, and enter the Keyword in the Keyword text field.** In the Keyword Is pop-up menu, choose how OS X should listen for the keyword:

   - **Optional Before Commands** tells OS X to listen for commands continuously, even if you don't speak the keyword. This option can result in inadvertent commands being executed if you're not careful in what you say.

   - **Required Before Each Command** tells OS X to ignore what you say until it hears the specified keyword and then to interpret what you say next as a command.

   - **Required 15 Seconds After the Last Command** tells OS X to not require you to speak the keyword for 15 seconds after the last command it heard. This lets you pause in a sequence of commands without having to say the keyword for each command.

   - **Required 30 Seconds After the Last Command** works the same way, just with a longer pause period.

7. **In the Commands subpane, choose from the available command sets based on what kinds of commands you want OS X to understand.** For some items, the Configure button is available to let you select specific names and words to listen for in commands.

8. **Close the System Preferences application.** The Speakable Items control appears, displaying the listening key or the keyword at the center. When listening, the microphone icon appears in color and the bottom displays the intensity of the audio it hears. Figure 5.12 shows the Speakable Items control in use.

Genius

To see the available commands, click the Open Speakable Items Folder button, which shows a list of the commands for which OS X has the required files to understand.

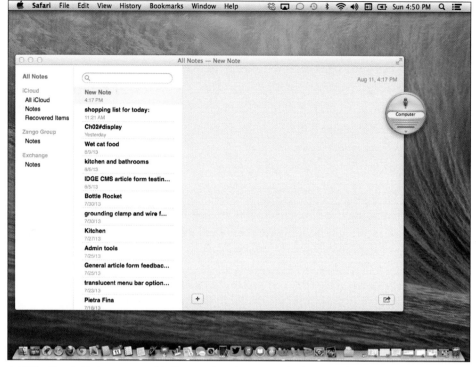

5.12 The Speakable Items control indicates when the MacBook is listening for voice commands.

Maintaining the Battery

To use your MacBook Pro efficiently, it (obviously) must be running. Like all devices with batteries, a MacBook Pro can operate only as long as its battery continues to provide power. Fortunately, with the current models, this is quite a long time. Still, when your battery runs out, your trusty MacBook Pro becomes so much dead weight. To get the most working time while you're mobile, you should practice good energy-management habits. These include a combination of using the OS X battery management tools, conserving battery power, and being prepared to connect to an external power source whenever you have the opportunity.

Saving power with App Nap

Apple works hard to make its devices power-efficient. OS X does lots of work behind the scenes to do that, shutting off or slowing down various components when not in use, and then bringing them back to full strength when needed. OS X Mavericks continues that effort, adding something called App Nap that has applications put themselves to sleep when idle. App Nap is designed so that you don't notice when apps are sleeping or see any delay when they wake back up.

To take advantage of App Nap, you don't do a thing. Application developers need to enable it, and when they do, it works automatically to save power.

Monitoring battery status

You can use the Battery menu to keep an eye on your MacBook Pro's power level. This way, you know how much working time you have left and can take action if you are going to run out of power soon. Perform the following steps to configure the Battery menu on your MacBook Pro:

1. **Open the Energy Saver system preference.**

2. **Select the Show Battery Status in the Menu Bar check box.**

3. **Open the Battery menu in the menu bar by clicking its icon.**

4. **To display the battery-life percentage along with the icon, choose Show Percentage from the Battery menu, as shown in Figure 5.13.**

5. **Quit the System Preferences application.**

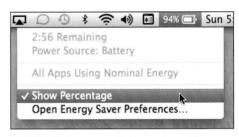

5.13 The Battery menu helps you know the power state of your MacBook Pro.

As you work with your MacBook Pro, keep an eye on the Battery menu, shown in Figure 5.13. At the top of the menu, you see the power status, such as time remaining or how long for it to be fully recharged, as the power source in use (battery or power adapter).

When the battery gets close to being discharged, warnings appear that provide an estimate of the remaining time and recommend that you save your work. If you keep going, the MacBook Pro eventually goes into Sleep mode and you won't be able to wake it until you connect it to a power source.

Although it can remain in Sleep mode for a long time, a MacBook Pro eventually runs out of even the low level of power required to keep it asleep and shuts off. The MacBook Pro goes into a hibernation mode and any open documents are usually saved (though there is a slight chance that any unsaved changes may be lost when this happens). In most cases, you can recover your open documents as soon as you power your MacBook Pro again. Beyond the very minor possibility of losing unsaved changes, there really isn't any risk if you let the MacBook Pro run completely out of power.

When you connect the MacBook Pro to a power source, the battery icon contains the lightning bolt symbol to indicate that it's being charged. When it is fully (or close to fully) charged (about 95 percent or higher), the battery icon shows the electrical plug symbol so you know you don't have to worry about recharging it.

Note When you connect the power adapter to the MacBook Pro, the status light on its magnetic plug is amber while the battery is charging. When fully charged, the status light turns green.

Note The MacBook Pro will vary the power charge between 95 and 100 percent when plugged in to a power source. It does so to optimize the battery's life; that small cycle of draining and recharging makes it last longer. All batteries can be recharged only so many times before they must be replaced, and you'll notice that the battery life decreases even when fully charged. You can expect a MacBook Pro's battery to last several years, and when it is time to replace it, the battery menu will show an alert to that effect.

Extending battery life

You can use the Energy Saver system preference to minimize power use while operating on battery power. You can also adopt simple practices to minimize the amount of power your MacBook Pro uses so that you get the most time possible from the battery.

Using the Energy Saver system preference

In the Energy Saver system preference, you can tailor how the computer uses power and extend the working life of the battery for as long as possible. There are two basic ways to configure power usage on a MacBook Pro: You can use the default settings or customize them. You configure settings separately for operating on battery power and for operating on the power adapter. After they are configured, the MacBook Pro automatically uses the settings for the power source you are using. Follow these steps to set up your MacBook Pro for minimum energy use and maximum working time:

1. **Open the Energy Saver system preference.**

2. **Go to the Battery pane, as shown in Figure 5.14, to configure energy use while operating on battery power.**

3. **Use the top slider to control the amount of idle time before the entire system goes to sleep.** The MacBook Pro uses the least amount of power (only slightly more than when it is shut off) when it is asleep. Of course, it wakes up much faster than it starts up, so sleep is a good thing. You want to set a time that conserves power but doesn't occur so frequently that it interrupts what you are doing.

4. **Use the lower slider to set the amount of idle time before the LCD screen goes dark.** The LCD screen is one of the highest drains on battery power, so you can extend its life by having it sleep after shorter periods of activity. Of course, if it goes to sleep too quickly, it can be intrusive and annoying, so you need to find a good balance between saving power and having your screen go dark.

5. **In most cases, you should leave the Put Hard Disks to Sleep When Possible check box selected.** If you notice that you have to pause frequently during tasks so the MacBook Pro can save data to the hard drive, try deselecting this check box.

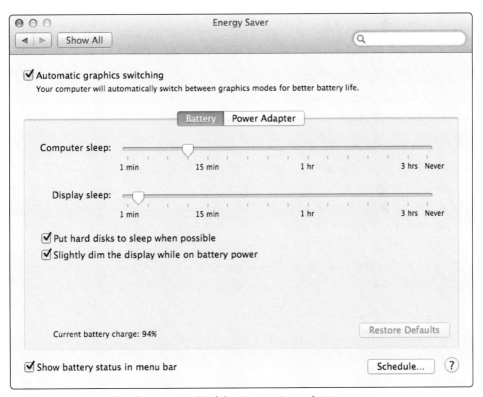

5.14 These options apply when your MacBook Pro is operating on battery power.

6. **Select the Slightly Dim the Display While on Battery Power check box if you want your display to have a lower brightness when operating on the battery.** Dimming causes the screen to go to a lower brightness setting so it uses less power. In my experimentation, it appears that this function reduces screen brightness by about two ticks on the brightness indicator.

Note

To return the energy configuration to what Apple considers optimal for most users, click Restore Defaults.

7. **Select the Automatic Graphics Switching check box.** When selected, the MacBook Pro varies the intensity of its graphics processor—a big power user like the LCD screen, main processor, and hard drive—based on battery charge level. You won't notice this switching in action unless you're running highly rendered or 3D-style games.

8. **Quit the System Preferences application.**

Automatically Starting or Shutting Down the MacBook Pro

You can configure the MacBook Pro to automatically start, sleep, restart, or shut down according to a schedule. Perform these steps to do so:

1. **Open the Energy Saver system preference.**

2. **Click Schedule.** The Schedule sheet appears.

3. **To set an automatic start-up or wake time, select the Start Up or Wake check box.** Next, set the time you want this event to occur using the adjacent pop-up menu and time box.

4. **To set an automatic sleep, restart, or shutdown time, select the lower check box on the sheet.** Choose Sleep, Restart, or Shut Down from the adjacent pop-up menu, and set the time you want the selected event to occur using the adjacent pop-up menu and time box.

5. **Click OK.** The sheet closes, and the schedules you set take effect. (If the lid of the MacBook Pro is shut, the schedule has no effect.)

Adopting low-energy habits

Although configuring the energy use of your MacBook Pro has some impact on how long you can operate on battery power, you can also adopt low-energy habits to further maximize battery life. The following tips can help you do this:

- **Lower the brightness of your display.** Because it makes high demands on battery power, set the brightness of the display at the lowest possible comfortable level to maximize battery life. To dim your screen, use the Brightness slider in the Displays system preference. You can also press F1 to decrease or F2 to increase the brightness.

- **Set the brightness level so it adjusts automatically.** In the Displays system preference, ensure that Automatically Adjust Brightness is enabled. This automatically dims the display in low-light conditions and increases it in brighter environments. If you use the MacBook Pro in bright conditions for extended periods, you may want to disable this and manually set the brightness level to the dimmest comfortable level possible.

- **Avoid applications that constantly read from the hard drive.** Although you probably won't have much choice on this, some applications have settings that affect hard drive use, such as autosave features. You can increase the amount of time between automatic saves to reduce hard drive use and, thereby, save energy.

- **Save your files less while working on them.** Each save takes power, and the "save often" mantra that many of us learned in the early days of computing is less necessary with today's more reliable computers.

- **Avoid applications that constantly read from a CD or DVD.** If you can copy the files that you need onto your hard drive, you use power at a lower rate than if your MacBook Pro is constantly accessing its optical drive. For example, when you want to listen to music or watch movies, add the content to your iTunes library so you don't need to use the optical drive.

- **Use an iPod, iPhone, or iPad.** Playing content in iTunes requires lots of hard drive activity, and iTunes is a heavy battery-power user. If you can use another device for these tasks, it saves your MacBook Pro for those you can only do (or do best) on it.

- **Configure keyboard backlighting.** When you are in low-light conditions, the backlit keys make your MacBook Pro much easier to use. However, backlighting also uses more power. Try to reduce the amount of time for which, and the level of brightness at which, the keys are backlit. These settings are in the Keyboard pane of the Keyboard system preference. You can also press F5 to decrease or F6 to increase the brightness of the backlighting.

● **Put your MacBook Pro to sleep whenever you aren't actively using it by closing the lid.** When you open the lid or press a key, the MacBook Pro wakes up quickly, so putting it to sleep frequently doesn't waste lots of time.

Genius

You can also set a hot corner for display sleep by clicking the Hot Corners button in the Mission Control system preference. If you aren't going to be using your MacBook Pro for a little while, move the pointer to that hot corner to put the display to sleep.

Powering your MacBook Pro while traveling

If you are traveling for a long time, the odds are good that you're going to run out of battery power, even if you tweaked your MacBook Pro for maximum operating time and practice low-energy habits. You can reduce the chances of running out of power by being ready to power your MacBook Pro while you are on the move.

Note

Most airports have power outlets available in the gate areas, but they aren't always obvious to see and can be hidden by chairs or other obstacles. Some airports have charging stations, which provide a handy way to top off your MacBook Pro's battery.

The following are some recommended items that can help you manage your power on the move:

● **Standard power adapter.** Whenever there's a power outlet available, use the MacBook Pro's power adapter to run it and charge its battery.

● **MagSafe Airline Adapter.** With this adapter, you can connect your MacBook Pro to the power outlet available in some airline seats. The seat must have an EmPower or 20mm power port.

Caution

Although the airline adapter looks like it might be compatible with the DC power port in automobiles, it isn't.

- **International adapters.** If you travel internationally, get a set of power adapters so you can connect the MacBook Pro power adapter to power outlets in a variety of countries. Apple makes a nice kit that provides a set of small plugs that go into the back of the power brick in place of your standard plug; it's more space-efficient than many universal adapters.

iCloud is a suite of web-based services that syncs your data across your devices via the Internet and stores data so you can access it from your MacBook Pro, iPhone, iPad, iPod touches, and even a web browser. This keeps e-mail, contacts, calendars, music, e-books, photos, documents, bookmarks, passwords, and so on in sync on all your devices, so the same information is available to you regardless of the device you're using. You can store documents on iCloud and work on the same version of them on each device. An iCloud account includes access to a website with applications so you can work with your information from any computer.

Getting Started with iCloud

To use iCloud, you need an iCloud account. The good news is that obtaining an iCloud account is fast, easy, and free. A free account includes access to most of the services described in this chapter, along with 5GB of online storage space. After you obtain an account, you sign into it on your MacBook Pro and iOS devices so iCloud services are available on each of them. Then you access the iCloud website to become familiar with the functions it provides.

You may already have an iCloud account and just don't realize it. For example, if you have shopped at the iTunes Store, you created an Apple ID. You use this same Apple ID for your iCloud account. If you don't have an Apple ID, creating one takes only a few minutes.

Follow these steps to create a new iCloud account:

1. **Open the iCloud system preference by choosing ⇨ System Preferences and clicking the iCloud icon.**

2. **Click Create an Apple ID.**

3. **Follow the on-screen instructions to complete the process.** When finished, you are logged in to your new iCloud account and can configure the services you want to use.

4. **In the dialog that appears, leave the two options (one is Use iCloud for Mail, Contacts, Calendars, Reminders Notes, and Safari, and the other is Use Find My Mac) selected and click Next.**

5. **Enter your MacBook Pro's Administrator password if requested.**

6. **Click Allow when asked for permission to use your location for Find My Mac.**

You're now ready to configure iCloud services, which I explain later in this chapter.

If you already have an iCloud account, just sign into the iCloud system preference using your Apple ID (or separate iCloud ID if you have one), and password, then click Sign In, then follow Steps 4 through 6 for creating a new account. You may also be asked to approve this device for use with iCloud Keychain; click OK if so. This feature is new to OS X Mavericks.

Note   When you create an iCloud account, you have the option of also creating a new iCloud e-mail address or using an existing one. If you choose to use an existing e-mail address, it becomes your Apple ID. This chapter assumes you are working with an iCloud e-mail address.

Synchronizing Data on Multiple Devices

One of the most useful features of iCloud is that you can make the same information available on your MacBook Pro, other Macs, iPhones, iPads, and iPod touches. This information includes e-mail, contacts, calendars, passwords, reminders, notes, and bookmarks. To use data synchronization, you configure the specific data you want to keep synchronized on each device.

Note iCloud also syncs music, podcasts, books, videos, and courses obtained through Apple's iTunes and related stores across your Macs and iOS devices. Books you buy in iBooks, as well as the annotations you make in them, are synced in iBooks in OS X and iOS. Music you buy on one device is downloaded to the others. The same is true for other media. The secret to syncing is to make sure it is enabled. On your MacBook Pro, open the Preferences dialog in iTunes, go to the Store pane, and select the Music and Apps check boxes. In both iBooks and iTunes, be sure you are signed in with the same Apple ID. On your iOS devices, open the Settings app, go to the iTunes & App Store pane, and turn on the Music, Apps, and Books switches (but turn off the Cellular Data switch to prevent eating up your cellular data plan due to automatic downloads).

Configuring iCloud on a MacBook Pro

Use the following steps to determine which information on your MacBook Pro (or any other Mac, for that matter) is synced on iCloud:

1. **Open the iCloud system preference, shown in Figure 6.1.**
2. **Select the check boxes for the information you want to sync.**
3. **Deselect the check boxes for information you don't want to sync.**

You can configure the following types of information to sync between your MacBook Pro and iCloud:

- **Mail.** This causes your iCloud e-mail to be enabled in the Mail application when selected—or disabled when deselected.

- **Contacts.** When you enable this setting, the contact information stored in the Contacts application is copied to iCloud. It can then be accessed there via the Contacts web application and on any other device that is set up to sync contact information. When changes are made to contacts on any iCloud-connected device, they are also made on your MacBook Pro.

6.1 Use the iCloud system preference to determine the types of information you want to sync on your MacBook Pro.

- **Calendars.** Use this check box to sync your calendars from the Calendar application.

- **Reminders.** Use this check box to sync reminders from the Reminders application so you can access them on any synced device.

- **Notes.** With this enabled, notes you manage in the Notes application are copied to iCloud. Likewise, any notes synced from other devices are copied to your MacBook Pro.

- **Safari.** This setting causes your Safari bookmarks and Reading List entries to be copied to and from iCloud. This is a great way to easily access your favorite websites from any iCloud-enabled device. Also, any web pages currently open or recently opened on any of your iCloud-connected devices are available in Safari on every other device, using the iCloud Tabs feature in Safari.

- **Keychain.** With this enabled, the passwords and credit card information saved in Safari are synced across all your iCloud-connected devices. This topic is covered in detail later in this chapter.

● **Photos.** With Photos enabled, your MacBook Pro can access the photo storage that is included as part of your iCloud account. After you enable Photo on the iCloud system preference, configure iPhoto (which is installed on a new MacBook Pro) and/or Aperture (which can be purchased and downloaded from the App Store) to sign into iCloud. Do so in the Preferences dialog in the applications, go to the iCloud pane, and select all the Photo Stream options. When new photos are added to your Photo Stream, they are automatically added to your photo library. Likewise, when you add new photos to the library, such as by importing them from a digital camera, they are added to the Photo Stream, and thus, moved onto the other devices on which Photo Stream is enabled.

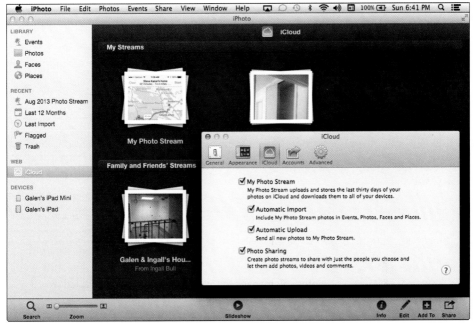

6.2 Photo Stream, which is being enabled in iPhoto in this figure, is a great way to protect photos you take with an iOS device because they are automatically downloaded to your MacBook Pro—just as any photos imported into iPhoto on your Mac from cameras, websites, and so on, are uploaded to Photo Stream and available on your iOS devices.

Genius

If you use an iOS device (such as an iPhone) to take photos, you should definitely use Photo Stream because it temporarily backs up your photos on iCloud and permanently stores them on your MacBook Pro. If something happens to the iOS device, it is unlikely that you will lose any photos. (Note that the iOS device must be connected to the Internet for photos to be copied to and from iCloud.)

- **Documents & Data.** This setting allows iCloud-enabled applications to store documents on iCloud so you can work with them from any iCloud-enabled Mac or iOS device. This topic is covered in detail later in this chapter.

- **Back to My Mac.** This lets you use your iCloud account to access services on one Mac from a different Mac, including file and screen sharing. For example, suppose you are traveling with your MacBook Pro and want to access files stored on your iMac in a different location. With Back to My Mac, you can connect to the iMac and use file sharing to get to the files you want, just as if you were sitting at that computer.

- **Find My Mac.** You can use this to locate or secure a Mac that is no longer in your control. It is explained in detail later in this chapter.

Caution   iCloud syncs data in iCloud accounts. Some applications—Calendars, Contacts, Mail, Notes, and Reminders—work with other services, such as Microsoft Exchange, IMAP-standard e-mail services, and Google's various services like Gmail. Data from those services is also synced across your Macs and iOS devices—*if* they are set up on all those devices. iCloud does not sync their data, just its own, so be sure you have set them up on all devices for which you want their data to stay up to date.

In the iCloud pane, click the Account Details button to change the name associated with the iCloud account as well as to connect to Apple to manage your Apple ID.

At the bottom of the iCloud pane, the iCloud Storage gauge (refer to Figure 6.1) shows how much iCloud storage is available. By default, your iCloud account includes 5GB of storage space. This is usually fine if you primarily use iCloud to sync information. If you use iCloud to sync documents, you may want to add storage to your account, which you do by clicking Manage. The Manage sheet appears, as shown in Figure 6.3. On the left side of this sheet, you see the various types of information currently stored on iCloud, such as backups and e-mail. You also see applications configured to store documents on iCloud, such as Pages or Numbers. When you select a type of information, details about it are displayed in the right pane.

You can manage how information is being stored in various ways. For example, you can select a document and click Delete to remove it from iCloud. You can also click Delete All to remove all of the selected type of information from iCloud. If you click Buy More Storage, a sheet appears where you can add storage space or downgrade if you don't need the space you have.

If you click View Account on the Manage Storage sheet, you can view and change certain information about your account, such as your Apple ID, your storage plan, payment information, and the country/region associated with your account.

6.3 Use this Manage sheet to work with your iCloud storage space, such as deleting individual files from iCloud.

Configuring iCloud on an iOS device

iCloud is a perfect match for iOS devices, which are iPhones, iPads, and iPod touches. If you have any of these, you can take advantage of iCloud by following these steps and configuring its services on the device:

1. **Open the Settings app.**

2. **Tap iCloud to open the iCloud pane.** If you haven't signed in, you are asked to do so or to set up an account. If you're prompted about merging information already on your iCloud account, tap Don't Merge if you don't want the information on your device to be moved to your iCloud account. Tap Merge if you do. If prompted about location, tap Allow to allow iCloud to access your device's location, or click Don't Allow if you don't want this to happen. You need to allow this for some features (such as Find My iPhone) to work.

3. **Set the slider to the On position next to each kind of information you want to sync on your device, as shown in Figure 6.4.** If you set a slider to the Off position, that information won't sync between your iCloud account and the device. The options you have on an iOS device are the same as those on a MacBook Pro (which are described earlier in this chapter), except there is no Back to My Mac or similar option for iOS devices.

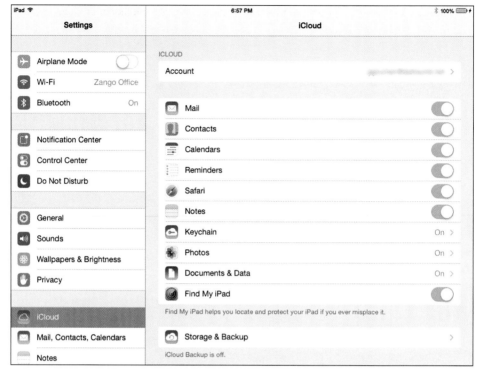

6.4 You can configure the information you want to sync on an iOS device by setting the switches to On for the data you want.

Using iCloud Keychain

iCloud syncs lots of information among your Macs and iOS devices. With the iCloud Keychain capability introduced in OS X Mavericks and iOS 7, it also shares passwords and credit card information in Safari, so when you save those items on one device, it's available on all your devices.

After iCloud Keychain is enabled in the iCloud system preference, you should set up the keychain restoration code that any device must have entered to access those saved passwords and credit card numbers. Do so by following these steps:

1. **Open the iCloud system preference.**

2. **Click Account Details to open the settings sheet, shown in Figure 6.5.**

3. **Select the Restore with iCloud Security Code check box, and enter a four-digit passcode that other devices must have entered to access iCloud Keychain.** This passcode is in addition to the Apple ID that must be entered.

4. **Enter an SMS-capable phone number in the field below.** An additional one-time verification code is sent to your Macs and iOS devices (received by Messages) when they try to restore access to iCloud Keychain.

6.5 Setting a restoration code lets you enable access to iCloud Keychain even when another connected device is not available to verify the connection request.

5. **Click OK when you're finished.**

6. **Quit the System Preferences application.**

When you enable iCloud Keychain on a Mac or iOS device, an alert appears on all devices connected to iCloud Keychain asking whether to approve the device trying to use the service. You can enter your Apple ID on any of those devices to approve it. But if none of those devices is handy, you can have them restore the iCloud Keychain. You must enter your Apple ID and your iCloud security code. Then wait for Messages to receive the one-time verification code, which you then must enter. All three steps are required to restore access when another device is not available to enable access. If you enter the verification code incorrectly, you must run the restoration process again.

After iCloud Keychain is enabled on your MacBook Pro and other devices, you can use it. When you enter a password or credit card, Safari asks if you want to save it. If so, when you click or tap a password or credit card field on a web page, iCloud Keychain offers to fill in the password or credit card information, as Figure 6.6 shows. (You still must enter the CVV code on the back of the card manually if required by the merchant; iCloud Keychain does not store this code, as a safety precaution in case someone gains access to your Mac or iOS device.)

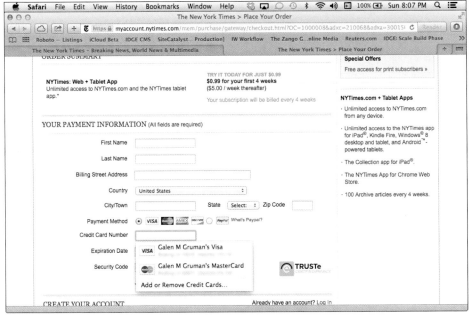

6.6 iCloud Keychain offers to fill in credit card information and passwords in web pages.

Genius

An easy way to get your credit card information into iCloud Keychain is to open the Preferences dialog in Safari (choose Safari ⇨ Preferences) and go to the AutoFill pane. Click the Edit button to the right of Credit Cards entry, and in the settings sheet that appears, click Add and enter the credit card information. You can also double-click a card's description to change it to something you prefer. To delete a card, select it and click Remove. To prevent Safari from storing or offering to provide passwords or credit card information, deselect the corresponding options in the AutoFill pane. Click Done when you're finished, and close the Preferences dialog.

Using iCloud with Documents

If you have multiple devices (and who doesn't these days?), you probably want to share documents on all of them so that you need not be concerned whether you are using the most current version of that document—or even have to remember to copy the documents from one device to another. You can store documents in iCloud. Applications that support iCloud document storage can then access those documents from any device you use, and you can access them from any computer.

Genius To see which apps on your MacBook Pro are using iCloud Documents, click the Options button to the right of Documents & Data in the iCloud system preference to open a settings sheet listing those apps. If you want to disable an app's use of iCloud Documents, deselect the check box next to the app's name.

The iCloud Documents capability isn't a general Internet-based storage site like Google Drive, Dropbox, or Box. Those services act like big hard drives, storing all files for access by any compatible application on any device. You can even browse their contents as if they were a local hard drive. By contrast, iCloud Documents is application-specific: For example, Apple's Pages on a MacBook Pro or iOS device can see and access Pages documents in iCloud, but other applications can't see or work with those files, and Pages can't see other file types like TextEdit documents.

Furthermore, only applications purchased from the Mac App Store or iOS App Store are allowed to use iCloud Documents. The only exceptions are some applications that come installed in OS X, including AppleScript Editor, Automator, Preview, and TextEdit.

In other words, iCloud Documents is not for general shared storage but for application-specific shared storage and syncing.

Because iCloud Documents is application-specific, you cannot attach documents in iCloud to an e-mail in Mail or to a message in Messages, or upload it to an Internet location via an application like Safari or an FTP client. You must move or copy the file from iCloud to the Mac first. However, from the Open dialog of an iCloud-compatible application, you can select one or more documents and use the Share button to send the files via Mail or Messages; doing so creates a new e-mail or message with the file attached—just like how iCloud Documents works in iOS.

When an application is iCloud-enabled, it has two buttons at the top of the Open and Save dialogs: iCloud and On My Mac, as Figure 6.7 shows. Click the button to see the available documents in each location and navigate them.

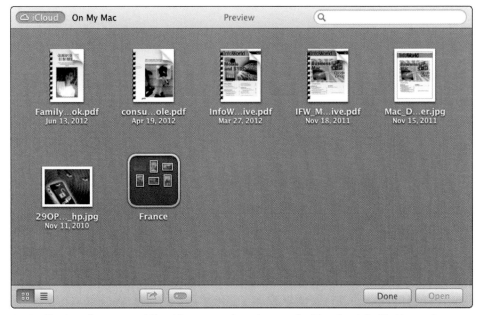

6.7 Applications that support iCloud Documents have buttons for iCloud and On My Mac to choose where they open files from and save them to.

When saving a document the first time, you can choose to save it in iCloud or on your Mac, but after that, each time you save the document, it's saved to the same location. To change that location, choose File ➪ Move To and select a new location. You can also drag files and folders into and out of the iCloud view of the Open dialog to move them between your Mac and iCloud. To copy, not move, documents between iCloud and your MacBook, choose File ➪ Duplicate after opening the document instead.

To delete a file from iCloud, right-click it in the iCloud view of the Open dialog and choose Move to the Trash from the contextual menu that appears. To delete a folder from iCloud, remove the documents from it by dragging and dropping them outside the folder. After the last document is removed, the folder is deleted.

When the document is open in the application, choose File ➪ Duplicate to make a copy of the document, and then choose File ➪ Save to save that copy, at the same or new location as the original. In the iCloud view of the Open dialog, you can also right-click a document and choose Duplicate from the contextual menu.

Working with iCloud's Web Applications

The iCloud website has applications you can use for e-mail, contacts, notes, reminders, and calendars—even when you're using someone else's Mac or even a Windows PC. You can also use the Find My iPhone feature to locate your MacBook Pro and secure it if it's out of your control. You can store, access, and even create and edit documents there, too, using web versions of Apple's iWork suite, if you also bought these applications for your MacBook Pro.

Note The iCloud Find My iPhone service lets you find a lost or stolen Mac—not just iPhones—and lock or even wipe the computer so its data can be protected, as Chapter 13 explains.

To access these features, follow the steps below to log in to the iCloud website:

1. **In your browser, go to www.icloud.com.**

2. **Enter your Apple ID and password.** To save your information on the computer so you can move directly into your website when you come back to this address, select the Keep Me Signed In check box.

3. **Click the right-facing arrow, or press Return.** You log in to your account and can work with the iCloud web applications or manage your account on the iCloud home screen, as shown in Figure 6.8.

Managing your iCloud account

One of the functions available on your iCloud website is the ability to manage your account. On the iCloud home screen, click the account link (which shows your name) at the top of the iCloud window. You then see the Account dialog.

You can do all of these things in the Account dialog:

● **Change the image associated with your account by hovering the pointer over it and clicking Edit when it appears.** In the pop-over that appears, you can change the zoom level of the image using the slider at the bottom. To change the image, hover your pointer over it and click Choose Photo when it appears to open a dialog from which you can select a new image on your MacBook Pro.

Safari File Edit View History Bookmarks Develop Window Help ✳ 奈 ◆ ⬔ Mon 1:54 PM Galen Gruman Q ☰

6.8 After you're logged in to iCloud.com, you see the applications available for your iCloud account.

- ⊙ **Change the language or time zone associated with your account.** Click the Language or Time Zone links, and change their settings in the pop-overs that appear.

- ⊙ **Control which services you get notifications from when logged into iCloud on the web.** Click Notifications to open a window that lets you select which services to display notifications for: Mail, Calendar, Reminders, and Find My iPhone.

- ⊙ **Get help from Apple's website by clicking the Help button**. You can also get help from the iCloud Home screen by clicking its Help button (the ? icon).

- ⊙ **Click your Apple ID to open the My Apple ID website, where you can manage its settings.**

After you finish making changes, click Done. Your changes are saved, and the dialog closes.

Note

If you ever forget your password or want to reset it, go to http://appleid.apple.com. Here, you can reset your password or manage your account. You can also create another iCloud account.

Working with iCloud's e-mail and information management applications

The iCloud website lets you use five applications that you likely regularly use on your MacBook Pro and on your iPhone or other iOS device: Mail, Contacts, Calendar, Reminders, and Notes. Click an application's icon to open it. To go back to the iCloud Home screen, click the iCloud icon button in the upper left of each application window.

Note

If you configured your MacBook to sync this information with your iCloud account via the iCloud system preference, these applications let you access, change, and add to the synced information. If you don't allow syncing, you can still use these applications, but the information they contain is available only on the website. iCloud on the web cannot access data from other sync services, such as Google or Exchange, that you may have set up on your MacBook Pro.

As Figure 6.9 shows, working with the iCloud web applications is similar to working with their OS X and iOS counterparts. You'll see familiar layouts and buttons, so if you know how to use them on your MacBook, you know how to use them on iCloud.com.

The one application that works differently is Mail. Sending, receiving, replying to, forwarding, and deleting messages, as well as creating mail rules, work as they do on the MacBook Pro (see Chapter 7). But the web version offers two handy tools not available for the OS X or iOS versions, especially when you are traveling:

- Automatic e-mail forwarding
- Vacation messages

To get to these controls, click the Settings button (the gear icon) at the upper right of the Mail window and choose Preferences in the pop-over that appears.

Go to the General pane to have your messages sent to your iCloud address forwarded to a different e-mail address, such as that of a colleague when you are on vacation, as shown in Figure 6.10. Select the Forward My Email To check box and enter the e-mail address to forward e-mail to in the adjacent text field. You can have iCloud delete the e-mails from your iCloud after forwarding them by selecting the Delete Messages After Forwarding check box, but I suggest you keep a copy in iCloud for later reference.

6.9 The iCloud web versions of Mail, Contacts, Calendar (shown here), Notes, and Reminders work very much like their OS X versions.

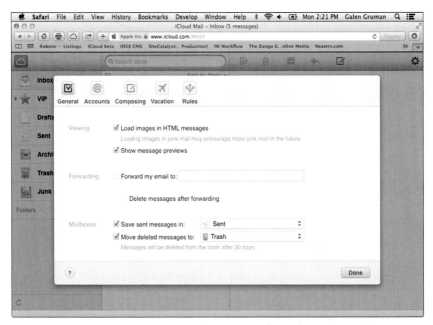

6.10 The Mail application on the iCloud website lets you forward e-mail to another account—when you are on vacation, for example.

Go to the Vacation pane to have an automatic reply sent to anyone who e-mails your iCloud address. Select the Automatically Reply to Messages When They Are Received check box, and enter the text you want in that automatic reply in the text field below.

Click the Done button when you've changed the preferences. And be sure to undo the forwarding and vacation replies when you're back.

Using iWork in the Cloud

If you have purchased any of Apple's iWork applications—Pages, Numbers, or Keynote—from the Mac App Store, you can use them at the iCloud website from a Mac or Windows PC. That's right: You don't need to have the applications installed on your computer, and you can finally use these OS X-only applications from a Windows PC.

Apple has made the applications available on it its iCloud website, so you should see them when you sign in to iCloud.com on the home screen. As this book went to press, the three web iWork applications were not finalized, so only prerelease versions, known as betas, were available. And not all users will see these applications when they sign in to iCloud until the final versions are available; Apple has been slowly adding people to the beta access program.

Caution Because the tools aren't final, it's not clear what functionality the web iWork tools won't have that the OS X and iOS versions do, nor if there will be any formatting that will be removed for files opened and saved on the web. So you should work on copies of your documents until these compatibility issues are fully known.

Just as the web versions of Mail, Contacts, Calendar, Notes, and Reminders are very much like their OS X and iOS versions, so too are the web versions of Pages, Keynote, and Numbers. As with the OS X versions, you can drag iWork, Microsoft Office, and other compatible files from the Desktop into the document window that appears when you open an application from the iCloud website. Doing so copies them to iCloud. Figure 6.11 shows a document window.

The document window contains any compatible documents stored in iCloud—meaning those you created in iCloud from the iWork application on your MacBook Pro, saved to iCloud from iWork on your Mac, or created or saved in iWork on your iOS device.

6.11 The document window for the web version of the Keynote application at iCloud.com.

Here are the key differences to note:

- You cannot drag files from the web iWork document windows to your Desktop to copy them from iCloud to your MacBook Pro. Instead, select one or more documents, and choose Download Document from the Settings pop-over, which you open by clicking the Settings button (the gear icon) in the document window. You can also e-mail selected documents from your iCloud account (not from other accounts) by choosing Send a Copy from that same pop-over.

- Use the iCloud icon button at the upper right of an iWork web application's document window to close that window and return to the iCloud home screen; any documents for that application remain open. To close a document itself, use the standard Close button in the upper left of its window. Closing a document saves any changes.

● Formatting and other controls are accessed via the Format panel on the right side of an open document, as Figure 6.12 shows. Clicking a button in the toolbar at the top usually opens its controls in that panel, but it may open a pop-over under the toolbar.

● The Share button at the upper right of an open document lets you send a copy of the document in its native iWork format, in the equivalent Microsoft Office format, or as a PDF file attached to a message from your iCloud e-mail account (not from other accounts).

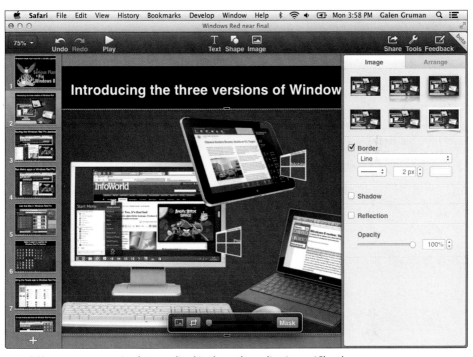

6.12 A Keynote presentation being edited in the web application at iCloud.com.

Your MacBook Pro comes with the software needed to help you keep in touch. The Contacts application stores contact information that you can use in many applications, including Mail, Safari, and Messages. You also can access your contacts from your iPhone, iPod touch, or iPad, thanks to Contacts' ability to synchronize across devices. E-mail is a great way to communicate, and the Mail application offers a flexible set of tools to do so.

Using Accounts in Contacts

The Contacts application is a central repository for all your contacts. That means it can connect to multiple accounts and access address cards from each, as well as update the cards in those accounts. This is how contacts stay synced across all your devices; devices signed into the same accounts get their contacts synced across all those accounts. Although you can store contacts just on your MacBook Pro on the On My Mac "account," the only reason to do so is for private contacts you don't want available on your iPhone or other devices.

When you set up accounts in the Internet Accounts system preference, you can specify whether to sync their contacts to the Contacts application. If so, the contacts in those services—Facebook, LinkedIn, Google Contacts, work contacts from a business's Microsoft Exchange server, and of course your iCloud account—become available in the Contacts application.

As Figure 7.1 shows, the left side of the Contacts application shows all the accounts it's connected to. Click All Contacts to see all the contacts available, or click the name of an account to see just those contacts. Some accounts may have groups of contacts, and those groups appear under the account name, so you can select it and see just the members of that group.

7.1 The Contacts application shows all connected accounts, and their groups, on its left side.

Note

OS X Mavericks gets rid of the multiple Contacts views of previous OS X versions. It shows the full, or Cards, view, and no longer has options to display the Lists and Card Only views. But it does have an option to hide the accounts/groups list at the left: Choose Hide⇨ Hide Groups or press ⌘+1.

Setting Up Internet Accounts

The Internet Accounts system preference (called Mail, Contacts & Calendars prior to OS X Mavericks) is where you should set up your contacts, e-mail, calendar, to-do list, notes, and social networking accounts. Although you can set up many of these accounts in the applications that use them, such as Contacts and Mail, doing so means you're not getting the full value of the MacBook Pro. By using Internet Accounts for setup, you're making the data in all those accounts accessible to all applications that can work with them, making it easier to find and exchange information.

To set up an account and its related services, follow these steps:

1. **Open the Internet Accounts system preference by choosing ⇨ System Preferences and clicking Internet Accounts.**

2. **Click the name of the account you want to add, such as iCloud, Google, or Exchange**. If those accounts are not listed at the right, click the Add (+) button below the installed-accounts list at the left to have them appear. To add an unlisted e-mail account, such as the one provided by your Internet service provider, click Add Other Account and select the type of account to be added (such as Mail or Messages).

3. **In the settings sheet that appears, enter the requested information, such as name, e-mail or other account address, and password.** Then click Set Up, Sign In, or Next (the button varies based on the service).

4. **For accounts that support multiple types of services, a settings sheet appears that lets you select the ones you want the MacBook Pro to use, as shown in the figure below.** Select them, and click Done. The services available vary from account to account. iCloud, Google, Exchange, and e-mail accounts using the IMAP protocol all support multiple types of services. LinkedIn, Twitter, and Facebook let you sync their contacts with your MacBook's Contacts application.

continued

continued

5. **Repeat Steps 1 through 4 for each account you want to enable on your MacBook Pro.**

6. **Quit the System Preferences application when you're finished.**

You can change the configuration for a service by clicking its name in the left pane and adjusting the settings in the right pane.

Adding Contact Information to Contacts

The Contacts application uses an address card model, which originated with the Rolodex and Filofax paper card systems way back in the analog era. Each contact, be it a person or an organization, is represented by a card containing contact information. Contacts' address cards are flexible, letting you can store a variety of information on each one and even link cards together for related people.

In fact, each card in Contacts can hold an unlimited number of physical or e-mail addresses, phone numbers, dates, notes, and URLs. Because cards are flexible, you don't have to include each piece of information for every contact; you can include just the info that you have. Contacts (with a few exceptions) displays only fields that have data in them, so your cards don't have lots of empty fields.

Configuring the card template

When you create a new card, it is based on the Contacts card template, which determines the data fields that are on the card initially. You can change what information is included on the template and thus on the cards you create. You should configure the template before you start creating cards so they include the specific information you want.

Note If you've been using a Mac or other computer and have imported or synced contacts data to Contacts, your cards include any information those other cards did, whether or not you adjusted the Contacts card template.

Follow these steps to configure the Contacts card template:

1. **Open the Contacts Preferences dialog by choosing Contacts ⇨ Preferences.**

2. **Go to the Template pane, shown in Figure 7.2.**

3. **You can modify the template in any of the following ways:**

    - **Remove fields you don't want by clicking the Delete (–) button.**

    - **Add more fields of an existing type by clicking the Add (+) button next to that type.** Choose the label for the new field on the pop-up menu to its left.

    - **Rename any field in the template by choosing a different label on the pop-up menu to its left.**

    - **Add types of fields that don't appear on the template by opening the Add Field pop-up menu at the top of the dialog and choosing the type you want to add.** Fields that are already on the template are marked with a check mark and grayed out. After you make a selection, the new field appears on the template in the appropriate location based on the type of field you added (for example, the Nickname field appears at the top of the card, just below the first and last names).

4. **Close the Preferences dialog.** Both new cards that you create and cards that already exist include the template's fields.

Genius

I recommend that you add the Profile and Related Names fields to your template. The Profile field lets you add social media addresses for your contacts, such as for Twitter or Facebook. The Related Names field lets you enter the names of people related to the person (such as parent, manager, spouse, or sibling), providing a way to trace your contacts when needed, such as to find a colleague's manager when that colleague is on vacation.

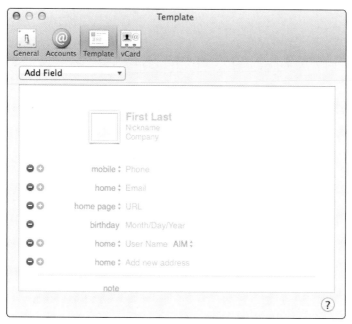

7.2 Configure the Contacts template so it contains the fields you want on your cards.

Creating and editing contact cards

Adding a contact card is really easy. There are four basic methods, one you do in Contacts, one you do in Mail, one you do from any of several applications, and one you do from the Internet Accounts system preference:

- **In Contacts, choose File ➪ New Card to open a blank card, as shown in Figure 7.3.** Fill in the information you have for that person, and click Done.

- **In Mail, click a person's name or e-mail address from the header at the top of the message, right-click it, and choose Add to Contacts from the contextual menu that appears.** The Contacts application opens, displaying a blank card for you to complete. Click Done when you're finished.

- **From any application that can include file attachments, such as Mail and Messages, you can take a vCard file someone sends you and import it into Contacts.** Drag the vCard file (its filename extension is .vcf) from the application into Contacts, or save the file onto your Desktop and drag it into Contacts from there. Either way, Contacts creates a new card.

Note   To send someone a vCard of a card stored in Contacts, right-click the card in Contacts, choose Export vCard from the contextual menu that appears, and follow the prompts. Then send the card to whomever you want to share it with. Even easier, click the Share button under the selected card's details and choose the desired sharing Method: Email Card, Message Card, or AirDrop Card. (Chapter 4 covers sharing methods.)

- **In the Internet Accounts system preference, select the account whose contacts you want to access and click Contacts in the pane at the right.** All contacts in those accounts appear in Contacts in their own contacts cards.

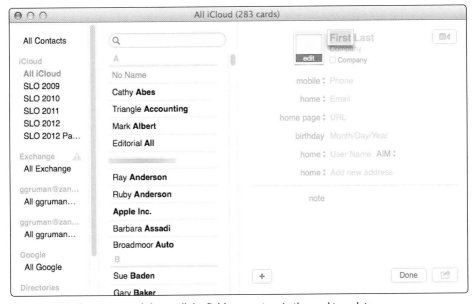

7.3 A new, blank contact card shows all the fields you set up in the card template.

To edit a card, select it and click Edit at the bottom of the card. You get the same view as for a new card, except the card you're editing displays any information it already has.

Note If you have multiple accounts set up in Contacts, such as iCloud, Google Contacts, Facebook, LinkedIn, and/or Exchange, first select the account from the list at the left before adding the card, so Contacts knows which account to put the new card into. If you don't choose an account—which you can't do when adding contacts from Mail—the new contact goes in the default account. You can change that default in Contacts' Preferences dialog using the Default Account pop-up menu in the General pane.

When creating or editing a card, the process is mostly straightforward, but there are a few tips and tricks to note:

- **Use the pop-up menu next to a field to select the type of contact information you want to enter, and type the information for that field.** For example, choose Mobile from the pop-up menu next to a Phone field, and type the mobile phone number. The label of a pop-up menu can be confusing. For example, the one labeled Mother is what shows by default for the Related Names field, but if you open that pop-up menu, you see Father, Brother, Sister, and many more relationships. Likewise, the pop-up menu for Profile may show Twitter, but click it to choose other social accounts such as Facebook and LinkedIn.

- **Many fields can have more than one entry, even though only one entry shows initially.** For example, the Related Names field shows Mother by default. It may seem you can choose only one relationship, but note the Add button (the green + icon) to its left: Click it to add another pop-up menu for the Related Names field, such as Father. You can add as many as you like. And you can add more than one instance of each field, so if Heather has two mommies, for example, her card can have two Mother fields.

- **To remove a field from the card, click its Delete button (the red – icon).** The Delete button appears only after you have entered information for a field.

- **If the information you want to enter isn't available on a pop-up menu, choose Custom in that pop-up menu.** Type the label for the field you want to add, and click OK. You return to the card, and the custom label appears on it. Type the information for that field to add it to the card. You could use this to add different relationships to the Related Names field or new social networks to the Profile field.

- **To add or change a person's image or its placeholder, double-click it.** A pop-up opens where you can choose a new one, as well as crop and resize it by clicking Edit and using the crop window and sizing slider that appear. Note the Linked section of the pop-up shown in Figure 7.4; this section shows images of that person from linked social accounts. You can also just select the image or placeholder and paste an image into it or drag an image onto it, or you can choose Card ⇨ Choose Custom Image to open a dialog from which to select an image for that card.

Note

The image for a contact appears next to his or her name in Mail, FaceTime, and Messages, and it syncs to your iPhone so that person's picture appears on the screen when he or she calls you.

- **If a card is for a company rather than a person, choose Card ⇨ Mark as a Company or press ⌘+\.** Doing so makes the Company Name field the top field, displaying in place of the First Name and Last Name fields, and ensures that the company name appears in the names list.

- **If a person is listed in more than one account, you'll see the Cards entry at the bottom of the card listing each account.** You can delete the entries for any account by clicking the Delete (–) button to its left in that section. In fact, this is a good way to identify duplicates whose unique information you can put in your master card for that person before deleting the duplicates.

- **To move a contact card to a different account, select the account you want to move it from in the list at the left, and drag the person's name (in the list to its right) to the account you want to move it to.**

Your Contact Card

One of the most important cards in Contacts is your own. When you first set up your MacBook Pro and worked through the registration process, the information you entered was added to a card in Contacts. This card identifies your contact information in various places, including the Safari browser's AutoFill feature that lets you quickly complete web forms. You should review and update your card as needed so its information is always current.

To jump to your card in Contacts, choose Card ⇨ Go to My Card. Your card is selected on the list and appears in the pane at the right. Notice that your card is the only one in the names list with the silhouette icon and the text label *Me* in the card image. Review the information on your card, and make any necessary changes.

You can make any card in Contacts yours by selecting it and choosing Card ⇨ Make This My Card.

7.4 You can add, change, and edit images for a contact.

Finding People in Contacts

After Contacts has the contact information with which you want to work, you start to get many benefits from the work you've done. You can browse your contact information or search for specific information. You can also change how you see contact information.

Setting format and sort preferences

Make sure that Contacts displays names and sorts cards according to your preferences. Follow these steps to get it set up:

1. **Choose Contacts ⇨ Preferences.**

2. **Go to the General pane, shown in Figure 7.5.**

3. **In the Show First Name section, click Before Last Name if you want names to be shown with the first name followed by the last.** Click Following Last Name if you prefer last names to appear first.

4. **From the Sort By pop-up menu, choose Last Name to have cards sorted by last name or choose First Name to be sorted by first name.**

5. **From the Address Format pop-up menu, choose the country with the formatting you want to be used for physical addresses.**

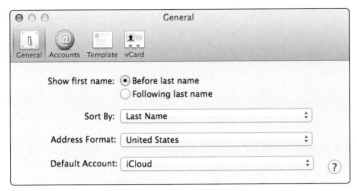

7.5 Configure the order in which Contacts should display a first and last name.

6. **On the Default Account pop-up menu, choose under which account you want contact information to be stored by default.** For example, if you have an iCloud account, you can choose it so that whenever you create a new contact, it is available from any device that can access your iCloud account.

7. **Close the Preferences dialog.**

Browsing for cards

Follow these steps to browse for cards:

1. **Move into the Groups view, and select the group that you want to browse from the list of groups on the left page.** To browse all your contacts, click All Contacts. The contacts in the selected group appear on the Contacts list.

2. **Scroll the list of contacts.**

3. **Select the contact whose card you want to use.** The card you select is displayed on the right page.

Searching for cards

When you search for cards in Contacts, it searches all fields on all your cards simultaneously. Perform these steps to search for cards:

1. **Select the account or group in which you want to search.** To search all your contacts, select All Contacts.

2. **Type the text for which you want to search in the Search box.** As you type, Contacts starts searching all the fields in the cards. As it finds matching cards, it shows them in the list of names. The more information you type, the more specific the search becomes.

3. **Click the card that you want to use when it appears in the names list.** The card opens on the right pane, as shown in Figure 7.6.

To end a search, click the Clear button, which is the X within the gray circle in the Search bar. All the cards within the selected group appear again.

Note To see multiple cards at the same time, select a card you want to see in its own window and then choose Card ⇨ Open in Separate Window or press ⌘+I). The card opens in its own window. Do that for each card you want to see at the same time.

7.6 When you search, Contacts highlights the search term in the cards that it finds.

Acting on Card Information

Contacts has several capabilities for cards that may not be so obvious at first but are quite handy:

- **You can share any contact's card by viewing it, clicking the Share button, and choosing the option you want to use to share the information: Email Card, Message Card, or AirDrop Card.** This sends a vCard file to the chosen destination.

- **If you hover the mouse pointer over a physical address in a card, the Show Map label appears to its right.** Click it to open that address in the Maps application. Prior to OS X Mavericks, you would right-click the address and choose Show Address in Google

Maps from the contextual menu, which would open the Safari browser and display the address location in the Google Maps website.

● **Click the FaceTime icon (the camera icon) to the right of the person's name in a card to start a FaceTime video chat.** If the icon is grayed out, that means the person's contact card does not include an e-mail address associated with that person's FaceTime service or that the person doesn't have a Mac or iOS device with which to participate in FaceTime chats.

● **If you right-click on any text in a card, a contextual appears.** Its options depend on what is right-clicked, but include these:

   ● **Look Up.** Searches OS X's Dictionary app for the term you right-clicked.

   ● **Search with Google.** Opens up the Safari browser and searches the term there using the Google search engine.

   ● **Create New Contact** and **Add to Existing Contact.** Lets you create a new card from the right-clicked field or add its information to someone else's card.

   ● **Open URL.** Opens a right-clicked website address in Safari.

   ● **Add to Reading List.** Bookmarks a right-clicked website address in Safari's Reading List.

   ● **Large Type.** Displays a right-clicked phone number in very large type on the screen so you can more easily read it.

   ● **Copy Map URL.** Creates a URL for the Google Maps of the physical address you right-clicked.

   ● **Share.** Lets you share via your social media accounts such as Facebook in addition to the AirDrop, Email, and messages options also available via the Share button.

   ● **Tweet** (if you have a Twitter account set up in the Internet Accounts system preference). Lets you tweet that person.

Organizing Cards with Groups in Contacts

Groups are useful because you can do one action and it affects all the cards in that group. For example, you can create a group containing family members whom you regularly e-mail. Then you can address a message to the one group instead of addressing each person individually. There are two kinds of groups in Contacts:

● Manual groups are those you create and then manually place cards into.

● Smart groups are a collection of criteria, and Contacts automatically places cards into smart groups based on these criteria.

Creating groups manually

Here's the simplest way to create a group:

1. **Select the account you want the group to be added to.**

2. **Select all the cards you want to be in the group.** To select multiple cards, ⌘+click each one.

3. **Choose File ⇨ New Group from Selection.** A new group named "untitled group" appears under the account name.

4. **Click the group name to make it editable, type in the name you want for it, and press Return.**

To add cards to the group later, just drag them in. If a card is already in the group, you won't be able to drag it in again.

You can also create a group before knowing whom you want to add to it by following these steps:

1. **Select the account you want the group to be added to.**

2. **Choose File ⇨ New Group.** A new group appears beneath the account name with its default name of "untitled group" ready to be edited.

3. **Type the name you want for the group, and press Return.**

4. **Select the group containing the cards you want to add to the new group (select All Contacts to browse all your contacts).** Browse or search for the first card you want to add to the group.

5. **Drag a card from the names list, and drop it onto the group to which you want to add it.** To add multiple cards to a group at the same time, hold down the ⌘ key while you click each card that you want to add, and drag that selection onto the desired group.

Note

To remove a person from a group, select the group, and then select the person's name from the names list. Choose Edit ⇨ Remove from Group. To delete a group, select it and press Delete—but be careful when selecting to not make the name editable, because pressing Delete then deletes the name but not the group.

Creating smart groups

Smart groups are also collections of cards. However, unlike regular groups, you don't have to manually add each card to the group. Instead, you define criteria for the cards you want included in the smart group, and Contacts automatically adds the appropriate cards. For example, suppose you want a group for everyone with the same last name. Simply create a smart group with that criterion, and Contacts automatically adds all the people with that last name to the group. These steps walk you through creating a smart group:

1. **Choose File ⇨ New Smart Group.** The New Smart Group sheet appears, as shown in Figure 7.7.

2. **Type the name you want to give the smart group.**

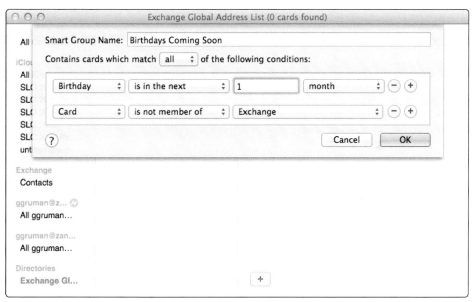

7.7 This smart group includes everyone whose birthday is in the next month but is not in the Exchange account (my work account).

3. **Choose the first field you want to include in the criteria on the leftmost pop-up menu (which is Card by default).** For example, to base a criterion on name, choose Name.

4. **Choose how you want the information you enter to be included on the center pop-up menu.** For example, the options for Name include Contains, Does Not Contain, Is, and Is Not, while the options for Birthday include Is in the Next, Is Within, Is Not Within, Is Set, and Is Not Set.

5. **Type the information that you want to be part of the criterion in the adjacent fields and pop-up menus.** If you select Name and Contains, for example, type the name you want the criterion to find. If you select Birthday and Is in the Next, type the duration of the period you want to use and the select the choose the period type (Day, Week, or Month).

6. **Click the Add (+) button at the right of the criterion to add another criterion for the smart group; to delete a criterion, click the Delete (–) button.**

7. **If the group has at least two criteria, choose All from the top pop-up menu if you want all criteria to be met for a card to be included in the smart group.** Choose Any if only one criterion must be met for inclusion in the smart group.

8. **Click OK.** The smart group is created, and all the cards that meet the criteria you defined are automatically added to it.

Note

To edit a smart group, select the group, choose Edit ⇨ Smart Group, and adjust the criteria as desired. To delete a smart group, select it and press Delete—but be careful when selecting to not make the name editable, because pressing Delete then deletes the name but not the group.

Configuring E-mail Accounts in Mail

One of the benefits of Mail is that you can configure many e-mail accounts in it, and you can easily work with all (or just one) of them at any point in time. When you set up accounts in the Internet Accounts system preference, as described earlier in this chapter, you can enable their mail services and have them available in Mail, where you then configure their settings in detail.

Mail works with the following kinds of e-mail accounts:

- **iCloud.** If you have an iCloud account, you also have an iCloud e-mail account. This is convenient because you can use Mail to access your e-mail, or you can use the iCloud website to work with it almost as easily, as Chapter 6 explains.

- **POP.** Post Office Protocol e-mail accounts are one of the most common types provided by many Internet service providers and other organizations that provide e-mail services. POP is a client-based protocol, meaning that e-mail is typically downloaded to the computer or device on which it is read and removed from the e-mail server (most include an option to leave e-mail on the server).

- **IMAP.** Internet Message Access Protocol is primarily a server-based protocol, meaning that e-mail is usually left on the server after it is downloaded to a client such as your MacBook Pro. The iCloud, AOL, and Gmail e-mail services are based on IMAP, even though you set them up directly, not via the Add Other Accounts option in the Internet Accounts system preference.

- **Exchange.** Microsoft's Exchange Server technology is dominant in the business world for managing e-mail.

Although there are technical differences among these kinds of accounts, they are seldom important when it comes to performing e-mail activities. The differences show up primarily in how you configure Mail in its Preferences dialog to work with the various types of accounts. There are a number of attributes that you need to know to configure an e-mail account in Mail. The following are the most common attributes; however, they vary from type to type:

- **E-mail address.** The e-mail address is a unique identifier for you.

- **Incoming mail server address.** Mail that you receive is delivered through an incoming mail server.

- **Username.** This is usually everything before the @ in your e-mail address but can be the whole e-mail address.

- **Password.** Sometimes, you have two: one each for the incoming and outgoing mail servers.

- **Outgoing mail server address.** To send e-mail, you need to configure the outgoing mail server through which it is to be sent.

- **User authentication.** To configure an authenticated account, you need a username and password. Accounts use different kinds of authentication. You don't need to understand the technical details; you just need to know which specific kinds of authentication your accounts use so you can configure them correctly.

When you obtain an e-mail account, you should receive information for each of the attributes that need to be configured. If not, you can usually get it from the provider's website.

To configure e-mail accounts:

1. **Open the Preferences dialog in Mail by choosing Mail ⇨ Preferences.**

2. **Go to the Accounts pane.**

3. **Select an account to configure.**

4. **Adjust the settings in the subpanes.** Most e-mail services have settings in three subpanes: Account Information, Mailbox Behaviors, and Advanced.

5. **Repeat Steps 3 and 4 for each account you want to configure.** You will be asked to save your changes when you click another account.

6. **Close the Preferences dialog.**

Setting Account Information preferences

Use the Account Information subpane, shown in Figure 7.8, to adjust the basic account details, such as the e-mail address, password, the name you want people to see in e-mails they receive from you, and so on. Although the fields vary based on the service, here are the main ones:

- **Enable This Account.** If checked, you will be able to send and receive e-mail using this account.

- **Description.** The name you see in the accounts list in Mail.

- **Email Address.** Your e-mail address; if grayed out, the service won't let you change it from Mail.

7.8 Configure basic connection information in the Account Information subpane of Mail's Preferences dialog.

- **Full Name.** The name that people who receive e-mails from you will see as the sender.

- **Incoming Mail Server.** The server address used to get e-mail from. If grayed out, the service won't let you change it from Mail. Most e-mail services display the User Name and Password fields needed to connect to the incoming mail server as well.

- **Outgoing Mail Server (SMTP).** The server address used to send e-mail from. (SMTP is the Simple Mail Transfer Protocol.) If grayed out, the service won't let you change it from Mail. The address appears in a pop-up menu, from which you can choose another server or edit or create a new entry using the Edit SMTP Server List option. Normally, you would use the outgoing mail server specified by your e-mail provider, but some Internet service providers allow you to use their outgoing servers only when connected to their broadband service, so when you travel, you need to select a different outgoing mail server. Deselect the Use Only This Server option to have Mail try other outgoing mail servers if it can't establish a connection with the default one for this account.

- **TLS Certificate.** Some e-mail services require a verification that you are who you say you are, in the form of a digital certificate that OS X creates. If so, choose the certificate from the TLS Certificate pop-up menu.

Your iCloud account also has the Alias pop-up menu that lets you choose another e-mail address to appear as the source when you send e-mails. iCloud lets you set up aliases for two reasons. One is to use a special e-mail address such as for online shopping that you can then filter for to reduce the spam messages you're sure to get from merchants. The other is to use an older Apple e-mail address that people may know you as, such as the me.com or mac.com addresses used by Apple's predecessors to iCloud. You set up iCloud aliases by choosing Edit Aliases in the Alias pop-up menu, which opens iCloud.com in the Safari browser (see Chapter 6).

Exchange doesn't have the Incoming Mail Server or Outgoing Mail Server (SMTP) fields. Instead, it has Internal Server and External Server. The internal server is one you would use at your office, to connect to the Exchange server over your internal corporate network; the external server is a Web-connected server that you use when not at the office, such as when you're at home or traveling. In some cases, your company may use a Web-connected server as both the internal and external server, so the two fields could have the same server address. Both fields handle your incoming and outgoing messages for Exchange.

Setting Mailbox Behaviors preferences

Use the Mailbox Behaviors subpane, shown in Figure 7.9, to adjust how mail is stored. The options vary slightly based on the account type:

- **Drafts.** To save draft messages—those you have not yet sent—on the server so you can retrieve them from another computer or device later, select the Store Draft Messages on the Server check box. It's a good idea to leave this option selected. The Drafts section does not appear for a POP account, because POP does not support saving draft messages on a server.

● **Sent.** To save messages you've sent on the server, so you can see them in the Sent folder on any computer or device using this e-mail account, select the Store Sent Messages on the Server check box. To keep your e-mail server from getting overly full, you can choose how long the messages are retained on the server using the Delete Sent Messages When pop-up menu.

● **Junk.** This option works just like the Sent option, except that it applies to messages marked as Junk. You might save junk messages on the server for a week as a safety valve in case an e-mail is misidentified as junk, so you can retrieve it from any device using that account when you realize that's what happened.

7.9 Configure mail handling in the Mailbox Behaviors subpane of Mail's Preferences dialog.

● **Trash.** Again, this option works like the Sent option, except that it applies to messages you deleted. You might save deleted messages on the server for a week or a month as a safety valve in case you realize later you still want a deleted message, so you can retrieve it from any device using that account. Note that IMAP accounts have an additional option here: Move Deleted Messages to the Trash Mailbox, which if selected moves deleted messages to the Trash folder rather than leaving them in your inbox either grayed out or hidden from view.

Setting Advanced preferences

You won't often need to change the settings in the Advanced subpane shown in Figure 7.10, but in case you do, here's what they do:

- **Include When Automatically Checking for New Messages.** If this checkbox is deselected, Mail will retrieve e-mail for this account only when you click the Get New Mail button (the envelope icon) or choose Mailbox ⇨ Get New Mail or Mailbox ⇨ Get All New Mail. The automatic mail checking frequency you set up in the Preference dialog's General pane is ignored if this check box is not selected.

- **Compact Mailboxes Automatically.** Available for some IMAP-based e-mail services, this option if checked saves on storage space by compressing messages and eliminating duplicate copies of file attachments.

7.10 Configure attachment handling and secure-connection settings in the Advanced subpane of Mail's Preferences dialog.

- **Automatically Download All Attachments.** If not selected, you'll need to click file attachments in individual messages to retrieve them, which can save you on data charges when using a cellular modem on the road or make e-mail download times

tolerable when using a dial-up modem connection by letting you download only those files you really need to open. This option is not available for POP accounts.

⦿ **Remove Copy from Server After Retrieving a Message.** Available only for POP accounts, this option controls how long messages are kept on the server for access by other devices you may have. Normally, POP accounts delete the message after a device retrieves it, making it unavailable to other devices. So it's a very good idea to select this check box. To keep the POP server from getting too full, use the pop-up menu below it to set how long messages are kept after the first time they are accessed.

⦿ **Prompt Me to Skip Messages Over __ KB.** Available only for POP accounts, enter a value in the field to have Mail ask you whether to download large messages. (Leave the field blank to download all messages.) This setting can be helpful if you're using a cellular or dial-up modem to reduce data charges and mail download times, respectively.

⦿ **Port**, **Authentication**, and **Use SSL.** These settings relate to the server's settings for securing e-mail transmissions. If for some reason, the initial settings at your provider have changed or were misconfigured (preventing e-mail access), update them using these controls. Note that Exchange accounts provide the Internal Port, External Server Path, External Port, and Use SSL options for its secure-transmission settings.

⦿ **IMAP Path Prefix** and **Use IDLE Command If the Server Supports It.** The IMAP Path Prefix option is specific to an IMAP-based e-mail provider's internal configuration and is often unused. But do select the Use IDLE Command If the Server Supports It check box, to let Mail get new messages more quickly. For Exchange accounts, the equivalent to the path prefix is set in the Internal Server Path and External Server Path fields, which are typically set automatically for their required values.

Testing e-mail accounts

After you configure your e-mail accounts, expand the Inbox by clicking the disclosure triangle next to it. Under the Inbox, you see an inbox for each e-mail account that you configured, as shown in Figure 7.11. If you don't see a warning icon containing an exclamation point (!), the accounts are properly configured and ready to use.

If you do see this icon, you need to correct the account configuration. Click the warning icon to get more details on the issue, and check the settings in the Preference dialog's General pane to make sure none is misconfigured. Some problems could be due to outages at your e-mail provider, so don't assume a connection problem is on your end.

As a final test, send e-mail to and from each address to make sure that it is configured as you want it to be. If you find any problems or want to make any changes, do so in the Accounts pane of the Preferences dialog.

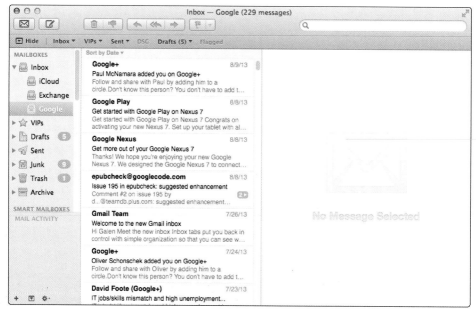

7.11 No caution icon means that these three e-mail accounts have been successfully configured in Mail.

Working with File Attachments in Mail

E-mail is one of the easiest and fastest ways to exchange files with other people. Using Mail, you can attach files of any type to e-mails that you send.

Note One limitation of sending files through e-mail is that most gateways limit the size (typically 5MB or 10MB) of file attachments. A service such as Dropbox or Box can get around such limits, because you just send a link to the files. Of course, the person receiving it must have or set up an account on the sharing service to get the file.

Sending files through e-mail

I'm going to recommend something here that many people don't do as standard practice, which is to compress files before attaching them to e-mail messages, even if you are sending only one file with a message. There are three reasons why this a good idea: Sending a compressed file requires less bandwidth; compressed files are less likely to be screened out by spam or virus filters on the recipient's e-mail (although some e-mail systems are configured to screen compressed attachments); and a compressed file gives the user a single file to deal with instead of an attachment for each file.

Follow these steps to compress the files you want to send:

1. **Open or go to a Finder window showing the files you want to send.**

2. **Select the files you want to send.** Remember that to select multiple files, you hold the ⌘ key down while clicking the files.

3. **Choose File ⇨ Compress # Items (where # is the number of files you selected).** The files you selected are then compressed into a Zip file, which is the dominant compression standard on Windows too.

4. **Rename the Zip file.** The default name for Zip files is always Archive.zip when you compress more than one file. If you compress a single file, it takes the name of the file you compressed and adds the filename extension .zip.

You can use any of the following techniques to attach a file (compressed or not) to an e-mail message:

- **Drag the file onto the New Message window.**

- **While the message to which you want to attach files is active in Mail, choose File ⇨ Attach Files.** Then use the Choose File sheet to select the file you want to attach.

- **While the message to which you want to attach files is active, press Shift+⌘+A.** Use the Choose File sheet to select the file you want to attach.

- **Click the Attach button (the paperclip icon) on the New Message window's toolbar.** The Choose File sheet appears; use it to select the file you want to attach to a message.

Note

OS X and Windows handle files very differently, and that can prevent Windows users from using the files you send from your MacBook Pro. There's a simple solution, though, that works most of the time: When attaching files to an e-mail, be sure the Send Windows-Friendly Attachments check box is selected in the Choose File sheet. After you select it, it stays selected for all future attachments (unless you later deselect it, of course).

Of course, people often attach files that haven't been compressed (I do it more than occasionally). When you place a file that hasn't been compressed in a new message window, you see a thumbnail preview of the file with its icon, the filename, and its size in parentheses. If the file type is one that can be displayed in the message, such as a JPEG image or a PDF file, you actually see the contents of the file embedded in the body of the message. The recipient may see the file as an attachment icon or in the message body itself, depending on how his or her e-mail client works.

You can use the Photo Browser button (the icon of a picture) in the New Message toolbar to easily find photos in your iPhoto, Aperture, and/or iCloud Photo Stream library. In the panel that appears (shown in Figure 7.12), drag them into a new message window to attach them to an e-mail.

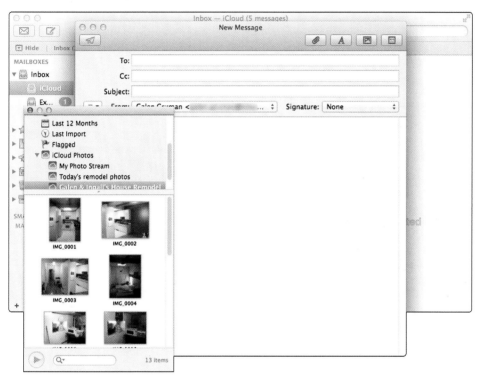

7.12 Mail lets you drag files from your iPhoto, Aperture, and iCloud Photo Stream libraries into a message for use as a file attachment using the Photo Browser panel.

Working with received files

When you receive a message that has files attached to it, you usually see icons at the bottom of the message for each attachment; these icons show the filename and the file size. If Mail can display the content of the attached files, that content appears in the message body. Messages that have attachments also show the paperclip icon to the right of the sender's name in the header at the top, as you can see in Figure 7.13.

Genius

If the contents of the file are displayed in the message body and you would rather see just its icon, right-click the preview and choose View as Icon in the contextual menu that appears. To view the file's content again, right-click the file icon and choose View in Place from the contextual menu.

In OS X Mavericks, if you hover the pointer over the message's header, a tray of icons appears below the subject, as Figure 7.13 shows. If the message has file attachments, the rightmost button is a paperclip icon with a numeral (indicating how many files are attached) and a menu indicator. Open that Attachments pop-up menu to see a list of files, as shown in Figure 7.13, as well as the Save All and Quick Look options. You may also see the Export to iPhoto option if the attachments are image files. (In previous versions of OS X, you would see a text note indicating how many attachments there and their total size, as well as the Save and Quick Look buttons, at the bottom right of the header.)

7.13 The icon tray below the message header includes the Attachments pop-up menu if files are attached to the e-mail.

The following list includes various ways in which you can work with file attachments:

- **Download and use the attachment.** If a file is not yet downloaded to your MacBook Pro, click its icon (the downward-facing arrow) in the message body to download it. When the attachment has been downloaded, the download icon is replaced by an icon representing the file type. After the file has been downloaded, double-click its icon to open the document in the associated application.

- **Choose File ⇨ Save Attachments.** Use the sheet that appears to choose the location where you want to save the files.

- **Click the Save All menu button in the Attachments pop-up menu at the top of the message.** All the files are saved to your MacBook Pro's Downloads folder.

- **Select one or more files' icons at the bottom of the message, right-click the selection, and choose Save Attachment to specify where to save those selected files.** Or choose Save to Downloads Folder to save the files in the Downloads folder.

- **Drag file icons from the message onto a folder or Desktop in the Finder to save them there.**

- **Select one or more files' icons at the bottom of the message, right-click the selection, and choose Open to open in the application the MacBook Pro has designated as the default for the file type.** Or choose Open With to select a different application to open the file in. You can also double-click a file icon to open the attachment in its default application.

- **Choose Quick Look from the Attachments pop-up menu.** The Quick Look window opens and you can preview the contents of the files, as shown in Figure 7.14. (Use the ← and → buttons to move among multiple attachment previews.) Or select the attachment icon at the bottom of the message, and press the spacebar to open the Quick Look window. Either way, if you have an application that can open the file, click the Open With button in Quick Look to open the file in that application.

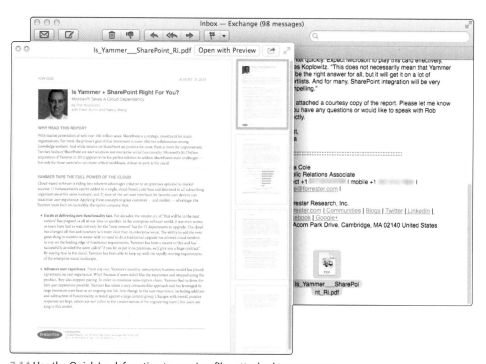

7.14 Use the Quick Look function to preview files attached to a message.

Organizing E-mail in Mail

As you send and receive e-mail, you end up with lots of messages that you need to manage. Fortunately, Mail provides two ways to organize your e-mail: mailboxes (folders) and smart mailboxes. Using rules can automate some of that organization effort.

Using mailboxes

You can create your own mailboxes to organize your messages. These are much like folders in the Finder. The mailboxes you create are shown in the Mailbox pane below the inbox and other special mailboxes. You can also create nested mailboxes to create a hierarchy of mailboxes in which to store your messages. Follow these steps to create a mailbox:

1. **Choose Mailbox ⇨ New Mailbox.**

2. **In the New Mailbox sheet that appears, choose a location for the folder using the Location pop-up menu.** The Location pop-up menu shows all accounts and any folders within each. Select an account to put the new folder at the top level of folders for that account; select a folder to put the new folder as a subfolder in the selected folder.

3. **Enter a name for the new folder in the Name field.**

4. **Click OK.** The mailbox is created and appears in the Mailbox pane in the location you selected. If you created a subfolder, the top-level folder has a disclosure triangle next to it; click it to expand the folder hierarchy so you can see the subfolders it contains.

Genius

After you create folders, you can move them within their account's folder hierarchy. For example, you can move a folder into another folder, or you can pull a subfolder out of a folder and make it a top-level folder in the account.

You can move messages to mailboxes, as well as move them from one mailbox to another, in any of these ways:

- **Drag a message from the Message List pane onto a mailbox.** This moves the message from the current location (such as the inbox) into the folder. Hold the Option key while dragging to copy the message instead of move it.

- **Select messages, and choose Message ⇨ Move To.** From the menu, choose the mailbox to which you want to transfer the messages.

- **Select messages, and choose Message ⇨ Copy To.** From the menu, choose the mailbox in which you want to place a copy of the selected messages.

● **Select messages, and choose Message ⇨ Move Again to move the selected messages to the same mailbox into which you most recently transferred mail.** Or press
Option+⌘+T.

● **Select messages, and choose Message ⇨ Apply Rules.** Choose a rule that transfers the
messages to your desired destination.

● **Right-click a message in the Message List to open its contextual menu, and choose
the Move To, Copy To, Move Again, or Apply Rules option.**

You can create and use rules to have Mail handle your e-mail automatically. For example, you can
have e-mail from a specific person stored in a designated folder and color-coded. You create and
manage rules in the Rules pane of the Preferences dialog. In that pane, click Add Rules to add a
rule, and then specify the criteria and resulting actions in the settings sheet that appears. Figure
7.15 shows an example. Click OK when you're finished. Select the check box to the left of a rule in
the Active column to have the rule automatically applied as new messages are received.

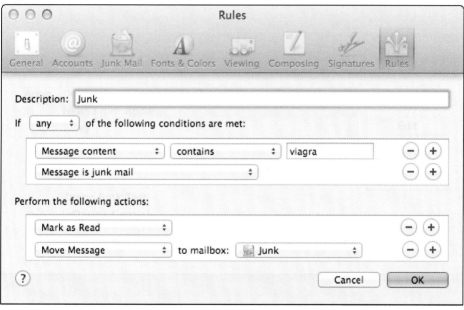

7.15 Create an e-mail rule to filter and act on messages based on your criteria.

Note When you configure e-mail rules, they're synced automatically to Mail on any other
Mac that you've signed into with the same iCloud account. This makes it easier to
have Mail on multiple Macs work the same way.

Using smart mailboxes

You can use smart mailboxes to organize your e-mail automatically based on criteria you define. For example, you might want to collect all the e-mail you receive from a group of people with whom you are working on a project in a specific folder. Rather than having to place these messages in the folder by dragging them out of your Inbox individually, you can create a smart mailbox so that mail you receive from these people is automatically placed in the appropriate folder.

However, when mail is shown in a smart mailbox, it isn't actually stored there. Because a smart mailbox is a set of conditions rather than a place, it shows aliases to messages stored in other locations. So, if a message in an inbox matches a smart mailbox's conditions, it is shown in that inbox and also appears in that smart mailbox.

You create a smart mailbox by choosing Mailbox ⇨ New Smart Mailbox, specifying the rules in the settings sheet that appears, and clicking OK. You choose the criteria the same way you do e-mail rules and smart groups in the Contacts application, explained earlier in this chapter.

Smart mailboxes are stored in the Smart Mailboxes section of the Mailbox list, below the inbox section. Hover the pointer over the Smart Mailbox label, and click the Show label when it appears to display the list of smart mailboxes. If you want to organize your smart mailboxes into a folder, choose Mailbox ⇨ New Smart Mailbox Folder, enter a name for the folder, click OK, and drag the smart mailboxes you want to group into that folder, which appears also in the Smart Mailboxes list. You can have several smart mailbox folders.

Making Mail Work Your Way

The Preferences dialog for Mail lets you customize how Mail displays messages and other aspects of e-mail. I urge you to explore its options. This section explains some options you may be most interested in configuring.

The General preferences

The options here are self-explanatory, but there are three I recommend you consider adjusting:

- **Check for New Messages.** Choose how often you want Mail to contact your e-mail servers for new messages. The default setting of Automatically checks for new mail the most frequently, but it can use more power, a concern if you're running the MacBook Pro off its battery.

- **Add Invitations to Calendar.** Make sure this is set to Automatically so any calendar invitations (.ics files) sent to you via e-mail display in the Calendar application as well.

- **Downloads Folder:** You may not want e-mail attachments saved in the Downloads folder on your MacBook Pro. If not, change the default folder for storing e-mail attachments here.

The Junk Mail preferences

More than half the e-mail sent is junk, also called spam, and it can clog your inboxes fast. Be sure that the Enable Junk Mail Filtering check box is selected, so Mail can identify likely spam and dispose of it for you. It won't catch it all, but it can catch lots of it.

I recommend you select the Move It to the Junk Mailbox or the Perform Custom Actions option in the When Junk Mail Arrives section, so potential spam is not left in your inbox.

The first option moves likely junk mail to the Junk mailbox, which you can access like any other mailbox in the Mailboxes pane, such as when you think a legitimate message has been erroneously tagged as junk. (Click the Not Junk button that appears at the top of the message when you select it to help Mail better filter your e-mail.)

The second option lets you create rules for identifying spam. Click the Advanced button to define those rules; its settings sheet works the same way as those for e-mail rules and smart mailboxes.

The Viewing preferences

Visual cues can be very important aids in managing your e-mail, and this pane lets you adjust those cues.

Many people find the bullet that Mail places next to new messages too subtle a cue. If you're one of those people, check the Display Unread Messages with Bold Font to get a more visually distinct cue as to which e-mail is unread.

Likewise, people have strong personal preferences about how conversations, also called *message threads*, are displayed. Mail normally organizes messages and replies into conversations, which groups them as one entry in the Message List. A numeral indicator at the right shows how many messages are in the conversation, and you can reveal all the messages in the conversation by clicking its disclosure triangle, as shown in Figure 7.16.

To disable conversations, choose View ⇨ Organize by Conversation to remove the check mark next to that option. If conversations are disabled, you can still identify related messages by selecting the Highlight Messages with Color When Not Grouped check box in the Viewing pane of the Preferences dialog, and select the highlight color using the adjacent color picker.

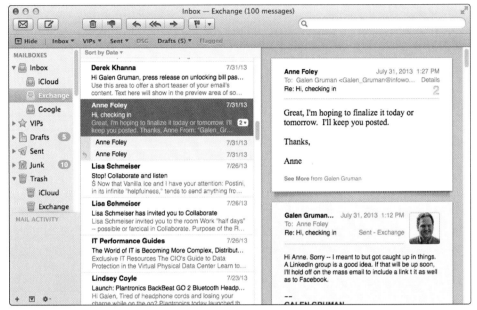

7.16 The conversations feature groups related messages so they appear in one place.

If conversations are enabled, you can expand the scope of the conversation to include messages that were forwarded or had changes to the subject line when replied to or forwarded by selecting the Include Related Messages check box in the Viewing pane. I suggest you select the Show Most Recent Message at the Top check box to ensure that the conversation's most recent message is the one that displays in the Message List, sorted so the conversation appears with messages received around the same time as the most recent message in the conversation; otherwise, the thread appears with the subject of and in the timeline of the original message.

The Composing preferences

These days, pretty much every e-mail client can support rich text, meaning text with formatting like boldface and text size. Choose Rich Text from the Message Format pop-up menu to see e-mails in all their formatted glory.

I don't know about you, but I am a lousy typist. So I select As I Type from the Check Spelling pop-up menu to identify errors quickly.

The Signature preferences

Many people don't add signatures to their e-mails—their name, or a more formal signature that includes name, company, address, and contact information—but it's a particularly good idea to do so for business communications. You create signatures in this pane and associate them to e-mail accounts, so they are added automatically as you create messages. Figure 7.17 shows an example.

7.17 Create signatures for your e-mail accounts to provide useful information such as contact details, especially for business use.

Follow these steps to create a signature:

1. **Click the Add (+) button below the center pane.**

2. **Enter a name for the signature in the center pane.** Its name is automatically highlighted for editing when you add a new signature.

3. **Enter the signature text in the pane at the right.**

Genius

To format the signature text, choose Format ⇨ Show Fonts to open the Fonts panel, where you can apply fonts and text size to your text selections. To apply color to text selections, choose Format ⇨ Show Colors to open the Colors panel, which provides a color picker for applying a desired color.

4. **Drag the signature onto the account name in the left pane to add it to that account's list of possible signatures.** When you create a new mail message, you see a pop-up menu below the header that lets you select the signature from those assigned to the e-mail's account.

5. **If you want a signature added automatically to each new message, select the account in the left pane and choose the default signature from the Choose Signature pop-up menu.** You can do this for each account. You also can have no automatic signature by choosing None (the default) or have Mail cycle through the available signatures by choosing the At Random or the In Sequential Order options.

Messages

To: Ingall W. Bull III

Search

 Ingall W. Bull III   6:05 PM
Leaving work now

 ggrumaniw
Away

Zack Farwell   7/19/13
Ok. Thanks for the reminder.

Tim Haigh   7/18/13
Please talk to hunter. He
paid for the carpet cleanin...

 Eric Knorr   6/25/13
Galen plz give Andrew
access to the CMS or help...

 +1 (661) 210-9850   4/18/13
Thanks for calling about 196
Craig, SLO. All details: ww...

Bill Snyder   12/31/12
Sure. I'm traveling too but
will have email

+1 (408) 510-2416   11/9/12
Cheap on Amazon. There's
something on my wish list,...

 3 Accounts
Away ▾

Today 9:29 AM

> Feliciano will finish the kitchen painting today.
> First coat is on, he'll be back later today to do
> the second coat.

 How's it look? Will the orange be hard to match
since the original wall had about 7 coats?

> the orange will probably need additional coats
> after today, but Feliciano says he'll do that for
> the part that is visible when he does the rest of
> the house. Probably two more needed; easier
> to tell once it's dry.

Today 5:46 PM

I sent a text to James to see if he is fine with
Stephen coming. See if Stephen is up for it

> sure, he'll come
> Delivered

Today 6:05 PM

James texted back. He is not available after all.
So we're dining at home

 Leaving work now

---

iMessage

With your MacBook Pro, you can take advantage of OS X's real-time communication applications, which are FaceTime and Messages. FaceTime enables you to have video chats with other Mac, iPhone, iPod touch, and iPad users. Messages enables you to conduct text, audio, and video chats with users of several chat services, and to share files and even screens while you chat.

Conversing with FaceTime

FaceTime is a great way to communicate because you can both see and hear the person with whom you are chatting. You can use FaceTime to video chat with anyone who uses a Mac, iPhone, iPod touch, or iPad. Using FaceTime is simple, fun, and free; all you need is an Apple ID, which you can get at no cost, if you don't already have one.

To be able to chat on FaceTime with someone, both people must be running the FaceTime application. It is currently available only for Macs, iPhones, iPod touches, and iPads. Also, the devices involved in a FaceTime chat must be connected to the Internet. (iPhones may support FaceTime over a cell connection in the future.) Only two devices can be involved in a FaceTime chat (unless you're using Messages—in which case, more than two devices can be involved in chats). You also must know the person's e-mail address or iPhone number. Before you can start chatting on FaceTime, you must configure some basic settings. After these are in place, conducting FaceTime chats is easy.

Configuring FaceTime

There's a little setup to do before you can use FaceTime to initiate and respond to video call requests:

1. **Launch FaceTime.** The first time you launch FaceTime, it prompts you to type your Apple ID and password; do so, and click Sign In.

2. **Confirm or update your e-mail address in FaceTime's Preferences dialog.** People will use your e-mail address to request a FaceTime session, so the application must be configured with the correct e-mail address. Choose FaceTime ⇨ Preference, and select the addresses and phone numbers by which you can be contacted for FaceTime calls. If an item is checked, a person can use it from his or her FaceTime to contact you. Note that phone numbers work only with iPhones, so be sure to list an e-mail address as a way to contact you for FaceTime calls. Click Done when your contact settings are correct.

3. **Add favorites to FaceTime.** In the Favorites pane, you can add people you will FaceTime with often. If the pane is not visible, click the Favorites button at the bottom of the screen. Click the Add button (the + icon at the upper right of the window) to open a list of your contacts (taken from the Contacts application), and click one that you want to add to your FaceTime favorites. If a person has multiple addresses, click the one you want to use to initiate a FaceTime call. Add additional people the same way. (To delete a person from favorites, click the Edit button, and then click the Remove button [the – icon] to the left of the person's name. Click Done when you're finished removing people.)

Starting a call

To request a FaceTime call, choose one of these options to select the person with whom you want to communicate:

- **Go to the Favorites pane, and click the person you want to call.**
- **Go to the Recents pane, and click on a contact with whom you've recently communicated.**
- **Click the Contacts pane, browse your contacts, and click the contact information you want to use to place the call.** This can be an e-mail address or a phone number (if the person has an iPhone).

A FaceTime request is sent to the person you select. While the call is being placed, you see the name of the person you are calling at the top of the FaceTime window, as Figure 8.1 shows. You also hear the ringer indicating a call is being placed. If the person accepts your request, the FaceTime session starts, and you can hear and see the other party while conducting the call. If the person declines or is not available, you see a "Not Available" message.

Receiving a call

When someone wants to chat on FaceTime with you, a window appears on your MacBook Pro's screen. In the top-right corner of the window, you see the person who is trying to contact you, as Figure 8.1 shows. At the bottom of the window appear the Decline and Accept buttons. To start the conversation, click Accept and conduct the call as described in the next section. To decline the call, click Decline. The person who sent the request then receives the "Not Available" message.

Note   On a Mac, the FaceTime application doesn't have to be running to receive calls. If someone tries to call you and your FaceTime application isn't running, it opens so you can accept or decline the FaceTime session.

Conducting a call

These controls are available while you conduct a FaceTime call, as shown in Figure 8.1:

- **Drag the preview window (which is the view of you that the other person is seeing) to change its location.**
- **If you hover the pointer over the preview window, the Rotate button appears; click it to rotate the window.**

8.1 FaceTime is a great way to keep in touch with people, be they close or far away. Left: Placing a call. Center: Receiving a call invitation. Right: Engaging in a call.

- **Mute the audio and darken the video in the preview window (the other person can still see you) by clicking the Mute button (the microphone icon).**

- **Click End to end the FaceTime session.**

- **Click the Full Screen button (the icon of diagonal arrows) to enlarge the view to a full-screen FaceTime window.**

- **After a few moments into a call, the title bar and buttons on the FaceTime screen disappear.** Move the pointer over the window to have the title bar and buttons reappear temporarily.

Caution Like other applications, FaceTime can be moved into the background. However, the other person can still hear and see you, even if you can't see the video call in your FaceTime window.

Messaging with Messages

With Messages, you can have text, audio, and video chats from your MacBook Pro with people via their computers or mobile devices. You can also share your MacBook Pro's screen, photos, and documents with other people. Messages enables you to chat with multiple people at the same time and conduct multiple chats simultaneously.

Configuring Messages

Before you can start chatting, you need to do some basic configuration to prepare Messages. Most important, you must configure the accounts you want to use to chat. The simplest way is to add chat accounts such as AOL Instant Messenger and Jabber—and to enable Messages for your chat-capable accounts such as Google, iCloud, and Yahoo!—is in the Internet Accounts system preference, as described in Chapter 7.

You'll also want to use various Messages preferences to tweak it and make it work as well as possible for you.

To chat, you must configure Messages with at least one chat account. You can use these types of accounts with Messages:

- iCloud
- AOL Instant Messenger (AIM)
- Google Talk
- Jabber
- Yahoo!

You can also use Apple's Bonjour technology built in to OS X and available for Windows to use Messages on a local network. Although this isn't really a type of account, it behaves in a similar way. The various devices that use Bonjour can automatically detect and connect to each other for many purposes, including chatting for computers and iOS devices.

Note

The capabilities available to you in Messages chats depend on the type of account you use, and the types of accounts and applications the people with whom you chat are using, and these services' capabilities can change over time. So what you see on screen may not always match what I describe here.

Trying to figure out which capabilities you can use for which types of accounts can be a bit confusing. The easiest way to determine whether you can chat with someone is to simply try it. If an option (such as audio chat) is available to you, you can use it. If not, either you or the other person (or both) must try to use a different account. You may encounter many combinations of account types and applications. You can use most of the Messages features if you have an iCloud or AIM account, as well as with Bonjour.

Like nearly every OS X application, Messages has the Preferences dialog in which you customize the software's operations. Choose Messages ➪ Preferences to open it. Its options are largely self-explanatory, but there are a few worth going over:

- **In the General pane, select the Save History When Conversations Are Closed check box so transcripts of your text chats remain available later on.**

- **Also in the General pane, you can set a different folder other than the default Downloads to place files sent to you during chats.** Change the folder using the Save Received Files As pop-up menu.

- **In the Accounts pane, you can enable Bonjour chats over the local network by clicking Bonjour and selecting the Enable Bonjour Instant Message check box in the right side of the pane.**

- **In the Audio/Video pane, you can select the audio input and output to use via the Microphone and Sound Output pop-up menus.** In an office, for example, you may want to use a headset rather than the MacBook Pro's built in microphone and speakers to maintain privacy and not disturb colleagues.

Using Messages to text-chat

For many people, text chats—also called *instant messaging* and *texting*—is the preferred method of communication. Text chats are easy to do, fast, and convenient. Using Messages, start your own text chats or answer someone's request to text chat with you. You can also chat with more than one person simultaneously.

Follow these steps to text chat with others:

1. **Click the New Message button (the pen-on-paper icon) located just to the right of the Search bar at the top of the Messages window.**

2. **Type the e-mail address or phone number of the person with whom you want to chat in the To field, or click the Get Contact button (the + icon).** If you click Get Contact, use the pop-up that appears to select a person from your contacts, and then choose the address or phone number to which you want to send a message. If the address you are typing is recognized as having a chat capability, Messages shows you the chat options, such as the type of service you can use with that person. When available, iCloud and AIM are the best options, because they support the most capabilities.

3. **Repeat Step 2 to send the message to more than one person.**

Note When you type a valid address or number in the To field, the contact's name is highlighted in blue. If you enter an address for which chatting isn't available for the contact, or if you choose an incompatible contact via the Get Contact pop-over, the contact's name is highlighted in red.

4. **Type the message you want to send in the message field at the bottom of the window, and press Return.** The message is sent, and you see it on the right side of the window along with a status, if available. When the person replies, you see it along the left side of the window, as shown in Figure 8.2. You also see the image associated with the person, if applicable.

Genius You can use the pop-up menu (identified with a smiley icon) at the end of the text bar to add emoticons to what you type. Emoticons are symbols representing emotional states.

5. **Type your reply to continue the conversation.**

6. **To send a file (such as a photo) to the person, drag it from the Finder into the conversation.** If you don't drop it into an existing message, a new message is created and the file is added to it. When you send the message, the person gets the file you sent.

7. **If a file is sent to you, double-click it to open a Quick Look preview, or click the down-facing arrow to download the file to your MacBook Pro.** When you view a file via Quick Look, you can open it in an application (such as to save it on your MacBook Pro) by clicking the Open With button that appears in the Quick Look window.

Your messages with the same person or people are all collected in one conversation. To move back to an existing conversation, select it on the list of conversations in the left pane of the Messages window (refer to Figure 8.2). You see the messages, photos, and other elements of the conversation.

When someone starts a new conversation with you, it appears on the conversation list. If a new message is sent for an existing conversation, it is added to that conversation. In both cases, you get whatever alerts you set in the General pane of the Preferences dialog. Conversations with new messages are also marked with a blue dot.

8.2 A text chat is underway.

Note

iCloud messages—also called iMessages—support status information at the message level. When someone is composing a message to you, you see the bubble with an ellipsis in it where the message will eventually display.

You can delete a conversation by hovering over it and clicking the Delete button (the X icon) that appears. If you click Delete at the prompt, the conversation is removed from Messages.

A status menu appears in the lower-left corner of the Messages window. Use this menu to change your status to something else (such as Offline) if you don't want to chat with other people. Not all accounts support this capability; iCloud is one that does not.

Note

When the text you type displays with blue backgrounds, you are using the iCloud iMessage service. When it is green, you are using a different service.

Note When you first launch Messages, you are prompted to log in with your Apple ID. That login message reminds you that you can send unlimited messages to people with Apple devices. It also provides the Send Receipt Notices option so you can opt in or out of such receipts before you begin using Messages.

Using Messages for audio chats or video chats

Messages also supports audio and video chats. However, to use these options, you and the people with whom you want to chat must be using a service that supports audio or video chatting (such as an AIM account). iCloud accounts don't support video or audio chats, except via FaceTime, of course.

If you are communicating with someone via iCloud and that person's account is configured for FaceTime chats, you can switch to a FaceTime conversation by clicking the Video button (the video-camera icon) at the top of the conversation window. Then choose the person's FaceTime e-mail address or phone number. The FaceTime application becomes active, and you can conduct the conversation as described earlier in this chapter. This button also lets you initiate an audio or video chat over another compatible service, such as AIM.

Follow these steps to conduct an audio chat:

1. **If you already have a conversation with the person with whom you want to chat on the conversation list, select it.** If not, start a new conversation using an account that supports audio or video chatting.

2. **Click and hold the Video button (the video-camera icon).** The available connection options are presented on a pop-over, as shown in Figure 8.3.

3. **Click Audio.** A chat request is sent to the person. If the person accepts your request, the chat starts and you see the audio chat window, shown in Figure 8.4.

As you chat, use these controls to manage your chat session:

- **Audio meter.** Use the Audio meter to gauge your own volume. As you speak, the green part of the bar should move to at least the halfway point. If not, you can use the Input level control on the Sound system preference.

- **Add.** Click the Add (+) button located in the lower-left corner of the window to add more people to the audio chat. Just as with text chats, you can add multiple people to an audio chat.

- **Volume slider.** Drag this to the right to increase the volume, or drag to the left to decrease it.

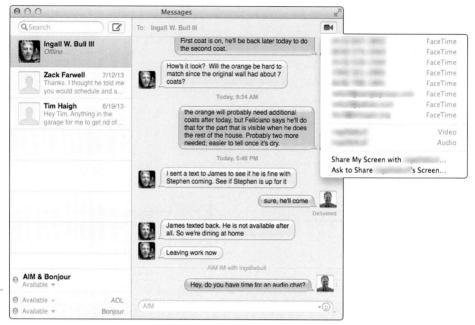

8.3 Messages presents the chat connection options available to you when you click and hold the Video button.

When someone wants to start an audio chat with you, you see a window with that person's name as its title and the Audio icon. Click the window, and then click one of these buttons:

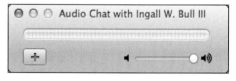

8.4 An audio chat in progress.

- **Text Reply.** Click this button to decline the audio invitation and start a text chat.

- **Decline.** Click this button to decline the audio invitation. The person who sent it to you sees a status message stating that you declined.

- **Accept.** Click this button to accept the invitation and start the chat.

Note

If you are listening to iTunes when you start a FaceTime audio or video chat, it automatically pauses. It starts playing again when the chat ends.

Conducting a video chat is very similar to an audio chat. First, move into an existing conversation or create a new one using an account that supports video chats, and click the Video button. In the menu that appears, choose Video. A video chat request is sent. When the person accepts your chat invitation, you see his or her image in the larger part of the chat window. The smaller, inset preview window shows you what the other person is seeing in his or her chat window, similar to how FaceTime works. Start talking and watching. As with audio chats, you have controls available in the video-chat window, shown in Figure 8.5.

8.5 A video chat in progress.

Genius

Video chatting in Messages allows as many as three people to participate, which the FaceTime video-calling service cannot do. Click the Add (+) button to invite other participants.

Here are some helpful video-chat control tidbits:

- **Mute.** To mute the audio on your end of the conversation, click the Mute button; click it again to unmute it. Note that you're still on camera.

- **Fill Screen.** To make the chat window fill the screen, click the Fill Screen button (the icon of diagonal arrows). To see the toolbar while in full-screen mode, move the pointer.

- **Effects.** When you click the Effects button, you see the Video Effects panel. You can browse the available effects and click one to apply it to your image. The preview updates, and the other participants see you as the effect changes.

- **Present documents.** Drag a document from the Finder into the chat window. In the prompt that appears, choose the Share with Theater option. The larger part of the chat window is taken up by the document so all participants can see it. You can then present the document by using the on-screen controls.

Note If the audio or video is sporadic, or you can't hear or see the other participants, the most likely cause is that one or more of the participants doesn't have sufficient bandwidth to engage in video chats.

Sharing your screen during a chat

You can share your screen with those with whom you chat. When you do this, the other person can also control your computer. That person sees your MacBook Pro's screen on his or her screen and can manipulate your computer using his or her keyboard and mouse (or trackpad). Using a similar process, you can share someone else's screen to control that person's computer from afar. Just like audio and video chatting, you must use an account that supports screen sharing and the other participant must also be using a Mac. (Chapter 4 describes how to share your screens without using Messages.)

Follow these steps to share someone else's screen and take control of his or her computer:

1. **Select an existing conversation, or start a new one.**

2. **Click the Video button.**

3. **Choose Ask to Share** *name***'s screen (where** *name* **is the other person involved in the conversation).** A sharing request is sent to that participant. If accepted, you see the other person's screen on your display. In the small preview window (labeled My Computer), you see your own screen. You can now work with the other person's computer just as if you were sitting in front of it. For example, you can make changes to documents or use commands on menus. An audio chat is started automatically so you can communicate with the other person.

Applying Backgrounds during a Video Chat

You can apply backgrounds to video chats that make it appear as if you are someplace else. A background can be a static image or a video. Messages includes some backgrounds by default, or you can also use your own images.

Follow these steps to add a default background:

1. **Start a video chat.**
2. **Click the Effects button.**
3. **Scroll to the right in the Video Effects panel until you see the background images and video provided by default.**
4. **Click the image or video that you want to apply as a background.**
5. **Move out of the camera view at the prompt.**
6. **When the prompt disappears, move back into the picture.** It looks as if you are actually in front of the background. The effect isn't perfect, but it is pretty amazing.

Follow these steps if you would rather add your own images or video as backgrounds:

1. **Choose Video ⇨ Show Video Effects.** The Video Effects panel appears.
2. **Scroll in the panel until you see the User Backdrop categories.**
3. **Drag an image file or video clip into one of the User Backdrop wells.**
4. **Click the image or video that you want to apply as a background.**
5. **Start a video chat, and apply the background you added.**

4. **To move back to your Desktop, click the My Computer window.** The two windows flip-flop, so your screen is now the larger window and you can control your MacBook Pro.

5. **Click back in the other computer's window to control it again.**

6. **When you finish sharing, click the Close button on the My Computer window.**

Note

Like video chats, screen sharing is very dependent on a high bandwidth Internet connection for the participants. If you try to use an insufficient connection, you may experience a large time lag between when one person performs an action and its effect on the computer being shared.

To share your Desktop with someone else, perform Steps 1 and 2, but instead of Step 3, choose Share My Screen with *name* (where *name* is the name of the person with whom you are chatting). If the person accepts your request, you see a message that screen sharing has started. The other user can now control your computer as if sitting in front of it. That person can also talk to you because when you share the screen, you also have an audio chat session going. Expect to see your MacBook Pro do things without any help from you. You can stop screen sharing by choosing Buddies ⇨ End Screen Sharing. (The Buddies menu is normally used for chatting via non-Apple services, as described in the next section, but it is also used here.)

Caution

When you share your screen, you are sharing control of your MacBook Pro. Someone who shares your screen can do anything remotely that you can do directly.

Using the Buddy List

Messages has another way of making chats and monitoring your friends' availability. It's called the Buddy List, shown in Figure 8.6, and it works for all chat accounts except iCloud. Choose Window ⇨ Buddies to see it.

In the Buddies List panel, you can control your availability on the various non-iCloud services you're signed into using the menus at the top of the panel. Below that are lists of each group, and any active members are displayed if the disclosure triangle is pointing down for that group. (Click the disclosure triangle to reveal or hide the group's available members.)

Double-click a name to invite the person for a chat. Or use the Add (+) button at the bottom of the panel. You'll also find buttons there to switch among the four kinds of available chats: text, audio, video, and screen sharing.

8.6 The Buddies List provides easy access to chatting with your friends and colleagues who don't use iCloud.

How Can I Manage
My Calendars?

With Calendar, you can manage your time by creating calendars that help you be where you're supposed to be, when you're supposed to be there. Calendar is very useful as a personal calendar tool, and even if that's all it did, it would be worth using. However, Calendar is also designed for calendar collaboration. You can publish calendars so others can view or share them on their Macs. Likewise, you can subscribe to other people's calendars so you can see all upcoming events of interest to you in one place.

Managing Calendars

Calendar is a complete calendar tool that lets you take control of your busy life and coordinate with other people. In this section, I cover how to get started with Calendar, from setting important preferences, to configuring your calendars, events, and reminders.

The best place to set up your calendar accounts is in the Internet Accounts system preference, as described in Chapter 7. These accounts sync across all your devices using any of the services you set up, such as iCloud, Google, or Exchange. You can have multiple accounts set up, so you can keep calendar entries such as work and personal separate (so your office's calendar server won't record your personal appointments, for example), but still be able to view them together on your MacBook Pro. Events for any accounts set up for Calendar access in the Internet Accounts system preference display in the Calendar application automatically.

Genius

Even if you want only to have a personal calendar set up on your MacBook Pro, I encourage you to do so using a calendar account, either iCloud or Google. That way, your calendar is automatically synced to that service, so it can be accessed from another computer or device. For example, if you're traveling, you can check and update your calendar at the iCloud.com website (see Chapter 6) or Google Calendar website. If you use a mobile device, you can access your calendar from there as well using either service on pretty much any device (iCloud works only on Apple devices).

Configuring Calendar preferences

Before you jump into managing your calendars, take a few moments to configure some of Calendar's preferences (choose Calendar ➪ Preferences) so it works the way that you want. Calendar's Preferences dialog has four panes: General, Accounts, Advanced, and Alerts.

The General preferences

You can set these preferences in the General pane, shown in Figure 9.1:

- **Days per Week.** From this pop-up menu, choose 7 if you want your calendars to include all seven days of the week. Choose 5 if you want only five days (the workweek, for example) to be shown.

- **Start Week On.** From this pop-up menu, choose the day that you want to be considered the first of your week. Choosing Monday groups your weekend days together in Calendar's Week and Month views, which can make them easier to plan.

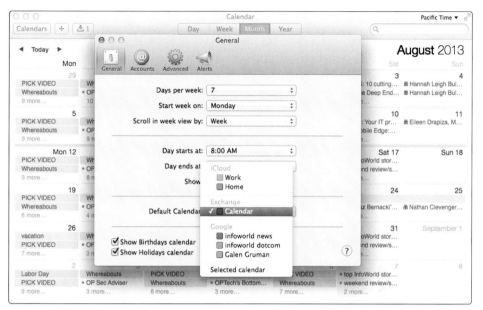

9.1 Use the Preferences dialog to customize Calendar's behavior to your liking, such as setting the default calendar for new appointments.

- **Scroll in Week View By.** This pop-up menu lets you choose to scroll by weeks or days when you view Calendar in the Week view. The Week, Stop on Today option makes Calendar pause scrolling when it reaches the current date.

- **Day Starts At**, **Day Ends At**, and **Show.** Use these pop-up menus to show when your workday starts and ends, as well as how many hours you want displayed on the calendar when you view it in Day or Week view. The start and end times for your days don't really matter; Calendar just shades the hours outside of this period.

- **Default Calendar.** When you manage more than one calendar—whether you have multiple calendar accounts or multiple calendars in the same account—this is where you choose which one you want to be the default when you create new events or reminders; you can always change the calendar with which any event is associated.

- **Show Birthdays Calendar** and **Show Holidays Calendar.** Select these if you want Calendar to display the birthdays of the contacts you're managing in Contacts (see Chapter 7) and/or the holidays for your country. This can be a helpful way to remember the birthdays of important people in your life because reminder events for them are automatically added to Calendar. Likewise, seeing the standard holidays in your calendar can help ensure you actually take them off!

The Accounts preferences

The Accounts pane lets you add accounts, but as noted earlier, it is best to do that via the Internet Accounts system preference. The Accounts pane is useful for these things:

● **Enable This Account.** When this check box in the Account Information subpane is deselected, the calendar entries for that service are no longer displayed in Calendar and the account's calendar is no longer synced. You might use this to temporarily disable a work calendar while on vacation.

● **Refresh Calendars.** Use this pop-up menu, also in the Account Information subpane, to set the schedule for how often the calendar is synced with its account's servers. The defaults usually are appropriate.

● **Delegation subpane.** Available for iCloud, Google, and Exchange calendars, this sub-pane lets you provide access to the account's calendars to people you specify, such as a family member or co-worker. It was designed for administrative assistants to have access to their bosses' calendars, but can be used by other people as well.

Genius

Delegation is available for secondary iCloud accounts, meaning those you create in the Internet Accounts system preference in addition to the basic iCloud account you set up on your MacBook Pro.

The Advanced preferences

These options are available in the Advanced pane:

● **Turn on Time Zone Support.** When you select this check box, Calendar automatically uses the current time zone set for your MacBook Pro for all appointments, if your appointments were made while you were in Pacific time but you're currently on the East Coast, they display in Eastern time while you are there. And any new appointments made while on the East Coast assume the current time zone, so you don't have to calculate what they would be in Pacific time.

Genius

Enabling time zone support also adds the Time Zone pop-up menu to the pop-over where you create new appointments, so if someone in another time zone asks you to agree to an appointment, you choose that person's time zone when adding the appointment, and let Calendar convert the time to your time zone—saving you that calculation effort. Even if you don't travel, it's good to enable this option.

- **Show Events in Year View.** Select this check box if you want to see specific entries for your events when you are viewing your calendar in the Year view. Normally, Year view shows a heat map of your appointments, indicating days with many appointments in red, those with a moderate number in yellow, and those with none in white. But it doesn't show the actual appointments. Because appointment details are very hard to read in Year view, enabling this option is often not useful.

- **Show Week Numbers.** When you enable this, you see numbers at the beginning of each week that indicate the number of the week relative to the 52 weeks in a year.

- **Open Events in Separate Windows.** When this is selected and you open an event, it appears in a separate window instead of as a pop-over attached to the event on the calendar. Enabling this setting can make events much easier to work with, so you might want to give it a try.

- **Ask Before Sending Changes to Events.** When you set up an event, you can invite others to it. When selected, this option asks whether you want to send any changes you make to an event to which others have accepted invitations. When deselected, invitees won't get notifications of minor changes to the event, such as the priority you've established for it or the calendar it is associated to, but they also won't get notifications of changes to date and time (the event simply moves in their calendar to the new date or time).

Note The Automatically Retrieve CalDAV Invitations from Mail option has been removed from OS X Maverick's Calendar application. Instead, to have OS X automatically add to Calendar any invitations sent to you via e-mail, go Mail's Preferences dialog and choose Always from the General pane's Add Invitations to Calendar pop-up menu. It replaces the Automatically Retrieve CalDAV Invitations from Mail option that used to reside in Calendar's preferences.

The Alerts preferences

Alerts notify you when events are coming up. You can determine the alert for a specific event when you create it. You can configure these default alerts on the Alerts pane:

- **Account.** Use this pop-up menu to choose the account for which you want to configure default alerts. When you create a new event on a calendar for this account, the default alert settings are used. You can set separate defaults for each account.

- **Events.** Choose the default alert time for events you create. Options range from at the time of the event to two days before the event.

- **All Day Events.** Choose the default alert time for all-day events you create. Options span from on the day of event to one week before.

- **Birthdays.** Use this pop-up menu to select when you want to be alerted about upcoming birthdays. The options are the same as for the All Day Events pop-up menu.

- **Use These Default Alerts Only on This Computer.** When this check box is selected, the default alerts set here are used only on your MacBook Pro. Other Macs and iOS devices use whatever settings they have for alerts. If this option is not checked, the alerts are synced across your devices. If you use a different computer or a website to create events, default alerts from those sources apply instead. Note that this option is available for iCloud and Google accounts only.

- **Notification Center section.** Select the Turn Off Shared Calendar Messages in Notification Center check box if you don't want alerts and messages originating from calendars you are sharing to appear in the Notification Center (see Chapter 1). Select the Turn Off Invitation Messages in Notification Center check box if you don't want these alerts about calendar invitations to appear in the Notification Center.

Managing calendars

To see the calendars you are managing in Calendar, click the Calendars button. A pane appears on the left side of the Calendar window, as Figure 9.2 shows. To hide the pane, click Calendars again. The pane lists the calendars by the account with which they are associated. If you have subscribed to calendars, they appear in the Other section. Calendar accounts that have multiple calendars show those calendars under the account name. To display a calendar's events and reminders, select its check box. If you deselect a calendar's check box, its events and reminders are hidden, but its information remains in the application.

Calendars are automatically assigned individual colors, to make it easier to know which calendar an event is associated to in the Calendar application's various views. You can change the color by selecting the calendar and choosing Edit ⇨ Get Info, which opens the Get Info settings sheet shown in Figure 9.3. Use the Color pop-up menu (the swatch to the right of the Name field) to change the color. You can change other options in the sheet as well; note that the options vary based on the type of calendar you've selected:

- **Name.** Type a new name for the calendar here. Note that you cannot change the name of the Birthdays calendar.

- **Description.** Type a description of the calendar in the Description field, to indicate what its purpose is. This field is not available for the Birthdays calendar or for subscribed calendars.

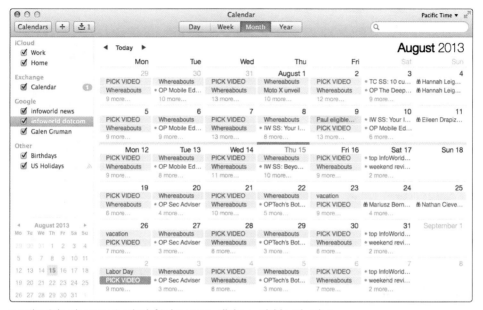

9.2 The Calendar pane (at the left) shows you all the available calendars.

- **Ignore Alerts.** If you want alert times for the calendar to be ignored, select this check box. Essentially, this option lets you override for the selected calendar the universal settings you made in the Settings dialog's Alerts pane.

- **Events Affect Availability.** Select this check box so people trying to see when you're available (for shared calendars) will see as unavailable any times for which you have events already set. This option is enabled by default and is available only for shared calendars.

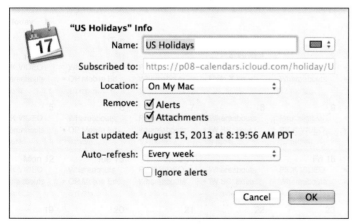

9.3 You can modify the behavior of individual calendars using the Get Info settings sheet.

● **Subscribed calendars.** Calendars you subscribe to, such as the US Holidays calendar that iCloud automatically subscribes you to, have several unique options in this settings sheet:

  ● **Location.** This pop-up menu lets you specify which account the subscribed calendar resides in. If you choose On My Mac, the calendar's entries are not synced to other devices.

  ● **Remove.** The Alerts and Attachments check boxes let you control whether any alerts or attachments are retained (deselect the check boxes to do so).

  ● **Auto-Refresh.** Use this pop-up menu to determine how often the subscribed calendar is updated. Options range from No (meaning no updating occurs) to Every Week.

To remove a calendar, select it in the Calendars pane and choose Edit ⇨ Delete. If you confirm the action when asked, the calendar and all its events and reminders are removed from Calendar. Most of the time, you're better off hiding a calendar so you can access its information later if needed. When you delete a calendar, all its information goes with it.

Calendars have various icons to show their status in the Calendars pane. For example, when a calendar has been published, it is marked with a radio-waves icon, as you can see in the bottom entry in Figure 9.2. If Calendar can't access the server on which a calendar is located, it displays the ~ icon. When a calendar's information is being refreshed, it is marked with the rotating-circle icon. When a calendar needs your attention, such as to respond to an invitation, it displays a badge icon showing how many items there are to which you need to respond, as you can see for the Exchange calendar in Figure 9.2.

Navigating calendars

Calendar has four views—Day, Week, Month, and Year—that you can switch among by using the buttons in the toolbar. The Day view provides the most detail for your events, but of course it limits how much of your calendar you can see.

To move through your calendar, click the Today button at the top to jump to the current date in whatever view you're using, and use the Back and Forward buttons (the left- and right-facing triangle icons, respectively) to move earlier and later. On your MacBook Pro, you can also navigate through your calendar using its trackpad. For Day and Week views, scroll up and down using one finger to move through the hours of the day or week. For Week views, you can scroll sideways with one finger to move through the weeks. For Month views, you scroll up and down using one finger to move through the weeks across the months. There are no scroll gestures for Year view.

Note The line across the calendar that appears in the Day and Week views with a pushpin at one end shows the current time. It helps you see where you are in your day. And note the red dot at its left that guides your eye to the current time adjacent to it.

Use the Search box to search for events, notes, titles, locations, or combinations of information. To start a search, type the search text in the Search box. As you do, items that match your search are found and displayed in the pop-up that appears at the right side of Calendar, as shown in Figure 9.4. The results are categorized, such as People and Notes. Click an item to get more information on it. For example, click a name to get a list of events for which someone was invited. Click the Event Contains option at the top of the pop-up to see all events containing the search term.

When you are finished with a search, click the Clear (X) button in the Search bar. The search is cleared, and the results pop-up pane closes.

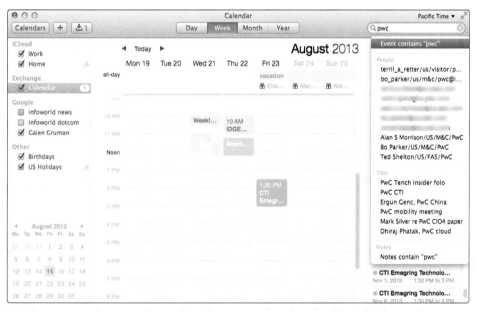

9.4 When you search, you see the results in the pane on the right side of the Calendar window.

Creating calendars

There are two levels of calendars that you deal with when you use Calendar.

The first level is the overall calendar, which is what you see inside the Calendar window. This calendar includes all the information being managed or shown by the application, from all visible accounts (those checked in the Calendars pane).

The second level is composed of the individual calendars in which you create events and reminders, as well as those you share or to which you subscribe. Each account has at least one calendar, but you can create additional calendars within most accounts, as Figure 9.2 previously shows is the case for some of my calendar accounts. There are many good reasons to create multiple calendars for your events and reminders.

The classic example is one calendar for work events and another for personal ones. When creating calendars, you should also consider publishing them. If there are some events you don't want shown in a published version, you can create one calendar for those events and another for those that you want to share. On the other hand, you don't want to create so many calendars that they become unwieldy.

Follow these steps to create a calendar:

1. **Choose File ⇨ New Calendar ⇨** *account.* For example, if you choose an iCloud account, the new calendar is created in your iCloud account. The Calendar pane opens, a new calendar appears under the chosen account, and its name is highlighted so you know it is ready to edit.

Note You can create multiple calendars for iCloud and Exchange accounts in Calendar. But you can't create multiple Google calendars. Google Calendar does support multiple calendars per account, but you have to create them at the Google Calendar website. After they are created, the Calendar application can work with them.

2. **Type the desired name for the calendar, and press Return to save it.** You can name a calendar anything that you want.

3. **If desired, adjust the calendar's settings using the Get Info settings sheet described earlier in this chapter.**

Adding events to calendars

You can use Calendar events to plan your time. For example, you can invite others to join a meeting by sending them an invitation. In addition to the time and date, you can include all sorts of useful information in Calendar events, such as file attachments, URLs, and notes.

There are two ways to create an event. One is the quick event, which is useful for simple entries, and the other is a standard event, which is useful when you want to set various parameters such as inviting people to the event, adding notes, and/or setting a repeating schedule. Either way, the event is initially placed in your default calendar.

These steps walk you through how to add a quick event to a calendar:

1. **Click the Add (+) button in Calendar's toolbar.** The Create Quick Event pop-over appears.

2. **Type information about the event, such as its title, date, and time, as shown in Figure 9.5.** Calendar tries to interpret what you type into a new event.

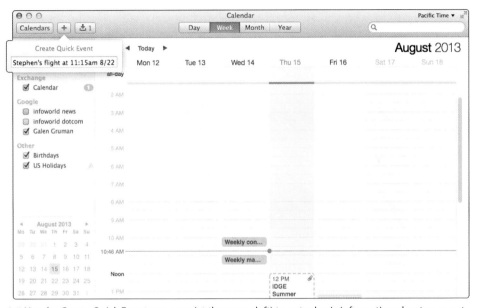

9.5 Use the Create Quick Event pop-over (at the upper left) to enter basic information about an event.

3. **Press Return.** The event is created in the calendar specified as your default in the General pane of the Preferences dialog, and its event info pop-over appears attached to the event (unless you enabled the separate info window preference in the Preference dialog's General pane), as shown in Figure 9.6. You're now ready to add more details to the event, as well as change the calendar it is in.

You can also add a default event by dragging the pointer over the calendar to indicate the time you want to set for the event; it's best to do this in Week or Day view, so you can more precisely set the event time. Or you can choose File ➪ New Event to add an event. Either way, you get the event info pop-over like that shown in Figure 9.6, except that the event has no details filled in yet.

In the event info pop-over, click a field to edit or add information to it. For example, click Add Invitees to enter names or e-mail addresses of people you want to invite to the appointment. Click outside the pop-over to close it and save your changes.

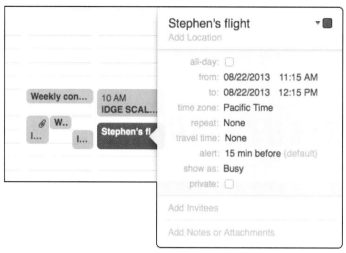

9.6 After you create a quick event, the event info pop over appears, where you can edit details and add more details.

Note

You can display the info window for existing events by double-clicking them. Then you can edit the event as needed. The event info window works just like the event info pop-over, except that you close the info window by clicking its Close (X) box, whereas you close the info pop-over by clicking elsewhere in Calendar.

You can use these fields:

- **Event Name.** Change the name for your event here.

- **Location.** Enter a location for the event, such as an address or conference room. If you enter an address, you can see the address on a map and even get driving directions for it, as described later on this chapter.

- **Calendar.** The color swatch to the right of the event name is a pop-up menu that lets you select a different calendar or account to which to move the event.

- **Date** and **Time.** Add or change the date and time by clicking either of them. The section expands to show several options, including All Day, From, To, Time Zone, Repeat, Travel Time, Alert, Show As, and Private.

  - Selecting All Day places the event in the All Day row in Calendar. That way, you can still see events scheduled during that day. For example, you might mark a conference as all day and set individual appointments at the conference as regular appointments.

- If you click Repeat, you can set a repeating pattern for the event, such as weekly or daily. Choose Custom to specify options such as every Tuesday or on the fourth Thursday of the month.

- Use the Travel Time option introduced in OS X Mavericks to specify travel time for your appointments, so you know when to leave for them. If you enter a location in the Location field, OS X tries to estimate the driving time to that address from your current location; you can override its estimate by entering your own value.

- Use the Show As option to specify how others see the event if they have access to the calendar. Your options are Busy, Free, Tentative, and Out of Office. Note that many calendar accounts do not support this feature, so it may not display for your events.

- Selecting Private hides the details of the event, so anyone who has access to your calendar sees only that the time is blocked but can't see any of its details.

Invitees. If an event has no invitees, click Add Invitees to add them; enter a name to pull contact information from Contacts or enter the person's e-mail address. The invitees receive an e-mail with a calendar invitation attached, which their e-mail or calendar applications should let them open to add to their calendars. If you've already invited people, you see their names listed; click one to open the list; from there, you can add people to the invitation and delete them from it. To delete a person, click the name and choose Remove Invite from the pop-up menu that appears. Click the Apply button to make the changes to the invitation, or click Revert to cancel them.

Note and **Attachments.** If an event has no notes or file attachments, click Add Notes or Attachments to expand this section. Then click Add Notes to open a text area for entering or pasting in your note. Click Add Attachment to open the Open dialog from which you select an attachment from your MacBook Pro. If you've added notes or attachments previously, they display in the event. Click them to edit them.

Status. If an event came from an invitation, its status appears here. If you have not yet acted on the invitation, the Status pop-up menu lets you Accept or Decline it.

Show. Click this button to have Calendar highlight the event onscreen. This button appears only in event panels. Event info pop-overs display next to their events, but event info windows display as independent elements onscreen, and so they may not be near the calendar entry.

Using Maps with Calendar

When viewing the info window or info pop-over for an event whose location includes an address, you can see a map of that address by selecting it, right-clicking the selection, and choosing Show Maps in the contextual menu that appears. The Maps application opens, centered at that address. You can use Maps to send driving directions to your iPhone, as Chapter 6 explains.

If the location includes a complete address, you can do more than open Maps from the contextual menu. You can see a map right in the event's info pop-over or info window, as the right side of the figure below shows. You also see the current weather for that location. (You do need an active Internet connection for this all to work.)

The key is to have a full address, and the way to do that is to let Calendar find it for you. As you type an address, person's name, or company name, Calendar checks both Contacts and Apple's mapping service to find likely addresses, which it displays in a list, as the left side of the figure shows. Select the correct location, and Calendar has the information it needs to display that map preview. Click the map preview to open it in the Maps application, where you can get driving directions and send them to your iPhone.

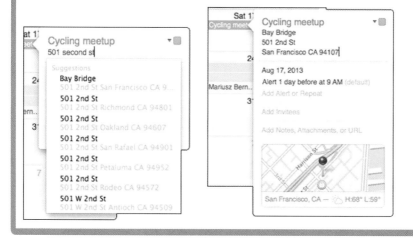

Working with event invitations and availability

As covered in the preceding section, you can invite people to your events, including meetings. Calendar sends them an invitation file via e-mail they can then accept in their e-mail or calendar program. Likewise, people can send you invitation files that you can accept in Mail or Calendar on your MacBook Pro. Because the .ics file format used for such invitations is an industry standard, invitations work with most computers' and mobile devices' e-mail and calendar applications.

The Invitees field in an event's info window or info pop-over is handy for managing who's invited to a meeting, but it just sends the invitation files without any personalization. Invitees do see the time and date, of course, plus the location and any notes or attachments.

If you want to send more personal invitations, right-click the event and choose Mail Event from the contextual menu that appears. This opens a Mail window in which you enter who you want to send the invitation to, as well as the subject and any message you want to include. The invitation file is automatically attached.

Calendar can help you determine whether someone is available for a meeting you are planning. Create an event and add invitees as explained earlier. Choose Window ⇨ Availability Panel. When the panel opens, you see the people you have invited. You see whether each person is available. If not, you can click the Next Available Time button to see the next time when everyone is free.

When you receive an invitation via e-mail (assuming you chose the Always option from the Add Invitation to Calendar pop-up menu in the General pane of Mail's Preferences dialog), you see the Notifications button (a tray icon) next to the Add button in the upper-left corner of the Calendar window. A numeral next to the icon indicates how many invitations you have not yet responded to, as well as any updates you have not viewed to previously accepted invitations.

Click the Notifications button to open a pop-over listing the invitations and updates you have received, as Figure 9.7 shows. Click the Maybe or Accept button next to an event in the pop-over to add an event to your calendar, or click Decline to reject it. The person inviting you is notified about your reply and sees your status in the event on his or her calendar.

9.7 The Notifications pop-over shows new invitations and unread updates to previously accepted ones.

Note
If you click Maybe, the event displays in gray on your calendar. If you click Accept, the event is added to your calendar in the calendar account associated with your e-mail address; an invite sent to your iCloud e-mail address appears in your iCloud calendar, for example. If the e-mail address is not associated to a calendar account (such as for a POP e-mail address), the event is added to your default calendar, as specified in the General pane of the Preferences dialog.

Printing Calendars

Although having your calendar in an electronic format is very useful and practical (because you can take your MacBook Pro with you), there may be times when you'd like to have a hard copy. You can use Calendar's Print command to create paper versions of your calendar information. Follow these steps to print a calendar:

1. **Choose File ⇨ Print.** The Print dialog appears, as shown in Figure 9.8. As you can see, it's not the standard Print dialog used in most applications.

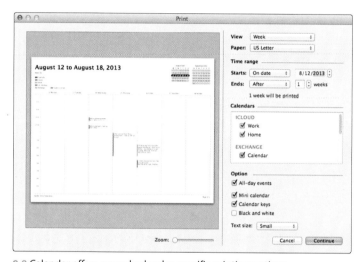

9.8 Calendar offers several calendar-specific printing options.

2. **Choose the view you want to print on the View pop-up menu.** Your choices are Day, Week, Month, List (you choose a range of dates to list events for), and Selected Events. (To select events, ⌘-click each in the calendar before you print.)

3. **Use the controls in the Time Range section to define the time period for the printed version.**

4. **In the Calendars section, select the check box for each calendar whose information you want included in the printed version.**

5. **Use the Option section's check boxes to set print options.** The options vary based on the time period you choose:

   - **All-Day Events.** If selected, the printout includes all-day events. This option is not available if you're printing the Selected Events view; you would need to select the all-day events you want included.

- **Timed Events.** If selected, the printout includes all events scheduled for specific times. You might deselect this option to print a calendar of all-day events, birthdays, holidays, and the like, to serve as the basis of a printed calendar that people can add appointments to. This option is not available for Day or Selected Event views.

- **Details and Phone Numbers.** These options are available only for the Day view. If selected, Details includes notes, locations, and other such information in the printout. If Details is selected, you can also select Phone Numbers to include those on the printout, drawn from the event's details.

- **Mini Calendar.** If selected, the printout includes a small calendar at the upper right for each month covered by the printout's period.

- **Calendar Keys.** If selected, the printout includes a color key for the events, indicating the calendar to which they belong.

- **Black and White.** If selected, the printout is optimized for black-and-white printers, with the colors converted to distinguishable shades of gray.

- **Text Size.** Choose the size for the printout's text from this pop-up menu.

- **Zoom.** Use this slider to zoom into the calendar preview shown in the pane at the left.

6. **Click Continue.** Calendar now generates and formats the printout's contents and opens the standard Print dialog.

7. **In that standard Print dialog, choose the printer, number of copies, whether two-side mode is enabled, and so on.**

8. **Click Print to print the formatted calendar or use the PDF menu button at the bottom to save the formatted calendar as a PDF file.**

Sharing Calendars

Calendar is designed to be a collaborative calendar tool, so you can publish or share your calendars—if you use iCloud. The difference between publishing and sharing a calendar is that when you publish it, a calendar is read-only. When you share a calendar, the people with whom you share it can make changes to it according to the permissions you set.

Note Although both Google and Exchange calendars can be shared, they can't be shared from Calendar. You can share a Google calendar from the Google calendar web page, and you can share an Exchange calendar from Microsoft's own Outlook application.

Publishing calendars via iCloud

With your iCloud account and Calendar, it's simple to publish calendars for other people to view (but not change). Follow these steps to publish a calendar:

1. **Right-click the calendar you want to publish in the Calendars pane, and choose Share Calendar from the contextual menu.** The Share With pop-over appears, as shown in Figure 9.9.

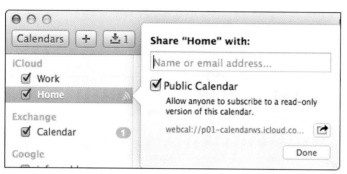

9.9 Select the Public Calendar option to publish an iCloud calendar on the web with read-only access.

2. **Select the Public Calendar check box.**

3. **Click the Share button (the icon of an arrow emerging from a tray) to send the web address of the published calendar via Mail, Messages, or Facebook.** Or right-click the URL and choose Copy from the contextual menu that appears to paste it into a document or message. People use the URL to open the calendar in their web browsers or, if they use iCloud, to subscribe to the calendar so it appears in Calendar on their Mac, iOS device, and or iCloud.com.

4. **Click Done.** The calendar is published, and the sharing icon (the radio waves) appears next to its name on the Calendar pane.

Sharing calendars via iCloud

When you share a calendar, rather than publish it, it becomes collaborative, meaning that people with whom you share it can also change it if you give them permission to do so.

The process for sharing an iCloud calendar is similar to the process for publishing it:

1. **Right-click the calendar you want to publish in the Calendars pane, and choose Share Calendar from the contextual menu.** The Share With pop-over appears.

2. **Enter a name or e-mail address in the text field at the top of the pop-over.** As you type, Calendar looks in Contacts and Mail for addresses that might match, and it displays them in a list you can select from. Press return after selecting or typing a name. To enter additional names, enter a new name or e-mail address after an existing one and press Return. Repeat for each name. If a ? icon appears to the left of a name, that person's address isn't connected to an iCloud account.

3. **Click the menu indicator (the down-pointing triangle) to the right of each name to set privileges: View & Edit, or View Only, as Figure 9.10 shows.** Repeat for each person.

9.10 Enter the names of people you want to share an iCloud calendar with, and choose the permissions for each.

4. **Click Done.** The calendar is shared and the sharing icon (the radio waves) appears next to its name on the Calendar pane. The people will receive an e-mail letting them know they can now share the calendar. In that e-mail, they need to click Join Calendar to be able to view and/or edit it on a Mac, iOS device, or browser at the iCloud.com website. If they don't have an iCloud account, they are invited to create one.

Note   If you've previously invited someone to share an iCloud calendar, you can resend that invitation by right-clicking the calendar in the Calendars pane, choosing Sharing Settings in the contextual menu that appears, clicking the pop-up menu to the right of the person's name in the Share With sheet, choosing Invite Again from its menu, and clicking Done.

Subscribing to public calendars

Many public calendars are available to which you can subscribe. For example, many professional sports teams have calendars that show games and other events. You can also find DVD release calendars, TV schedules, and many other types to which you can subscribe. Just like shared calendars, when you subscribe to public calendars, their events are shown in your Calendar window. Follow these steps to find and subscribe to public calendars:

1. **Go to the iCalendars: Most Recent web page in your browser.** You can find this at www.apple.com/downloads/macosx/calendars.

2. **Browse the available calendars by category, such as Most Recent, Most Popular, or Alphabetical.**

3. **Click Download for the calendar to which you want to subscribe.** The calendar is downloaded to your MacBook Pro.

4. **Choose the calendar to which you want the events on the public calendar added, or choose New Calendar to create a new one for the events.**

5. **Click OK.** The calendar is added to the Subscriptions or Other section of your Calendar window (if you selected the New Calendar option), and you can view it just like your own calendars. If you added the calendar's events to one of your existing calendars, you see its events when you view that calendar.

How Can I Make Better Use of the MacBook Pro's Audio Features?

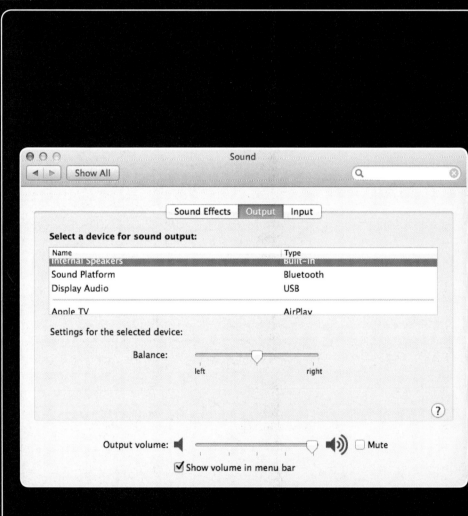

Sound is an important part of using a MacBook Pro. If you use iTunes, iMovie, QuickTime Player, GarageBand, or any other Mac digital media application, audio is a major part of the experience. Audio is also an essential component of communications applications such as FaceTime, Messages, and Skype. Therefore, understanding how to get the most from the MacBook Pro audio capabilities is fundamental to enjoying your MacBook Pro to the fullest. On its own, a MacBook Pro has reasonable audio capabilities. If you want to invest in a bit of hardware and some additional software, you can transform your MacBook Pro into an audio powerhouse.

Getting Sound out of a MacBook Pro

In this section, I cover the sound output options available to you. I also explain how to choose and use those options to ensure that you have a great audio experience as you work with your MacBook Pro.

Understanding sound output options

When it comes to audio, there are two fundamental options: analog and digital. As with any other device with these options, digital is better than analog from the quality perspective. However, taking advantage of digital sound is more expensive and requires a bit more work than analog sound. With your MacBook Pro, you can use both options in different situations. You have these methods for getting sound out of your MacBook Pro:

● **Built-in speakers.** The MacBook Pro includes built-in stereo speakers that actually do a decent job, considering their small size and basic capabilities. They're perfectly adequate for use in conferencing applications like Skype and FaceTime, for example. However, if the quality of the sound is important to you when you listen to music or watch movies or television shows, it's unlikely that the internal speakers will satisfy you. They are a bit on the tinny side, and their bass certainly isn't impressive compared to a home theater or car audio system.

● **Headphones, earbuds, and headsets.** You can connect any analog headphones or earbuds to the MacBook Pro's audio line-out port located on the left side of the computer (it's marked with the headphones icon). You can also connect analog headsets (headphones that have a microphone).

● **External speakers.** You can connect any set of powered (also called *computer*) speakers to your MacBook Pro's audio line-out port. The port works with both analog speakers and digital optical speakers, but to use the digital output, you need a Mini TOSlink adapter, shown in Figure 10.1. When you buy a digital audio cable, look for one that includes this adapter or that has a Mini TOSlink connector integral to it. You can also purchase the cable and adapter separately.

10.1 To connect to a digital sound system, use a digital cable with a Mini TOSlink adapter, like this one from Belkin.

Genius

You can use the earbuds included with iPhones and iPod touches to control iTunes running on a MacBook Pro. When you listen to iTunes via these headphones, use the switch on the right side to control the playback: Press the center part of the switch to play or pause. Press the upper part of the switch to increase the volume or the lower part to decrease it.

Note

The 13-inch and 15-inch Retina MacBook Pro models and the 13-inch MacBook Pro, as well as some older models, have only one audio port, which is used for both input and output. These MacBook Pros automatically detect the type of device connected to this port and configure themselves accordingly. The non-Retina 15-inch MacBook Pro model has separate line-in and headphone ports.

- **USB audio devices.** You can connect USB headphones, headsets, and other USB audio devices to the MacBook Pro's USB port. Some devices may require software to be installed to work properly. USB headsets are commonly used to make private Skype calls, for example.

- **AirPlay audio devices.** You stream audio over your local network from your MacBook Pro to one or more Apple TVs (which then relay them to TVs or receivers) and AirPlay-compatible speakers.

- **Bluetooth audio devices.** You can use wireless headphones, headsets, speakers, and other Bluetooth audio devices with your MacBook Pro. Chapter 4 explains how to connect Bluetooth devices. These devices can be very convenient because there are no wires to get tangled in, but the audio quality is not as good as with wired speakers, so you won't get a home theater level of quality from them.

When it comes to digital music and video, you need to connect an external speaker system (such as a 5.1 surround sound speaker system) to experience the best in sound quality for movies, television shows, and music. Fortunately, your MacBook Pro has the internal hardware required to support digital speaker systems, so all you need to add is the system itself. If you connect such a system, be sure to get the correct cable end for the external speaker—TOSlink (also called optical digital) or digital coax—as specified in its manual.

Controlling sound output

When you plug headphones or speakers into the MacBook Pro's audio line-out port, the sound automatically is directed to that device. You might think that's the end of the story, but it's not.

There are two issues to be aware of in controlling sound output: the volume of audio and where the output is directed when you have multiple audio devices connected (perhaps headphones, a Thunderbolt Display with its built-in speakers, and a Bluetooth speaker).

When it comes to sound output, be aware that there are as many as three types of volume levels:

- **System volume level.** This sets the base level of volume output from the MacBook Pro—that is, the intensity of the audio signal it generates—for each device.

- **Relative volume of applications.** When you adjust volume levels within applications, such as iTunes or DVD Player, you change their volume relative to the system volume level. In other words, they decrease or increase the volume only for the audio they generate, using the system volume level as their starting point.

- **Physical volume level of external speakers, headphones, and so on.** You control this with the system's volume controls. The speakers or other audio device take the audio volume received from the MacBook Pro as the base, and then you adjust the volume they emit using their volume controls.

Follow these steps to configure the MacBook Pro's system volume level for each audio device:

1. **Connect the audio device to your MacBook Pro.**

2. **Open the Sound system preference.**

3. **Go to the Output pane, shown Figure 10.2.** In this pane, you see the available output devices on the list at the top of the pane. When you select an output device, you see its audio controls below.

4. **Select the output device through which you want your MacBook Pro to play sound.** These are the most common options (the actual options are based on what you have connected):

   - **Internal Speakers.** If you have connected something to the audio line-out jack, you won't see the Internal Speakers option in the Sound system preference's Output pane. Disconnect the device (temporarily) to configure the internal speakers.

   - **Headphones.** Use this option for headphones, earbuds, or external analog speaker systems.

   - **Display Audio.** This option controls the speakers built into Apple's Thunderbolt Display.

   - **Bluetooth devices.** These include headsets and speakers connected via Bluetooth, such as the Sound Platform device shown in Figure 10.2.

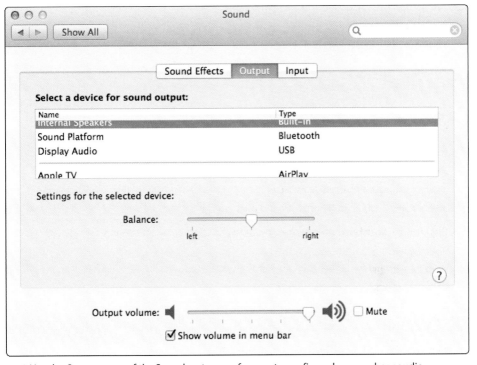

10.2 Use the Output pane of the Sound system preference to configure how you hear audio.

- **AirPlay devices.** These include Apple TVs, AirPlay-compatible wireless speakers, and speaker systems connected to Apple's AirPort Base Station router.

- **Digital Out.** Use this for an external, digital speaker system.

5. **Use the controls that appear for the selected device to adjust its sound:**

- **Use the Output Volume slider to set the system volume.** In most cases, it's best to set it at midlevel. If you are using an external speaker system, set its volume at a relatively low level.

- **Use the Balance slider to adjust the volume balance between the left and right speakers in your device.** Normally, you want both at the same level, which means the slider should be at the midpoint. Note that the Apple TV and single speakers don't have this slider.

- **Select the Show Volume in Menu Bar check box to have the Volume button (the speaker icon) appear in the menu bar.** Click the button to display a slider that lets you adjust the system volume without having to use the Sound system preference.

Note If you are using a digital system and see the message "The selected device has no output controls" when Digital Out is selected, you can use only the speaker system's controls to set volume levels. You also use it to make all other adjustments, including the bass level, balance, and surround sound field. You can still use an application's volume control to adjust the relative volume.

6. **Open an application that you use to play audio, such as iTunes.** Use that application's volume slider, as shown in Figure 10.3, to set its relative volume level.

7. **Play the audio, and adjust the system volume level accordingly.** Typically, you want to set the system volume at a

10.3 Use the volume slider in iTunes (to the right of the Fast-Forward button at the upper left) to set the application's volume relative to the system volume level.

level that allows you to control the volume with the application controls, so you can make it as loud or as quiet as you want. This sometimes requires experimentation to get the right balance between the system and application volume levels. If you use external speakers, their volume control is yet a third level to balance.

Note Most applications have keyboard shortcuts that enable you to adjust the application's volume level. In iTunes, press ⌘+↑ or ⌘+↓.

Note To mute all sound, select the Mute check box in the Output pane of the Sound system preference, set the Volume button's menu to the lowest level, or press F10. To unmute the sound, deselect the Mute check box, raise the volume in the Volume button's menu, or press F10. You can change the system volume level by pressing F11 (for quieter) or F12 (for louder). If you use a digital speaker system, these controls are disabled.

Creating and Using Sound Effects

OS X includes sound effects that the system uses to alert you or to provide audible feedback for specific events. You control these effects in the Sound Effects pane of the Sound system preference.

Configuring sound effects

Perform these steps to configure sound effects:

1. **Open the Sound system preference.**

2. **Go to the Sound Effects pane, as shown in Figure 10.4.**

3. **Click a sound in the alert sounds list.** The sound plays and becomes the current alert sound.

4. **If your MacBook Pro can output sound through different devices simultaneously (such as internal speakers and a sound system connected to a USB port), then select the device on which you want the sounds to be played via the Play Sound Effects Through pop-up menu.** If the MacBook Pro currently supports only one sound output device, the menu shows Selected Sound Output Device.

5. **Drag the Alert Volume slider to the right to make it louder, or drag it to the left to make it quieter.** This sets the volume of the alert sound relative to the system sound level. The default alert sounds have a relatively low volume level, so you'll probably have to set the slider to a high level to hear them over music or any other audio.

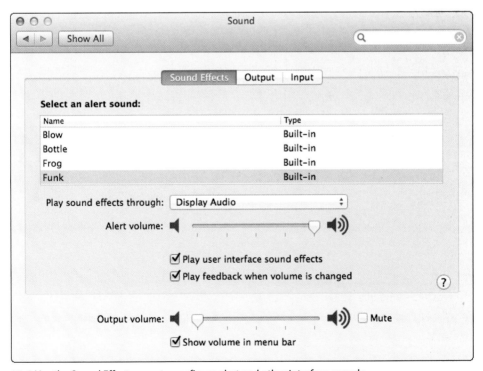

10.4 Use the Sound Effects pane to configure alert and other interface sounds.

6. **If you don't want to hear sound effects for system actions (such as when you empty the Trash), deselect the Play User Interface Sound Effects check box.**

7. **If you don't want audio feedback when you change the volume level, deselect the Play Feedback When Volume Is Changed check box.** When selected, your MacBook Pro plays a blip sound when you set a new volume level so you know what the new volume level is.

8. **Quit the System Preferences application when you're finished.**

Creating and using custom sound alerts

You can also create and use your own alert sounds if you want your MacBook Pro to communicate with you in a unique way. OS X's system alert sounds are in the Audio Interchange File Format (AIFF). You can use iTunes to record or convert almost any sound into an AIFF file and use that sound as a custom alert.

Creating a sound alert

You can create a custom alert sound in these ways:

- **iMovie and QuickTime Player.** You can use iMovie or QuickTime Player to create an audio track and save it as an AIFF file, or you can save part of a movie's audio track as an AIFF file. You can also record narration or other sounds to use as an alert sound. (I cover getting sound into your MacBook Pro later in this chapter.)

- **iTunes.** You can use iTunes to convert any sound in your library to an AIFF file, including sounds you record via the QuickTime Player application that comes with OS X.

- **GarageBand.** You can create a music snippet and save it as an AIFF file.

- **Record audio playing on your MacBook Pro.** Using an application like WireTap Pro from Ambrosia Software, you can record any audio playing on your MacBook Pro and use what you record as an alert sound.

Here's an example showing how to use QuickTime Player to create and save a sound as an alert from audio stored in your iTunes library. Use this technique to add just about any sound as an alert:

1. **Launch QuickTime Player.** It's in the Applications folder on your MacBook Pro.

2. **Choose File ➪ Open File to import an audio or video file with the audio track you want to use as an alert.** The playback window appears.

3. **Choose Edit ➪ Trim.** The trim bar appears at the bottom of the screen.

4. **Drag the sides of the trim bar to select the portion of the file you want to use as the alert sound, as Figure 10.5 shows.** Click Play to hear the portion you've selected, and adjust the trim bar's sides as needed. You may have to adjust and play the trim several times to get it exactly right.

5. **Click the Trim button on the Trim bar.** A copy of the file is made with just the portion of the file in the trim bar.

6. **Choose File ⇨ Save to save the trimmed portion as a new file.** Choose its location, give it a filename, and click Save.

7. **If your audio source was a video, choose File ⇨ Export ⇨ Audio Only.** Save the resulting .m4a file in whatever location you want, with the name of your choosing. Open the saved trimmed audio file in QuickTime Player.

8. **Choose File ⇨ Export ⇨ iTunes.** After a few moments, the file is added to your iTunes library.

9. **Quit QuickTime Player.**

10.5 Use the trim bar in QuickTime Player to select the audio for your alert sound.

10. **Launch iTunes.**

11. **Look for the added file, and select it.** It's usually in the Music library, but if you converted a video, it is in the Movies library. If you don't see the file, also look in the Podcasts and Home Videos libraries.

12. **If the audio came from a video file, press and hold Option, and choose File ⇨ Create New Version ⇨ Convert to AAC.** It's critical that you press and hold Option when choosing this menu option. In the Choose Conversion Destination dialog that appears, choose the location to save the file and click open.

13. **Quit iTunes.**

14. **In the Finder, open the folder containing the converted file.**

15. **Click the file, and change the filename extension to .aiff.** You are prompted to verify the change.

You can also record sounds in QuickTime Player, as described later in this chapter. If you record a sound in QuickTime Player that you want to use as an alert sound, follow Steps 3 through 5 and then 8 through 15 as just described for creating an alert-compatible file from an existing media file.

Adding a custom sound alert

You can add alert sounds to the system so they are available to all user accounts on your computer. To do this, you must authenticate yourself as an administrator. Follow these steps to add alert sounds to your system:

1. **Drag the AIFF file into the folder** *startupvolume***/System/Library/Sounds (where** *startupvolume* **is the name of your MacBook Pro's startup drive).**

2. **At the prompt, click Authenticate, provide an administrator account username and password, and click OK.** The custom alert sound is copied into the folder.

3. **If the System Preferences application is open, quit it, and open it again.**

4. **Open the Sound system preference, and go to the Sound Effects pane.** Your new alert sound appears in the list.

5. **Select and configure the custom alert sound just as you would one of the default sounds.**

Recording and Working with Sound

There are many situations in which you may want to put sound into your MacBook Pro. For example, you might want to add narration to iMovie projects or iPhoto slide shows; you need to have audio input for FaceTime chats; if you use GarageBand, you'll want to record instruments and vocals.

Note

You can also use your MacBook Pro's sound-input capabilities to take dictation and to command your Mac, as Chapter 5 explains.

On the simplest side, you can use the MacBook Pro's built-in microphone to record voice narration or other sounds, and it is certainly good enough for most audio and video chats. On the more complex side, you can add an external MIDI (Musical Instrument Digital Interface) keyboard or other device that enables you to record sound from musical instruments and other sources.

Caution   The MacBook Pro's audio-in port is not powered. This means that you can't just plug a standard analog microphone into it and record sound. Whatever you connect to the port must provide amplification to be able to record sound from it. To be able to connect a microphone to it, there must be a power source for the microphone.

Recording sound with a microphone

Using the MacBook Pro's internal microphone is easy and suitable for several purposes, such as audio and video chats, recording narration for iMovie and iPhoto projects, and other relatively simple projects. You can also use the microphone on a USB or Bluetooth headset for these purposes. For better audio recording, such as for home-movie narration, use a powered microphone you plug into the MacBook Pro's microphone port.

To record audio with a microphone, first follow these steps to configure it:

1. **Open the Sound system preference.**

2. **Go to the Input pane.** The Input pane has two default options—Internal Microphone or Line In—if you're using a non-Retina 15-inch model of the MacBook Pro. For all other current MacBook Pro models, it has only one option: Internal Microphone. Any other recording devices you have connected to the MacBook Pro also appear.

3. **Select the microphone you want to use.** Below the device list, you see the controls to configure the device selected in the list. As your MacBook Pro receives audio input through the selected microphone, the relative volume of the input is shown on the Input Level gauge, as shown in Figure 10.6.

4. **As you speak or play the sound, monitor the input on the level gauge.** The maximum level freezes briefly so you can see where it is.

5. **If the gauge shows input when you aren't speaking or playing a sound, select the Use Ambient Noise Reduction check box.** This applies a filter that screens out background sound.

6. **Drag the Input Volume slider to the left to reduce the level of input sound, or drag it to the right to increase it.** The higher the level, the more sensitive the microphone is. That can result in clearer recordings, but also in unwanted background noises being recorded, so experiment.

The microphone should now be ready to use to record sound in an application, using the application's own recording controls.

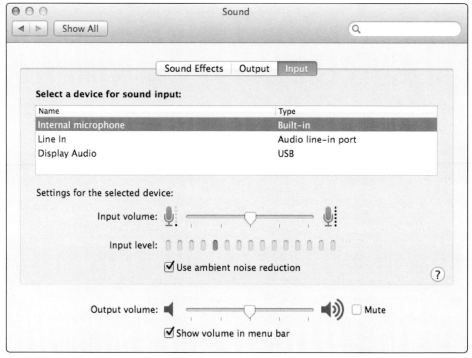

10.6 Use the Input Level gauge to assess the input level of sound coming into the MacBook Pro.

Recording sound with a video camera

Although it might not be obvious, a video camera can be a great way to record sound for your projects. You can then use iMovie to save that sound as a file to use in projects, add to your iTunes library, or for other purposes. Follow these steps:

1. **Connect the camera to your MacBook Pro.**

2. **Launch iMovie.**

3. **Choose File ⇨ Import from Camera, and add the clips containing the audio to the event library.**

4. **Choose File ⇨ New Project.** The New Project sheet appears.

5. **Name your project.** Again, the options don't matter because you are only using the audio.

6. **Click Create.** The new project is created and appears on the project list.

7. **Add the clips with audio you want to save to the new project.**

8. **Edit the clips until the audio track is the way that you want it.**

9. **Choose Share ⇨ Export Using QuickTime.** The Save Exported File As dialog appears.

10. **From the Export pop-up menu, choose Sound to AIFF.**

11. **Choose a location, and save the file.** The file is exported from iMovie.

12. **Launch iTunes.**

13. **Choose File ⇨ Add to Library.** The Add To Library dialog appears.

14. **Navigate to and select the sound file you created in iMovie.**

15. **Click Open.** The sound is added to your iTunes library where you can listen to it, or you can open it in other applications (for example, you can select it in iPhoto's Media Browser for use as a soundtrack for an iPhoto slideshow).

Recording sound from musical instruments

If you want to record sound from external microphones and musical instruments, you need an interface between those devices and the MacBook Pro. These devices can use either the audio port or USB port to connect to your MacBook Pro. USB is a more common interface, and in most situations, it is the easier method to work with.

You can use a variety of USB audio devices for this purpose. Some devices include a MIDI instrument, such as a keyboard, as part of the interface device. These are convenient because you get an input source (the instrument) and the interface in one unit. To use a device like this, connect it to a USB port on your MacBook Pro. Then connect the microphones or instruments from which you want to record sound into the various ports. After the device is configured, you can choose it as the input device in audio applications, such as GarageBand, so you can record the output of the microphones and instruments in those applications.

Recording sound in QuickTime Player

Despite its name, QuickTime Player can also record audio, video, and the activities on your MacBook Pro's screen. Here's how to record audio with QuickTime Player:

1. **Launch QuickTime Player.**

2. **Choose File ⇨ New File Recording to open the recording window, shown in Figure 10.7.**

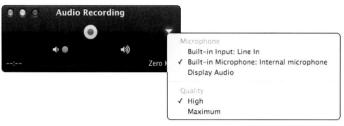

10.7 Select the microphone to use when recording audio in QuickTime Player.

3. **To select the input source, click the menu icon at right and choose the desired microphone or other device.** If you don't make a selection, QuickTime Player uses the microphone selected in the Sound system preference's Input pane.

4. **Click the Record button (the red circle) when you're ready to record.**

5. **Click the Stop button (the red square) when you're finished recording.**

6. **Choose File ⇨ Save to save the recording as an MPEG-4 (.m4a) audio file.**

Recording sound in iMovie

A common use of recorded sound is as narration in iMovie projects. Follow these steps to add your own narration to an iMovie project:

1. **Launch iMovie.**

2. **Select the project in which you want to record sound, and put the playhead where you want to start recording.**

3. **Click the Voiceover button (the microphone icon).** The Voiceover panel appears, as shown in Figure 10.8.

10.8 I'm recording narration for an iMovie project.

4. **From the Record From pop-up menu, choose the desired input source.** If you don't make a selection, iMovie uses the microphone selected in the Sound system preference's Input pane.

5. **Click the clip for which you want to record narration.** The timer starts a countdown. When the countdown stops, the project starts to play and iMovie starts recording.

6. **Speak in a normal conversational voice as the project plays.** As you speak, monitor the sound levels using the two input gauges under the Input Volume slider. You want the sound level to be as high as possible without going into the red. If it isn't, use the tools in the Voiceover panel to adjust the input volume. A red bar fills the clip you are recording over, and you see a large red dot and the *Recording* message in the Preview pane.

7. **When you finish speaking, press the space bar.** The recording stops, and an audio clip appears under the clip on which you recorded sound. The recording also stops when you reach the end of the project.

8. **Edit the recorded audio clip just like other audio clips.** For example, you can make it fade in, adjust its volume, and move it earlier or later in the project. Narration is shown in purple and is labeled with Voice Clip.

Recording sound with an iOS device

There are several recording apps such as WaveRecord for iOS devices whose audio you can then copy to your MacBook Pro. To copy their audio files:

1. **Connect the iOS device to your MacBook Pro via a cable or over Wi-Fi.** (You enable Wi-Fi syncing for each device in its Summary pane in iTunes.)

2. **In iTunes, select the device in the Devices pop-over.** If you're displaying the iTunes Sidebar (choose View ➪ Show Sidebar), select your device there instead.

3. **Go to the Apps pane.**

4. **Scroll down to the File Sharing section, and click the name of the app that recorded the audio.** A list of audio files should appear in the pane at the right, as Figure 10.9 shows. (If the app is not listed, its files cannot be transferred.)

5. **Select the files to copy to your MacBook Pro, and click the Save To button. In the dialog that appears, choose a location to save the files to and click Save To.**

6. **Quit iTunes.**

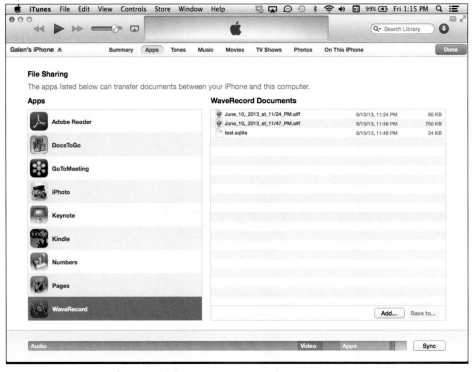

10.9 Use iTunes to copy from an iOS device to your MacBook Pro.

iPhones, as well as some iPod touch models, have the Voice Memos app that you can use to record sounds. To copy Voice Memos recordings to your MacBook Pro, you must set up iTunes to do so. After you do, the files are copied to iTunes each time you sync. To set up iTunes to sync the Voice Memos files:

1. **Connect the device to the MacBook Pro.**

2. **Launch iTunes.**

3. **Select the device from Devices pop-over (or, if visible, from the iTunes Sidebar) in iTunes.**

4. **Go to the Music pane.**

5. **Select the Include Voice Memos check box, and click Apply.** The device is synced, and the sound clips you recorded are moved into your iTunes library (the default name of each clip is the date and time you recorded it). From then on, voice memos are copied to the MacBook Pro when you sync the device.

You can work with these clips just like other audio files in iTunes, and you can add them from iTunes to iMovie and other Apple applications through their Media Browser panels.

How Do I Add and Manage Storage Space?

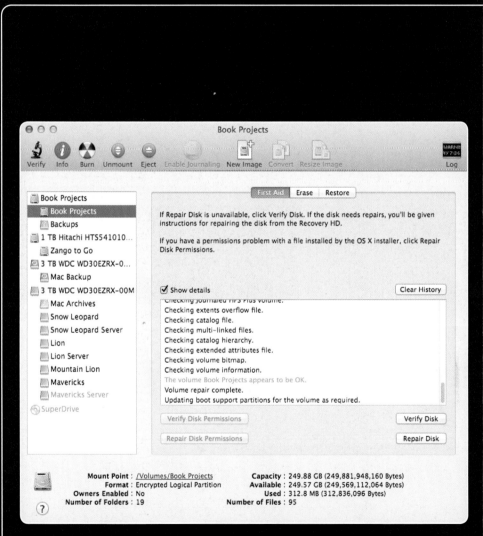

The two primary reasons to add more data storage space to your MacBook Pro are to back up your data or increase the data storage space. Time Machine, which requires an external hard drive, is the easiest way to back up data. Over time, you collect lots of data, and the MacBook Pro's hard drive is only so big. Adding more storage space enables you to work with more information. You may also want to carry data with you when you don't have your MacBook Pro, and a flash drive or SD card is ideal for this purpose.

Using External Hard Drives

Adding an external hard drive to your MacBook Pro system is an easy and inexpensive way of making more storage space available. It is also essential if you want to use Time Machine to back up your MacBook Pro over the long haul (see Chapter 13).

You should consider the following factors when choosing a hard drive to add to your MacBook Pro:

- **Which interface do you want to use to connect the drive to your MacBook Pro?** All current MacBook Pro models support Thunderbolt and combined USB 2 and USB 3 interfaces, and the non-Retina models also support FireWire 800. Older MacBook Pros might not support Thunderbolt or USB 3, but they typically support FireWire 400 and/or FireWire 800, as well as USB 2. Thunderbolt and USB 3 drives are the fastest, followed by FireWire 800, FireWire 400, and USB 2. Thunderbolt drives are by far the most expensive. Because USB 2 is the most common technology, those drives tend to be the least expensive, all other things being equal. Drives that support more than one kind of interface are more expensive, but they provide more flexibility.

- **How many devices are you using with your MacBook Pro?** If you already use two or more USB devices, you might want to consider a Thunderbolt or FireWire 800 drive so you don't need to get a USB hub—remember that the MacBook Pro has just two USB ports for direct connections to it. Also, USB can slow down when used with multiple devices via a hub. Devices that use Thunderbolt or FireWire interface allow daisy-chaining, so you can connect one to the other, all sharing that one initial connection to the MacBook Pro.

- **What size drive do you need?** Drives come in various sizes. Generally, you should get the largest one you can afford. Hard drive prices continue to fall, and even large drives (2TB or larger) are fairly inexpensive. Smaller drives, such as a 750GB, are even less expensive. For backup purposes, I don't recommend that you purchase a drive smaller than 1.5TB, but in all cases, a drive with more capacity is better than one with less storage space.

- **Does the drive need to meet specific performance requirements?** If you intend to use the drive for high-data-rate work, such as for digital video, you need to get a drive that spins at least 7200 rpm. Some drives spin even faster, which means they can transfer data at a greater rate. However, if you are primarily going to use the external drive for backing up, speed isn't really important. Because faster drives are more expensive, you can save some money by choosing a slower drive.

- **What format is the drive?** Many formats are available, and all drives come formatted for one system or another. Fortunately, it doesn't really matter which format the drive comes in because you can always reformat it to work with your MacBook Pro using the Disk Utility application (which I cover later in this chapter). Drives that are preformatted for Windows are generally less expensive than those that have been preformatted for Macs, even though they have the same physical drives inside the box.

- **How much can you afford to spend?** As with all things digital, you tend to get more by spending more. For most purposes, such as backing up, you should decide how much you can afford to spend and then get the largest drive you can afford for that amount of money. If you shop around a bit, you'll be amazed at how much the cost of external hard drives varies from retailer to retailer—and they are often on sale.

Connecting an external hard drive

Adding an external hard drive is about as simple as it gets. Follow these steps to get yours going:

1. **Connect the power supply to the drive and an electrical outlet, if the drive uses external power.**

2. **Connect the cable to the drive and the appropriate port on your MacBook Pro.**

Note If the drive is preformatted so your MacBook Pro can access it immediately, you might be prompted to configure Time Machine. Just click Cancel, and proceed to the next section. Time Machine is covered in Chapter 13.

3. **Power up the drive, if it has a power switch.** If the drive is formatted so it is compatible with your MacBook Pro, you see it in the Sidebar in the Finder window, with its default name. (It may also appear on the Desktop, depending on how you've set your Finder preferences, as Chapter 1 explains.) Figure 11.1 shows the new external drive named Untitled in the Sidebar and on the Desktop. If the drive is not formatted, you won't see the device.

Caution Data on external drives isn't part of your Home folder, so any user account can access the external drives' data, even those that can't access the data in your Home folder. You can encrypt external drives to protect their contents, as Chapter 13 explains.

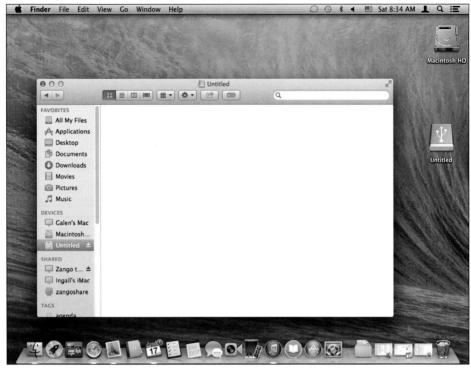

11.1 A mounted external hard drive appears in the Devices section of a Finder window's Sidebar, just as the internal hard drive does.

Preparing an external hard drive with Disk Utility

Before you use a hard drive, you should format it (assuming it was not preformatted for the Mac). You can also partition a hard drive to create multiple volumes on a single drive so it behaves as if it is more than one drive.

When you partition a hard drive, logical volumes are created for each partition on the drive. For most practical purposes, a logical volume looks and acts just like a separate hard drive. There can be some small performance advantages to partitioning a drive, but the best reason to partition it is to help you keep your data organized. For example, you might want to create one partition on the external hard drive for your backups and another for project files that you don't access often (so they're not taking space on your MacBook Pro's internal hard drive).

Generally, you should make your partitions as large as possible, so you have enough space on them for the long run. Of course, the purpose of the partition will help determine how much space it needs both now and in the future. You can change the size of a partition, but of course you can't make a partition any larger than the available room on the hard drive would allow, so if your partitions take the full space of the hard drive, you'd have to shrink one partition to enlarge another.

Follow these steps to format a drive with a single partition:

1. **Launch Disk Utility, located in the Utilities folder within the Applications folder (you can get quick access to it via the Launchpad).** In the Disk Utility window, you see two panes. In the upper part of the left pane, you see the drives connected to your MacBook Pro, including its internal hard and optical drives. Below each drive, you see the volumes (partitions) for each drive; a drive has at least one partition. In the right pane, you see information and tools for the drive or volume selected in the left pane.

2. **Select the drive you want to format.** At the top of the right pane are several tabs, each of which opens a subpane for various actions.

3. **Go to the Erase subpane, shown in Figure 11.2.**

4. **Select the format for the partition on the Format pop-up menu.** In most cases, you should choose Mac OS Extended (Case-sensitive, Journaled) to take advantage of the most sophisticated format option.

5. **Enter the name for the drive in the Name field.** This is what displays in the Finder window's Sidebar and with the disk icon on the Desktop.

6. **Click Erase, and then click Erase again in the confirmation sheet that appears.**

Genius

You can erase individual partitions on a drive by selecting the partition in Disk Utility, going to the Erase subpane, and clicking Erase. The other partitions are unaffected.

If you want to create more than one partition on a drive, you can do so. In Disk Utility:

1. **Select the drive you want to partition.** Be sure you are selecting the entire drive, not a partition on the drive. The icon for the drive itself is all the way to the left in the volume list, and partitions are indented slightly.

2. **Go to the Partition subpane.**

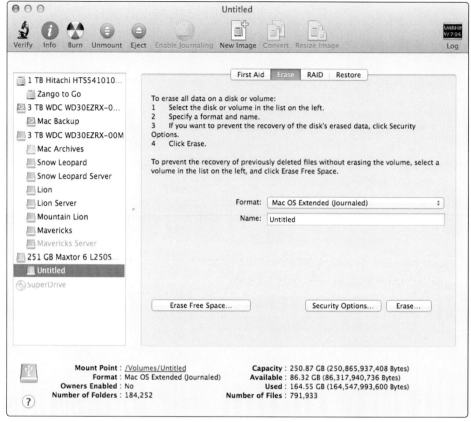

11.2 Erase a hard drive in Disk Utility.

3. **Choose the number of partitions you want, using the Partition Layout pop-up menu.** The preview of your drive's partition's updates to reflect the new split. You can also use the Add (+) and Remove (–) buttons below the partition list to add and delete partitions.

4. **Size the partitions.** You can do so by dragging the handle between the partitions in the preview, or you can select each partition in turn and enter a value in the Size field. Figure 11.3 shows a drive with two partitions to be created.

5. **Name each partition.** Select a partition, and enter a name for it in the Name field. Repeat for each partition.

6. **Specify the format for each partition, if you want them to differ from each other.** Select a partition, and choose a formatting option from the Format pop-up menu. Repeat for each partition.

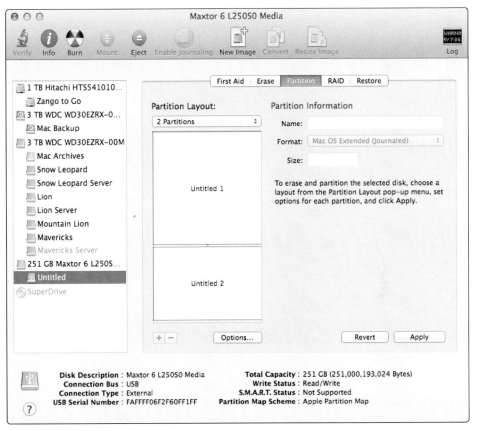

11.3 This drive will have two partitions.

Note

If the drive was formatted with encryption (see Chapter 13), only the first partition remains encrypted if you add partitions to it.

7. **Set the partition scheme for the drive by clicking Options.** In most cases, in the setting sheet that appears, you should select the GUID Partition Table option, but if you're formatting a drive for use in Windows as a startup drive, select Master Boot Record. The Apple Partition Map option ensures compatibility with very old Macs (those running on PowerPC chips or using OS X 10.3 or earlier), but drives formatted this way cannot be used as startup drives on Macs running on Intel chips. Click OK after selecting the desired option. Note this option affects all partitions on the drive.

8. **Click Apply.** In the confirmation sheet that appears, you see a summary of what will be done to the drive. After you click Partition, you return to the Disk Utility window, and a progress bar appears in the lower-right corner of the window. You can use this to monitor the process. After this process is completed, you should see the partitions you created under the drive's icon. The drive and its partitions are ready to use. You may be prompted to use the drive for Time Machine; choose the partition you want to use for Time Machine backups, and click Use as Backup Disk, Decide Later, or Don't Use.

Genius   You can change the partitions in an existing drive without having to reformat. In Disk Utility, select the drive and go to the Partition subpane. Change the size for the partitions you want to change. You'll see blue in each partition indicating existing data and white for free space. The new partition size cannot be less than the blue area. Click Apply when you're finished, and confirm the change in the settings sheet that appears.

Working with external hard drives

After it's configured, you can use an external hard drive in many ways to store files, as additional storage space, or as the location for your Time Machine backups (I cover Time Machine in Chapter 13). You open, save, move, name, copy, and so on the same way on an external drive as you do on the internal drive.

Note   There's just one operational difference to note when using external drives: When you drag folders and files from one drive to another, they are copied rather than moved. To move folders and files dragged from one drive to another, hold Option while dragging them.

Before you remove a hard drive or any of its partitions, you need to eject it. This ensures that all data has been written to the drive and that all processes affecting it are stopped so the data isn't damaged when you disconnect the drive. To eject a drive, select one of its partitions in a Finder window's Sidebar and click the adjacent Eject button. You can also select the drive and press ⌘+E. If the drive icon appears on the Desktop, you can drag it into the Trash, whose icon changes to the Eject symbol so you know you're not deleting the drive's contents. Note that dragging a drive from the Sidebar to the Trash removes the drive from the Sidebar's Devices list but does not eject it.

Sharing an External Hard Drive

An external hard drive is a great way to share files among multiple computers. This list includes some of the ways in which you can do this:

- **Physically connect the drive to different computers.** After a drive has been formatted, you can connect it to any Mac to access its files or write files to it. If you formatted the drive in the MS-DOS format, Windows PCs can access its files and write to it, too.

- **Share the drive over a network.** Like other resources, you can share the partitions and files on them with other computers over a local network, as Chapter 4 explains.

- **Share the drive from router.** If you connect a USB external hard drive to a router that has a USB port, any computer that can access the router's network can also access the drive, as Chapter 4 also explains.

When ejected, if the drive has only one partition, it is unmounted and disappears from the Finder window's Sidebar and from the Desktop, if they were visible there. If the drive has more than one partition, you are prompted to eject only the selected partition by clicking Eject or to eject the entire drive by clicking Eject All. Unless your goal is really just to unmount one partition and leave the rest available (meaning you aren't planning to disconnect the drive), you should always click Eject All, at which point all the drive's partitions are unmounted and disappear from the Sidebar and Desktop. You can then disconnect the drive from the MacBook Pro.

To start using a drive again, simply reconnect it to your MacBook Pro. After a few moments, it is mounted, you see all its partitions in the Sidebar, and it is ready to use.

Maintaining Hard Drives

Keeping your hard drives, whether internal or external, in good working condition goes a long way toward making your MacBook Pro reliable. In this section, I cover some of the more important drive maintenance habits you should practice to keep your drives in top form.

Managing free space on a hard drive

You can do much for the performance of your drives by simply ensuring that they have a good amount of free space. The more data you have on your drive, the less room there is to store new files. If drives get too full, their performance slows down significantly. You can also run into all kinds of problems if you try to save files to drives that are full to the brim; how full depends on the size of the files with which you are working, but having 10GB or less free space is a good indicator of when to be worried. With 1GB or less, you will start having performance and file-saving problems.

To keep an eye on their available space, right-click a drive in a Finder window's Sidebar or on the Desktop. The Info window appears, as shown in Figure 11.4. The Available entry tells you how much unused space remains.

Learn and practice good work habits, such as deleting files you don't need, uninstalling software you don't use, keeping your files organized (no duplicates), and archiving files you are finished with (such as to a DVD). Regularly removing files that you no longer need from your hard drives keeps them performing well for you, and it maximizes the room you have to store the files you do need.

11.4 This external drive has more than 360GB available, which is a comfortable amount.

Caution

If a drive is making an odd noise, such as becoming louder, you should expect it to fail soon, if not immediately. Unusual sounds typically (but not always) precede hard drive failure. Make sure to get any data you need off the drive right away, or it will be a very expensive hassle to recover it. Never store important data in only one location. Back up!

Note

Each partition and drive has its own Trash. If you empty the Trash while an external drive that has files in its trash is disconnected, the trash can icon becomes full again when you reconnect the drive. This is because the Trash for that drive still has files in it. Empty the Trash again after you've reconnected the drive to get rid of its deleted files.

Genius

Application installers waste drive space. If you're sure that the application version you want will continue to be available online, delete its installation files from the Downloads folder or wherever you saved it. If you paid for an application, archive its files in case you need to reinstall it. (If it came with an installation disc, that's your archive.) Some companies remove older versions from their download sites when newer ones are released, in which case you might have to pay an upgrade fee to download the application again.

Checking or repairing an external drive with Disk Utility

Two of the tasks for which you can use Disk Utility are to check or repair an external hard drive. If you start having problems with a drive, first make sure that it has plenty of available space. If it doesn't, get rid of files until it does. If it does have plenty of free space, follow these steps to use Disk Utility to check or repair it:

1. **Launch Disk Utility.**

2. **Select the drive or partition you want to check or repair.** In most cases, you should select a drive so the entire drive is checked or repaired, rather than just one of its partitions.

3. **Check the bottom of the Disk Utility window for information about the drive, volume, disc, or image you selected.** If you select a hard drive, you see the disk type, connection bus (such as ATA for internal drives), connection type (internal or external),

capacity, write status, S.M.A.R.T. (Self-Monitoring, Analysis, and Reporting Technology) status, and partition map scheme. If you select a partition on a drive, you see various data about the volume, such as its mount point (the path to it), format, whether owners are enabled, the number of folders it contains, its capacity, the amount of space available and used, and the number of files it contains.

4. **Go to the First Aid pane to see some information explaining how Disk Utility works.**

5. **Click Repair Disk.** The application checks the selected drive for problems and repairs any it finds. When the process is complete, a report of the results appears, as shown in Figure 11.5.

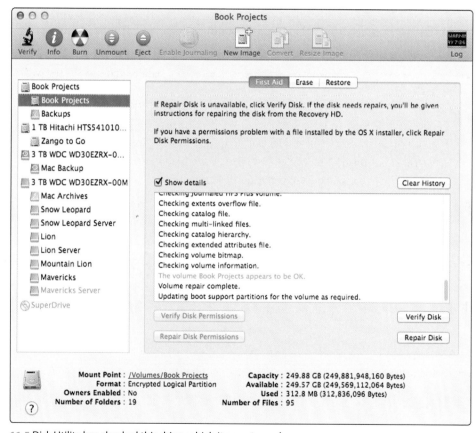

11.5 Disk Utility has checked this drive, which it reports as okay.

You can choose to verify a drive by clicking Verify Disk, rather than clicking Repair Disk. When you do so, the application finds problems with the drive and reports back to you. You then have to tell the application to repair those problems. So it's often quicker just to repair the drive; if Disk Utility finds no errors, you've basically just verified it's okay.

Note For most drives, the S.M.A.R.T. status provides an indication of the drive's health. This is Verified if the drive is in good working condition, or it's About to Fail if the drive has problems. If you see About to Fail, immediately copy important data onto another drive, CD, or DVD. If a drive doesn't support S.M.A.R.T., you see the status Not Supported. Your MacBook Pro's internal drive supports S.M.A.R.T., but many external drives do not.

Checking or repairing the internal drive with Disk Utility

Because you can't use Disk Utility to repair a drive with open files, and your startup drive always has open files (the Finder, for example), you can't use Disk Utility to repair the internal hard drive while you are started up from it. If your internal hard drive appears to have problems, you must start up from a different drive to repair them. You can use one of these options to accomplish this:

- **Start up from an alternate drive, and run Disk Utility from there.** If you have installed OS X on an external drive, you can start up from that drive and run Disk Utility there to repair the internal drive. (See the sidebar later in this chapter to learn how to start up from an alternate drive.) After you've booted up, use the steps for checking or repairing an external drive to select and repair the internal hard drive.

- **Start up from the Recovery HD volume.** Use the information provided in Chapter 14 to start up from the Recovery HD partition and run Disk Utility from there.

Note Although you can't repair the current startup drive, you can verify it. Although this doesn't fix any problems, it does identify whether there is a problem.

Erasing an external hard drive with Disk Utility

Perform the following steps to erase and reformat an external hard drive with Disk Utility:

1. **Launch Disk Utility.**

2. **Select a partition you want to erase.**

3. **Go to the Erase pane.**

4. **Choose the format you want to use for the volume on the Volume Format pop-up menu.** The format options are: Mac OS Extended (Journaled); Mac OS Extended (Journaled, Encrypted); Mac OS Extended (Case-sensitive, Journaled); Mac OS Extended (Case-sensitive, Journaled, Encrypted); MS-DOS (FAT); or ExFAT.

Genius You can use the Erase Free Space button to remove files that you have deleted from a drive or partition. This makes them harder (or impossible) to recover using data-recovery tools.

5. **Click Security Options.** The Secure Erase Options sheet appears, as shown in Figure 11.6.

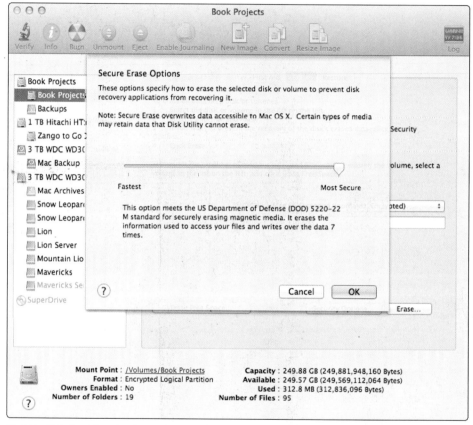

11.6 Use this sheet to select how you want data you are erasing to be handled.

6. **Select one of these options by dragging the slider to the right to make the erase more secure but slower or dragging to the left to make it less secure but faster:**

- **Directory erase.** This makes the data unviewable from the Finder but leaves it physically on the drive. As your MacBook Pro needs to write more files to the drive, it overwrites the erased space. Until the data is overwritten, it can be recovered (unerased) using an application designed to do so. This is the fastest, but least secure option.

- **One-pass erase.** This option writes zeros in all sectors on the drive. This is secure because it overwrites the entire drive, making the data harder to recover. However, this is slower than the first option.

- **Three-pass erase.** This option overwrites the drive three times. It takes even longer, but makes the data nearly impossible to recover.

- **Seven-pass erase.** This option writes data over the entire drive seven times. This takes a long time and makes the data virtually impossible to recover (hey, if it's good enough for the U.S. Department of Defense, it should be good enough for you).

7. **Click OK.** The option you selected is set, and the sheet closes.

8. **Click Erase, and then click Erase again in the confirmation sheet that appears to begin erasing the drive.**

Installing OS X on an External Hard Drive

You can install OS X on an external hard drive and start up from it, which is very useful for troubleshooting. Perform these steps to do so:

1. **Connect and format an external hard drive on which you want to install OS X.** You can use a partition on a hard drive that has several.

2. **Open the App Store application, go to the Purchased pane, and download the latest version of OS X.** After the application downloads, the OS X installer launches.

3. **Click Continue, and agree to the license.**

4. **Click Show All Disks.**

5. **Select the external hard drive or partition you configured in Step 1.**

6. **Click Install, and authenticate yourself.**

7. **Click Restart.** The installation process begins. Your MacBook Pro restarts, and you see the installation progress. When installation is complete, you're prompted to restart your MacBook Pro or wait and let it restart automatically. The MacBook Pro starts up from the external drive.

8. **Work through the screens of the Setup Assistant to complete the installation.** This is the same process as when you started a brand-new MacBook Pro.

Working with SD Cards and Flash Drives

Your MacBook Pro has an SDXC (Secure Digital Extended Capacity) card slot so it can read and write to an SD card. These cards are commonly used in digital cameras, so you can just pop the card into your MacBook Pro and import the photos it contains to your iPhoto library. However, you can also use these very compact storage devices in the same way that you would a drive: to transport or even back up files.

Follow these steps to use an SD card on your MacBook Pro:

1. **If the memory card includes an SD adapter (most do), place the card into the adapter.**

2. **Insert the card or, if it uses one, its adapter into the SD slot on your MacBook Pro.** It now appears in the Devices list in Finder windows' Sidebar, and it appears on the Desktop if you've adjusted Finder preferences to display external hard drives there (see Chapter 1).

USB flash drives are another popular way to move files around because they are very small and easy to carry. The capacity of these drives continues to increase rapidly; at this writing, you can get them in up to 512GB. However, large-capacity flash drives are quite expensive when compared to external hard drives. A smaller flash drive, such as a 32GB, is very inexpensive and can be quite useful. A flash drive can be a good way to transfer files among computers or to back up data when you are on the move.

To use a flash drive on your MacBook Pro, simply plug it into one of the USB ports. The drive is then mounted on your MacBook Pro for you to use.

Note

You can format SD cards and USB drives using Disk Utility just as if they were hard drives.

Caution

Remember to eject SD cards or flash drives before removing them from your MacBook Pro—just as you should do with external hard drives. It's critical to eject the storage before physically removing it so OS X can complete any information transfer and directory updates; if you don't eject the storage medium first, you may

How Can I Run Windows Applications?

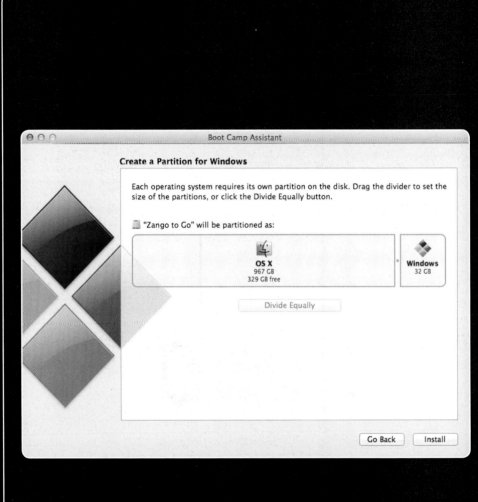

Some of us live in two worlds: the Mac world and the Windows world. Windows PCs dominate certain areas, particularly midsize and large organizations, and there are many applications that run only on Windows. With your MacBook Pro, you can run OS X and Windows on the same computer, which means you really can have the best of both worlds.

Choosing a Windows Option

There are two basic options for running Windows on Macs: Boot Camp and desktop virtualization. Each method has advantages and disadvantages, and you can use both methods when you need to.

Apple's Boot Camp

Boot Camp is the Apple technology that transforms Mac hardware into a fully capable Windows PC. You can choose to boot up your MacBook Pro into OS X or into Windows. When you boot up into Windows, you have a fully functional Windows PC on your hands.

The strengths of Boot Camp include great performance, maximum compatibility for hardware and software, and a lower cost because your only expense is a copy of Windows.

One downside is that it can be a bit more complicated to share data between the two operating systems because they can't be running at the same time, and OS X can only read files from the NTFS disk format used by Windows 7 and 8, so you can't copy files to the Windows disk when running OS X—you need to use a flash drive or a cloud storage service like Dropbox or Box as the intermediary for file sharing.

Also, Boot Camp can run just Windows 7 and Windows 8, not the popular but old Windows XP version. Boot Camp installs a Windows partition only on your MacBook Pro's internal drive, so you must have enough room for it. Also, you must restart your computer to switch between the operating systems.

Desktop virtualization applications

Under desktop virtualization, an application provides a virtual environment (also called a *virtual machine*) in which you install and run Windows. When you want to run Windows, you launch the virtualization application; the two available are VMware Fusion and Parallels Desktop, each of which costs $80. Within its windows, you run Windows and Windows applications. Both applications also have modes in which the Windows applications run as if they were OS X applications, meaning their icons appear in the Dock and their menus in the menu bar, not all in a separate Windows Desktop window.

Using the virtualization approach has several benefits. One is that you can run Windows and OS X at the same time because the virtualization software is just another application running on your MacBook Pro. In fact, you can run multiple instances of Windows at the same time, whether different versions or different configurations of the same version, as well as instances of OS X and Linux. For developers, trainers, and testers, this ability to run multiple operating systems simultaneously is a breakthrough.

Obtaining Windows

To run Windows on a Mac, you must purchase a full copy of Windows to install, whether you use Boot Camp or a virtualization application (or both). You can't use an upgrade (unless of course, you've previously installed a version of Windows on your Mac). The cost for the Windows software varies, depending on the version of Windows you purchase and how you purchase it. When you purchase Windows, try to get a version that is designed for builders, also called the Original Equipment Manufacturers (OEM) version. This version is significantly less expensive than the full retail version and is ideal for installing Windows on a MacBook Pro.

There are several versions of Windows 7, including Home, Professional, and Ultimate, and the differences are somewhat difficult to understand. For most MacBook Pro users running Windows as a second operating system, the Home version is likely to be sufficient. However, you should compare the versions to make sure one doesn't offer something you need to have. Visit http://windows.microsoft.com/en-US/windows7/products/compare for Microsoft's explanations of the differences between versions.

Other benefits include the good performance (if you're running just one instance, it isn't noticeably slower than running it under Boot Camp) and easy data sharing because OS X and Windows are running at the same time. Plus you can store the virtualization files for your operating systems on any hard drive, not just on your internal hard drive, so you get more storage flexibility with virtualization.

Virtualization does have two points against it: the cost of the virtualization software and the fact that it may not be compatible with all the hardware and software you want to run.

Running Windows with Boot Camp

To get Windows running under Boot Camp, use Boot Camp Assistant, which creates a partition on your hard drive for your Windows installation. After Boot Camp Assistant finishes its work, you install Windows in the partition it creates. During the process, Boot Camp Assistant downloads the files that you use to install the required drivers for your MacBook Pro hardware. When the installation is complete, you can run Windows at any time.

Configuring Boot Camp and installing Windows

Running the Boot Camp Assistant is mostly a matter of following the on-screen steps to work through the setup and using the Windows installer.

Note

If the MacBook Pro's internal hard drive is already partitioned into two or more volumes, Boot Camp Assistant can't create an additional partition for Windows.

These steps demonstrate how to install Windows 7 Professional; if you use a different version of Windows, the details might be slightly different, but the overall process is the same:

1. **Launch the Boot Camp Assistant application, which is located in the Utilities folder in the Applications folder.** You see the first screen of Boot Camp Assistant.

2. **Click Continue.** You see the Select Tasks window.

3. **Insert a USB thumb drive or connect an external hard drive to your MacBook Pro, and insert the Windows installation disc in your MacBook Pro's optical drive.** Note that the external hard drive must be formatted as MS-DOS (FAT), as Chapter 11 explains. The thumb drive or external hard drive needs 1GB of free space available. Boot Camp Assistant stores required installation software for Windows on the thumb drive or external hard drive.

4. **Select the Download the Latest Windows Support Software from Apple check box and the Install Windows 7 or Later Version check box, and click Continue.** You need a live Internet connection for the download to proceed.

5. **Select the destination for the support software, and click Continue.** If a USB thumb drive is inserted, that's the only location you can save the support software to. You see a progress bar appear as the support software is downloaded.

6. **At the authentication prompt that appears, type your administrator password and click Add Helper.** The Create a Partition for Windows window appears. On the left, you see the partition for OS X, and on the right, you see the partition for Windows, which can be no smaller than 20GB.

7. **Perform one of these actions to set the size of the Windows partition:**

   - **Drag the Resize handle (the dot) between the two partitions to the left to increase the size of the Windows partition, as shown in Figure 12.1.** You can set the partition to be any size you want, but you must trade off drive space for Windows versus what is available for OS X. I recommend that you allocate at least 50GB to Windows. If you plan to install lots of Windows applications and create large documents, you may need a larger partition.

   - **Click Divide Equally to divide the drive into two equally sized partitions.** I don't recommend this option, because it significantly reduces the amount of space available to OS X.

Caution After you've partitioned your drive, you won't be able to make the Windows partition larger without repartitioning the drive and reinstalling Windows, which is a time-consuming process. So make sure that you give the Windows environment plenty of space.

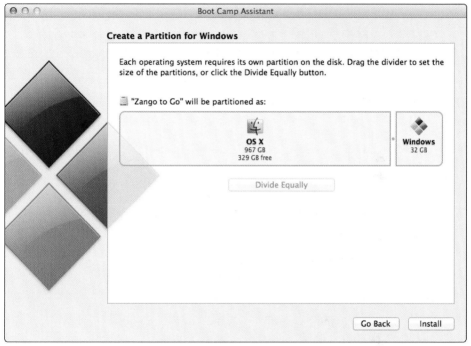

12.1 Use the Create a Partition for Windows window to set the size of your Windows environment (here, 32GB).

8. **Click Install.** Boot Camp Assistant creates the Windows partition on the MacBook Pro's hard drive, which can take quite a while. The MacBook Pro restarts after the partition is created, so save in and quit any applications that are open before the partitioning is complete.

The MacBook Pro then boots from the Windows installation disc. The Windows installation application starts installing files, and you see the progress at the bottom of the Windows Setup screen. You see the Windows Starting message as the Windows installer opens.

Note

Any Bluetooth devices such as the keyboard and mouse do not work during the Windows setup, because Windows doesn't load its Bluetooth drivers until the Windows Desktop or Start Screen appears, which occurs only after installation. You need to use the MacBook Pro's built-in keyboard and trackpad.

Follow these steps to work through the install process:

1. **At the prompt, choose the language, time and currency format, and keyboard method, and click Next.**

2. **Click Install Now.** The setup process begins.

3. **Accept the license, and click Next.**

4. **Select the new installation option.** Make sure you select the correct partition on which to install Windows. If you don't, you might overwrite a partition with OS X or your data on it, in which case that data is lost.

5. **Select the Bootcamp partition.** If you see an error message stating that Windows can't be installed on the selected partition, you need to format that partition by clicking Show Details, then clicking Format, and finally clicking OK in the confirmation dialog.

Note

If you have to reformat the partition, it may not be called Bootcamp after you do so. Note what it is called so you can select the correct partition.

6. **Click Next.** The installation process begins on the partition you selected. You see progress information in the Install Windows window and in the status bars at the bottom of the window. The install process can take quite a while, and your MacBook Pro may restart multiple times. Eventually, you see the Set Up Windows window.

7. **Work through the various windows of the Setup Windows application to configure Windows.** For example, you need to create a username and password, type the Windows product key, choose how Windows handles updates, and set the time and date. The computer may need to restart during the process as well. When the process is complete, you see the Windows Desktop.

8. **Eject the Windows installation disc.**

9. **In Windows Explorer (Windows 7) or File Explorer (Windows 8), open the flash drive or external hard drive containing the Apple Boot Camp support files and double-click the Setup.exe program there.** If asked, click Yes to allow it to install software in Windows. The Boot Camp Installer application opens.

10. **Follow the instructions on-screen to complete the installation of various drivers and other software that Windows needs to work with the MacBook Pro hardware.**

11. **When the Boot Camp Installer is complete, click Finish.**

12. **Click Yes at the prompt to restart your MacBook Pro.** It starts up in Windows.

Note You may be prompted to configure various Windows options (such as choosing a network location) while the Boot Camp Installer runs. You can minimize those until the Boot Camp Installer process is complete, or you can let the Boot Camp Installer run in the background and configure Windows while it runs.

13. **Type your password to log in to your Windows account, if you set one, and press Return.** Windows is ready to use.

Note Use Windows Update to install the current security and other updates for Windows. Windows Update should be enabled automatically, but to be sure, go to the Control Panel's System & Security group, open the Windows Update control panel, click Turn Automatic Updating On or Off, choose Install Updates Automatically from the Important Updates menu, and click OK.

14. **To return to OS X, open the Windows and choose Shut Down.**

15. **Restart the MacBook Pro, and hold the Option key down while it starts up.**

16. **Select the OS X startup volume, and press Return.** The Mac starts up under OS X again.

Note When OS X restarts, you may see Boot Camp Assistant because OS X restores open windows by default. Because you've already completed the tasks in Boot Camp Assistant, just quit it.

Running Windows using Boot Camp

After you install Windows, you can transform your MacBook Pro into a Windows PC. If you're currently running OS X and want to run Windows in Boot Camp instead, follow these steps:

1. **Open the Startup Disk system preference shown in Figure 12.2 by choosing ⇨ System Preferences and clicking Startup Disk.**

2. **Select the Bootcamp Windows startup disk.**

3. **Click Restart.**

4. **At the prompt, click Restart again.** The Mac restarts, and the Windows Login screen appears.

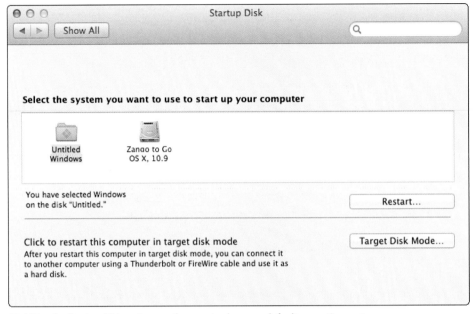

12.2 Use the Startup Disk system preference to choose a default operating system.

If the MacBook Pro is not turned on, press its power button and hold the Option key while it starts up. A row of available startup drives appears. Select the Windows drive and press Return.

Note

Right-clicking is a fundamental part of using Windows. To right-click with your MacBook Pro when running Windows, hold two fingers on the trackpad and click the trackpad button.

5. **Log in, and use Windows.**

6. **When you're ready to switch back to OS X, shut Windows down.**

7. **Restart the MacBook Pro, and hold the Option key down while it starts up.**

8. **Select the OS X startup volume, and press Return.** The Mac starts up under OS X again.

Caution Windows is constantly under attack from viruses, Trojan horses, and other attempts to steal or damage data. Running Windows on a MacBook Pro doesn't protect you from these threats. The Windows portion is susceptible to the same attacks it would be if you were running Windows on a PC. So you should use security software under Windows as soon as you get your Windows environment running, especially if you're accessing the Internet from it.

Running Windows Virtually

As covered earlier in this chapter, running Windows under a virtual environment has the significant advantage of allowing you to run Windows and OS X simultaneously. This makes it fast and easy to switch between the two environments and their applications.

The two most widely used virtualization applications are VMware Fusion and Parallels Desktop, both of which let you download a 30-day free trial from their websites (www.vmware.com/products/fusion/overview.html and www.parallels.com, respectively). Figure 12.3 shows Windows 7 running in Fusion, and Figure 12.4 shows Windows 8 running in Parallels.

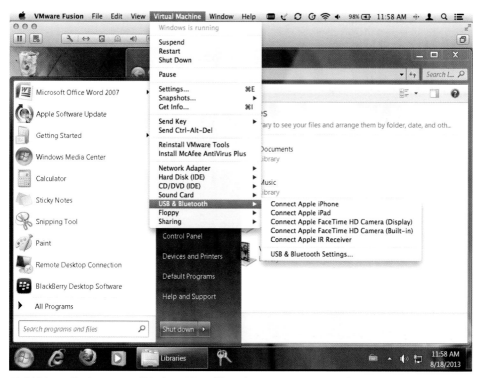

12.3 VMware Fusion can run Windows XP and later; here, it's running Windows 7.

12.4 Parallels can run Windows XP and later; here, it's running Windows 8.

Note

One of the great things about using virtualization software is that the Windows environment gets its network settings from the Mac. If the Mac on which you install Fusion is connected to a network and the Internet, so is the Windows environment—no further configuration is necessary.

After you install Fusion or Parallels, you create virtual machines for each operating system you want to run. Choose File ➪ New in either application, and follow the prompts. You'll need the disc or a downloaded installer for the operating system you want to install. After you've installed Windows, you follow the same setup as you would for Windows on a new PC. After Windows is running in Fusion or Parallels, the virtualization application downloads its special drivers—similar to the Windows support software in Boot Camp—to let Windows use the MacBook Pro hardware. Windows needs to restart before Fusion or Parallels can run it properly.

There isn't much difference between running Windows in a virtual machine and running it on a Windows PC. But consider these issues:

- **When running Windows in its own window, the pointer may stay in that window.** In Fusion, press Control+⌘ to make the pointer available in OS X. In Parallels, press Control+Option.

- **When running Windows, the Mac's ⌘ key is treated like the Windows key on a PC.** Control is treated as a PC's Ctrl key, and Option is treated as Alt.

- **You move among Windows and OS X applications by clicking in an application's window, choosing it on the Dock, or using any of the other standard ways of switching among applications.**

- **You can usually copy files from Windows to the Mac or vice versa by dragging them from one environment to the other.** You can also copy information from one environment to the other with standard copy-and-paste commands. If those options aren't enabled in the virtualization application's settings, you see the Mac as a network drive within Windows and can open that "drive" to share files. Both Fusion and Parallels also let you set the standard OS X folders such as Pictures to be shared with the Windows equivalents such as My Pictures, so files stored in one are available to the other.

- **Only one environment can use a CD, DVD, flash drive, iPhone, and so on at the same time.** When you insert a disc or connect a device, you are prompted to choose the OS that should use it. If you've inserted a CD or DVD or you connected another device but don't see it in OS X, the odds are that Windows is running, and the disc or device is mounted there, making it unavailable to the Mac. Use the Devices menu in Fusion or Parallels to control which operating system devices are available. Both Fusion and Parallels also have quick-access icon menus at the bottom of their windows to access device settings.

- **You can use the Unity mode in Fusion or the Coherence mode in Parallels so the Windows window disappears.** All you will see on the Mac Desktop is the VMware Fusion menu or Parallels menu in the menu bar and any Windows applications you are running in their own application menus.

- **You can view Windows in full-screen mode to have it fill the screen and hide OS X.** In this mode, a toolbar appears at the top of the screen when you hover the pointer there from which you can exit full-screen mode and use menus. If you have two displays, you can run Windows in full-screen mode on one, as if it were a separate PC.

- **When you quit Fusion or Parallels, the Windows environment is suspended, not shut down.** When you reopen that environment later in Fusion or Parallels, Windows acts as if it were never shut down, so applications remain in their previous state. It's as if Windows went to sleep while the virtualization application was not running. You can of course shut down Windows in the virtualization application to actually shut down Windows.

How Can I Protect My MacBook Pro's Data?

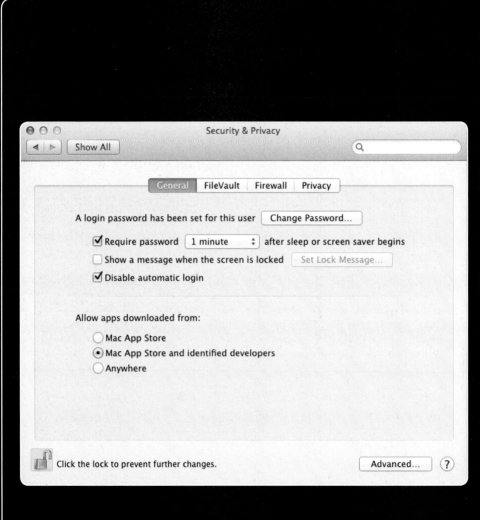

Your MacBook Pro is valuable, and protecting it is important, but this chapter is about protecting the *data* on your MacBook Pro, which is even more valuable. If you lose a document on which you've been working, all the time and effort you've invested is lost. Although you can redo work on documents, you can't replace photos. Think about how bad it would be if you lost your photo library. Then there's personal data, such as financial information, that needs safeguarding. For all these reasons, you should take precautions to secure your MacBook Pro and its data.

Keeping Software Current

There are two good reasons to keep the software you use current. One is that software developers frequently develop revisions to improve the features of their applications and remove bugs. The other (and the reason this topic is included in this chapter) is that many applications, and most definitely OS X itself, play a large role in how secure your MacBook Pro and its data are. The bad guys—people who develop viruses and attempt to hijack your computer or steal your data—are always working on new ways to penetrate your computer. Most software developers try to limit your exposure to attacks in their software as much as possible. To keep up with all new attempts to compromise your computer, take advantage of the security improvements that are part of software updates.

There are two basic categories of software that you need to keep current: the kind that is updated via the App Store and third-party software. The first category is updated via the App Store application, which includes OS X, along with any applications you have downloaded from the App Store. The second category is the third-party software you have installed in some other way, such as from an installer you downloaded from the Internet or from a DVD or CD.

Keeping OS X and Mac App Store software current

The App Store application makes it easy to find, download, and install applications from Apple and third-party developers. Thousands of applications are available. The App Store application also tracks all the applications you download and notifies you when updates are available. You can also use the application to update any software you've downloaded from the App Store.

Because it is the largest factor in how secure your MacBook Pro and its data are, OS X is the most important software to keep current, and by default OS X Mountain Lion and later automatically install any security updates. The better news is that in OS X Mavericks, OS X keeps itself, the Apple applications that are preinstalled with OS X, and any Mac App Store apps (from any vendor) you downloaded current with the latest updates, not just the OS X security updates.

You can have OS X Mavericks also download to your MacBook Pro any applications purchased from the Mac App Store that were purchased from another Mac using your Apple ID. To do so, open the App Store system preference, shown in Figure 13.1, by choosing ➪ System Preferences and clicking App Store, and then select the Automatically Download Apps Purchased on Other Macs check box. (The App Store system preference replaces the Software Update system preference in previous versions of OS X.)

13.1 The App Store system preference lets you change OS X's automatic-updates behavior.

You can also use the App Store app to manually check for updates:

1. **Launch the App Store application, and go to the Updates pane.** (A quick way to do so is to choose Software Update.) When it opens, it checks the status of all the applications you've downloaded. If updates are available, you see the number available on the App Store icon on the Dock and a list in the Updates pane, as shown in Figure 13.2.

2. **To install an application's update, click Update.** To install all updates, click Update All. Click the More link next to any update to get details on it.

3. **If prompted, type the Apple ID and password under which the application was obtained, and click Sign In.** The updates you selected begin to download to your MacBook Pro. You can see the progress next to the updates. When the process is complete, the update is moved to the list of previously installed updates pane and the number of updates available is reduced by the number you installed.

If a restart is required, your MacBook restarts and continues the installation process. When the Desktop reappears, you are using the updated software.

13.2 You can monitor the status of an update on the Updates pane.

Keeping other applications current

It's likely that your MacBook Pro has software installed on it that you didn't get from the Mac App Store. You also need to keep this software current. Each such application provides its own tools to download and install updates. Most also support manual or automatic updates.

The details of updating an application that you obtained outside of the Mac App Store depend on the specific application. But many applications—such as Microsoft's Office products Word, Excel, PowerPoint, and Outlook—have the Check for Updates option in their Help menu to look for and install updates. Likewise, Adobe's Creative Suite applications—including Dreamweaver, Illustrator, InDesign, and Photoshop—have the Updates menu option in their Help menu. Both Office and Creative Suite applications also check for updates periodically on their own, and they alert you to their availability.

Google Chrome, Mozilla Firefox, and Microsoft Skype use their application menus to access updates. Choose Chrome ⇨ About or Firefox ⇨ About. Chrome updates itself automatically, while Firefox presents the Update button for you to initiate the update from the About window. In Skype, choose Skype ⇨ Check for Updates.

Many applications check automatically for updates, while some give you that option in their Preferences dialog.

Many hardware vendors use Apple's App Store to keep drivers for their hardware current, because the App Store installs the updates automatically. Major printer and scanner providers, such as Brother, Canon, Epson, and Hewlett-Packard, do this, for example. Other hardware may require you to check the manufacturers' websites periodically for updates.

Protecting Your MacBook Pro with General Security

OS X includes general security settings that are particularly useful if you use your MacBook Pro in a variety of locations, some of which might allow it to be accessed by someone else. Follow these steps to configure these settings:

1. **Open the Security & Privacy system preference.**

2. **Go to the General pane, shown in Figure 13.3.**

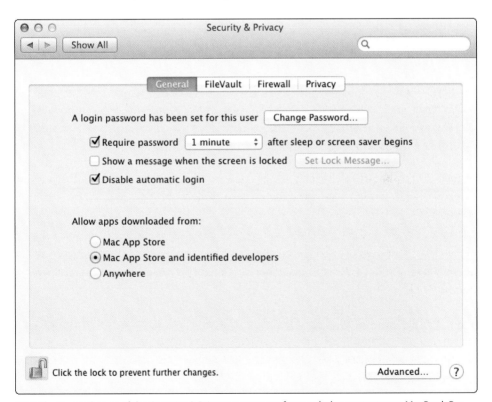

13.3 The General pane of the Security & Privacy system preference helps protect your MacBook Pro from unauthorized access.

3. **Select the Require Password after Sleep or Screen Saver Begins check box to require a user to type his or her login password to stop the screen saver or wake the MacBook Pro.** From the inline pop-up menu, choose the amount of time the computer is asleep or in screen saver mode before the password is required.

4. **To show a message on the screen when the MacBook Pro is locked, select the Show a Message When the Screen Is Locked check box.** Click Set Lock Message, type the message you want to be displayed, and click OK. This is handy in an office or living room environment as a way to let colleagues or family members know when you'll be back.

5. **To prevent someone from being able to use your computer just by starting it, select the Disable Automatic Login check box.** This prevents a user from being automatically logged in. To use your MacBook Pro, someone must know the password for at least one user account. (Chapter 2 explains how to set up user accounts and their passwords.)

6. **Choose the Gatekeeper option you want to use in the Allow Apps downloaded From section of the General pane.** Gatekeeper is designed to prevent malicious applications from being downloaded and run on your computer. Select one of these radio buttons:

   - **Mac App Store.** This is the safest option because it allows only applications that you've obtained from the App Store to be used.

   - **Mac App Store and Identified Developers.** This is a very safe option—and my recommended one—because it limits applications to those you've either downloaded from the App Store or those who have gotten credentials from Apple that OS X uses to verify their legitimacy when you try to install their software.

   - **Anywhere.** This option allows any application to run. Unless you are quite sure of your ability to monitor the source of applications being installed on your computer, I don't recommend this option as it provides no protection.

Genius

If you get software from an unknown developer and have selected the Mac App Store and Identified Developers option, or if you get software from anywhere but the Mac App Store and have selected the Mac App Store option, you get an alert box when you run its installer saying that you can't install the software. But you can; the trick is to right-click the installer and choose Open. You still get that alert box, but now it has the Open button that lets you override the installation protection you set up in the Security & Privacy system preference for this specific installer.

Are Viruses a Big Deal?

I believe that viruses are less of a problem than they appear to be from the tremendous amount of media hype they receive, especially for Mac users. Most of the time, you can protect yourself from viruses by being very careful about the files you receive in e-mail or download from the web. Because the most common way for a virus to get onto your computer is for you to accept a file in which it is contained, you can protect yourself from most viruses by using common sense. For example, if you receive an e-mail containing an oddly titled attachment (such as the famous I Love You file), you should either request more information from the sender before you open the file or simply delete the message.

When you see a prompt asking if you want to open an application (which happens the first time you open an application downloaded from the Internet), make sure that application is one you intended to open. Also, use the Gatekeeper feature in the Security & Privacy system preference to limit the applications that can be downloaded and run on your MacBook Pro.

There are cases in which malware has reportedly been downloaded when users browse certain websites. That's why OS X updates itself automatically each day with any security updates: Apple adds mechanisms to block any malware quickly after they are discovered. Disabling Java (via the Java system preference, if it's been installed) and Flash (via your browser's Preferences dialog) are also a good idea, because these two applications are the most common entry points into OS X for viruses and other malware that do get onto Macs. If you do run Java, as some applications require you do, be sure to enable automatic updates in the Java system preference.

Adding and using an antivirus application can make you safer, but my long experience with OS X is that you don't need it if you are careful about what you install. And some antivirus software can actually increase your risk: Symantec's software requires Java to be enabled, for example, providing a potential entry point for some malware that Symantec may not yet have identified. An antivirus application—even one that uses Java—is definitely a good idea if you share your computer with inexperienced users who are more likely to be naïve in what they download and install.

Preventing Internet Attacks

When you use your home network, you should shield your MacBook Pro from Internet attacks through your cable modem or DSL modem, or when you're using networks outside of your control, such as those available in cafés and other public places.

Shielding your MacBook Pro with a router

You can protect all the computers on your local network from attack by placing a barrier between them and the public Internet. Chances are good that you have one of these devices already, either as a separate router or a router built into the cable modem or DSL modem that connects you to the Internet. Be sure that the router is configured to use network address translation (NAT) and that its firewall is enabled.

How you set up the router depends on your router, so check its manual.

Caution These two features will block most attacks that try to come directly through the Internet. However, they do not protect you from malware you download in apps or websites.

Shielding your MacBook Pro with the OS X firewall

Even if your MacBook Pro is protected via your router, make sure that you configure OS X's own firewall to protect it from Internet attacks. After all, when you travel, you're not using your router any more, and even at home, having OS X's firewall in addition to the router's provides that much more protection.

Here's how to enable the OS X firewall

1. **Open the Security & Privacy system preference.**

2. **Go to the Firewall pane.**

3. **Click Turn On Firewall.** If the button is disabled, click the Lock icon and authenticate yourself as an administrator to enable it. The firewall starts running with the default settings.

4. **Click Firewall Options.** The Firewall Options sheet appears, as shown in Figure 13.4.

5. **To provide the maximum protection, select the Block All Incoming Connections check box.** This prevents all connections, except the most basic ones required for network access, such as DHCP and Bonjour. After configuring the firewall, if an action you normally perform doesn't work, deselect this check box and perform Step 6 instead.

6. **Add any applications for which you are sure you want to allow incoming connections.** To block all incoming connections, click the Add (+) button below the action list, select the application you want to add, and configure its pop-up menu to allow or block incoming connections. Applications that are allowed have a green indicator, while those

that are blocked have a red indicator. Any blocked applications cannot receive incoming traffic from the network or Internet, so functions that rely on receiving communication from outside your MacBook Pro are prevented. When you've not allowed a specific application through the firewall and it tries to communicate with your MacBook Pro, you're prompted to allow or prevent it.

7. **To allow applications that have a valid security certificate to receive incoming connections, select the Automatically Allow Signed Software to Receive Incoming Connections check box.**

8. **Select the Enable Stealth Mode check box.** This further protects your MacBook Pro by making sure that uninvited connection requests aren't acknowledged in any form so that the existence of your computer is hidden. Note that this can block the IT department in a work setting from troubleshooting your MacBook Pro over the network.

9. **Click OK.** Your settings are saved and the sheet closes. Your MacBook Pro is protected by the firewall.

13.4 Use the OS X firewall to protect your computer from Internet attacks.

Protecting Data with Time Machine

The most important thing you can do to protect your MacBook Pro and its data is to back it up. To back up simply means that you have at least one copy of all the data on your computer in case something happens to it. What could happen? Lots of things: an accidental deletion of files, a hardware or software problem that makes the data unavailable, a spill on the MacBook Pro that damages its electronics so it won't start up, and so on. There shouldn't be any question in your mind that something like this will happen, because no matter how careful you are, at some point data you want to keep is going to disappear from your computer.

If you have everything backed up properly, this is a minor nuisance. If you don't have good backups, this could be a disaster. To drive this point home, consider the photos that you manage in iPhoto or Aperture. Many of them are irreplaceable, but without a backup in place, you could lose them and never get them back. Then there are documents you've created, financial records, and so on.

The good news is that with an external hard drive, you can use OS X's Time Machine to back up with minimal effort on your part. In fact, after you set it up, the process is automatic. Time Machine makes recovering files you've lost easy and intuitive as well.

Time Machine backs up data on your internal hard drive and, if you want, external hard drives connected to your MacBook Pro—but not networked drives that your Mac sees—for as long as it can until the backup hard drive is full. It stores hourly backups for the last 24 hours, daily backups for the last month, and weekly backups until the backup drive is full. When the drive is full, it deletes the oldest backups to make room for the new. To protect your data for as long as possible, use the largest hard drive you can afford and exclude files that you don't need to back up (such as software installers that you can download from the Internet again) to save space on the backup drive.

To use Time Machine, you need an external drive. You can use an external hard drive that connects to your choice of a Thunderbolt port, FireWire port (if your MacBook Pro has one), and USB port. Or you can use a hard drive connected to your router's USB port and available over the network, or a router/drive combo device like Apple's Time Capsule.

Note

It's best if you don't use a backup hard drive for any purpose beyond backing up your data. You want to keep as much space as possible available for your backups. Using the drive for other purposes leaves less room for backing up, which means that your backups don't go as far back in time as they might. Also, you can share a backup drive among multiple computers, but if you do this, make sure it is a very large one.

Setting up Time Machine

Perform these steps to configure Time Machine:

1. **Open the Time Machine system preference.**

2. **Drag the slider to the On position.** Time Machine activates, and the Select Drive sheet appears, as shown in Figure 13.5.

3. **Select the drive on which you want to store the backed-up information.**

4. **If you want the backup encrypted so a password is needed to view it or restore it, select the Encrypt Backup option for the selected backup drive.**

5. **Click Use Backup Disk.** If you selected a Time Capsule or another location that is protected by a password, type the password, and click Connect. The sheet closes, and you return to the Time Machine system preference. The drive you selected appears at the top of the pane, and the timer starts the backup process, which you see next to the text *Next Backup.*

Genius

You can back up to multiple drives for extra safety. To do so, click Select Disk in the Time Machine system preference, select an additional drive in the list that appears, and click Use Disk. A dialog appears asking if you want to use the new drive instead of the previously selected one or as an additional backup drive. Click Replace to use the new drive instead of the previous one, or click Use Both to use both drives. You can add more drives as backup destinations by clicking Select Disk, clicking Add or Remove Backup Disk, selecting the additional drive from the Available Disks list, and clicking Use Disk, but note that you'll no longer be prompted as to whether to use the additional drive as a replacement or additional drive. To remove a drive as a backup drive, click Select Disk, click Add or Remove Backup Disk, select the drive from the Backup Disks list, click Remove Backup, and click Stop Using This Disk in the confirmation sheet that appears.

13.5 Use this sheet to select the drive that Time Machine uses to store your backed-up data.

6. **Click Options.** The Exclude items sheet appears, as Figure 13.6 shows. This sheet enables you to exclude drives, folders, and files from the backup process. For example, you can exclude the Downloads folder if you have those files available elsewhere, such as from developers' websites.

7. **Click the Add (+) button, navigate to the item you want to exclude in the sheet that appears, and click Exclude.** Repeat this step for all items you want to exclude. To include an excluded item, select it and click the Remove (–) button in the sheet.

Note

If you select the System folder, a confirmation sheet appears. In it, click Exclude System Folder Only to exclude only files in the System folder, or Exclude All System Files to exclude system files no matter where they are stored. If you exclude system files, you should choose to exclude them no matter where they are located.

8. **If you want to be warned when old backups are removed from the backup drive, select the Warn after Old Backups Are Deleted check box.** This is a good idea, because it lets you know when your backup drive fills up.

9. **Click Save.** You return to the Time Machine pane, which displays information about your backup. The timer starts, and when it expires, the first backup is created.

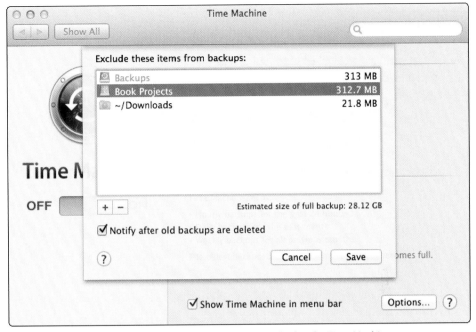

13.6 Use this sheet to exclude specific items from being backed up by Time Machine.

Backing up to Time Machine

After it's set up, Time Machine automatically backs up your data to the selected drive. New back-ups are created every hour. And if your Desktop is set to display connected drives (see Chapter 1), the backup drive displays with the Time Machine icon, a clock with a counterclockwise circular arrow.

Note

After you disconnect an external backup drive or move out of range of a Time Capsule, the next time you connect to it, a backup is performed automatically. Make sure you connect to the hard drive or Time Capsule frequently because your back-ups are only as fresh as the last time you connected to the backup drive.

If you want to manually force Time Machine to back up, make sure the backup drive is connected, click the Time Machine icon in the menu bar, and choose Back Up Now from its menu. Use the same menu to stop a backup in progress. At the top of the menu, you also see the date and time of the most recent backup. Choose Open Time Machine Preferences to open the Time Machine system preference.

Time Machine backups happen automatically, but you should follow these suggestions to ensure that things are working properly:

- **Every so often, open the Time Machine system preference and check the status of your backups.** This includes the name of the current backup drive, the amount of drive space available, the oldest backup stored on the drive, the latest backup, and the time at which the next backup will be performed. The latest backup date and time tell you how fresh your current backup is; it shouldn't be more than one hour old unless there is a problem, you've disabled Time Machine, or you haven't connected the backup drive to your MacBook Pro in a while.

- **As the backup drive gets full, you see warnings when old backups are deleted if you enabled that preference.** Make sure that there aren't files in the old backups that you might need. This can happen if you delete a document or folder from your MacBook Pro but don't restore it for a long time. Eventually, the only copy left might be in the oldest backup that gets deleted when the backup drive gets full.

- **When your backup system has worked for a while, check the status of the backup hard drive.** If it is filling up rapidly, consider removing some of the system and application files that might be part of it to reduce the space required. The most important files to protect over a long time are those you've created, changed, or purchased. Files that are already on a disc are relatively easy to recover, so there's no need to include them in a backup unless the disc is the only place that they exist.

- **If there are files you want to keep, but don't use anymore, consider moving them onto a DVD or CD for archival purposes.** Then delete them from the MacBook Pro's hard drive, and over time, they'll be removed from the backups; or you can exclude them from Time Machine to reduce the amount of drive space required. If the files are important, you should archive them in a couple of ways in case the disc you saved them on is lost or damaged.

- **Test your backups periodically to make sure that things are working properly by trying to restore some files (this is explained later in this chapter).** If you don't discover a problem until you need to restore important files, it is too late, so make sure your backup system is working properly. Create a couple of test files for this purpose, and let them exist long enough to get into your backups (at least one hour, assuming you are connected to your backup drive). Delete some of the test files, and empty the Trash. Make and save changes to some of the test files. Then try to restore both the deleted files and the original versions of the files you changed. If you are able to restore the files, your data is protected. If not, you have a problem and need to solve it so your data isn't at risk.

Restoring files with Time Machine

If you only have to use the information in this section to test your backups, it's a good thing. However, there may come a day when you need to use this information to recover files that are important to you. These might be photos from your last vacation, favorite songs you ripped into iTunes, or even documents you've put lots of work into. Maybe you accidentally deleted files or realized that you wanted a previous version of a file, or maybe something just went haywire on your MacBook Pro and you lost some important files.

The reason this function is called Time Machine is that you can use it to go back in time to restore files that are included in your backups. You can restore files and folders from the Finder and recover individual items from within some applications (such as photos in iPhoto, contacts in Contacts, and messages in Mail).

Restoring files in the Finder

If the folders or files you want to restore are included in your backups and available in the Finder, you can perform these steps to restore them:

1. **Open a Finder window showing the location where the files you want to recover were stored.** This can be the location where files that have been deleted were placed, or it may be where the current versions of files are stored (if you want to go back to a previous version of a file).

Note

You can launch Time Machine first and then navigate to the location from which you want to recover files using the Finder windows you see while in Time Machine.

2. **Launch the Time Machine application in one of these ways:**

   - Click its icon (the clock with the arrow showing time moving backward) on the Dock if it is installed there (it isn't by default).

   - Double-click its icon in the Applications folder.

   - Click the Time Machine icon in the menu bar, and choose Enter Time Machine from its menu.

3. **The Desktop disappears, and the Time Machine window fills the entire space, as shown in Figure 13.7.** In the center of the window, you see the Finder window that you opened in Step 1. Behind it, you see all the versions of that window that are stored in your backup, from the current version to as far back in time as the backups go. Along the

right side of the window, you see the timeline for your backups starting with today and moving back in time as you move up the screen. Gray bars indicate backups stored on the MacBook's hard drive, while the magenta bars indicate backups stored on your backup drive. At the bottom of the screen, you see the Time Machine toolbar. In the center of the toolbar, you see the time of the window that is currently in the foreground. At each end, you see controls that you use to exit Time Machine (Cancel) and the Restore button (which is active only when you have selected a file or folder that can be restored).

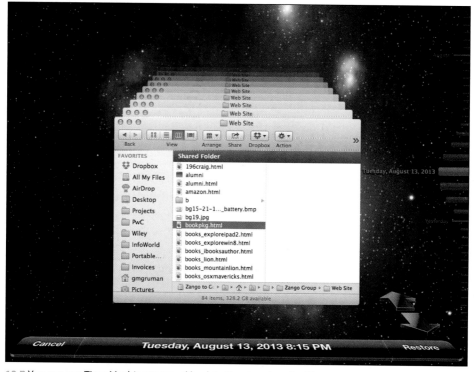

13.7 You can use Time Machine to travel back in time to when the files you want to restore were available.

4. **Move back in time by doing one of the following:**

- Click the time on the timeline when the files you want to restore were available. As you hover over a line, the time and date of the backup is shown.

- Click the back arrow (pointing away from you) located just to the left of the timeline.

- Click a Finder window behind the foremost one.

5. **When you reach the files you want to restore, select them.**

6. **Click Restore.** The files and folders you selected are returned to their locations in the condition they were in the version of the backup you selected. If the files still exist (meaning you are restoring older versions), a prompt asks you if you want to replace the newer files or keep both copies. After the files are restored, Time Machine quits. You move back to the Finder location where the restored files were saved. You can resume using them as if you'd never lost them.

Restoring files in applications

Some applications that work with individual files, such as iPhoto, Mail, and Contacts, provide Time Machine support so you can restore files from within those applications instead of by selecting the files in the Finder. This makes restoring files from certain kinds of applications easier because you can find the files to restore using the application's interface instead of using the Finder (which is difficult for some applications, such as iPhoto files because of the way that application names and organizes your photos).

The process is very similar to that for Finder windows, except that you open the application first and show the data you want to recover, such as a mail folder, photos, or contacts. Then follow Steps 2 through 6 detailed in the preceding section for restoring items from Finder windows.

Restoring your entire MacBook Pro

Time Machine can also restore an entire OS X environment, such as when you are replacing your MacBook's internal hard drive or want to transfer your applications and documents to a new Mac.

If you replace your internal hard drive because it failed or because you wanted a larger one, start your MacBook Pro with the Time Machine backup drive attached, and hold the Option key. You see a row of drive icons that the Mac can be started from. If you see Recovery HD, choose that, and click the Restore from Time Machine button to begin restoring all files and folders from the backup drive to your new drive. If Recovery HD is unavailable, the Internet Recovery service appears (if your MacBook was made in 2011 or later); sign in to your Wi-Fi network, and enter your Apple ID and password to download the OS X installer from Apple's servers.

If you bought a new Mac, or if you had to run Internet Recovery to install OS X on a new drive, you're asked in the Transfer Information to This Mac window during OS X's installation whether to restore from another disk. Choose that option, select your Time Machine drive as the source, and click Continue.

Protecting Data with Online Backup Services

Time Machine is great because it is easy to set up and use to recover files. However, it does have several significant downsides. One is that no matter how large your backup drive is, it does have limited space. Another is that your backup drive must be in the same general location or at least network as your MacBook Pro. This means that if something catastrophic (such as a fire, flood, or theft) happens, both your MacBook Pro and the backup drive may be damaged, leaving you without your data. And when you are away, your files aren't backed up.

That's why using an online backup service in addition to using Time Machine is a good idea. Most online backup services allow you to configure the software so it works in a low-priority way. This is so the backup process doesn't significantly slow down your other activities. You may also be able to set the backups to only occur at specific times, such as the middle of the night when you aren't using your connection.

These services usually offer significant backup space for an affordable annual fee. When you sign up for a service, you download and install software that enables automatic backups of the data you select and that can restore your data. The first time you back up, it can take a long time, depending on how much data you are backing up and your connection speed. After that, only incremental changes are backed up so the process is much faster—just like how Time Machine works.

Two popular providers of online backup services for Mac users are Carbonite (www.carbonite.com) and Mozy (www.mozy.com). Both offer free trials, so you may want to try them both out and sign up for the one that best suits your needs.

Using the OS X Document Protection Features

OS X includes two features designed to preserve versions of documents that you are using: Auto Save and Versioning. These features ensure that specific documents with which you are working are protected while Time Machine protects groups of documents. You use both at the same time to provide as much protection as possible.

Note Applications must be written to support Auto Save or Versioning. Not all applications support these features.

Using Auto Save

Applications designed to work with OS X's Auto Save feature automatically save your open documents every hour and as you make substantial changes to them, so you don't need to bother saving documents manually. To determine whether an application supports Auto Save and Versioning, open its File menu. If you see Save As, the application does not support these features. If you see Save a Version or Duplicate, it does.

Note If you want to create a new version of a document, choose File ➪ Duplicate. A copy of the file is created. Save the copy with a new name. You now have two documents, and changes you make in one do not affect the other.

Restoring documents with Versioning

As documents are automatically saved, each save results in a version of the document. Versions are saved every hour and as you make significant changes. Hourly versions are kept for 24 hours and early versions are available daily until they are a month old, from which point they are maintained weekly. When you delete a document, all its versions are deleted, too.

Note You can create a version of a document at any time by choosing File ➪ Save a Version.

Perform these steps to view or recover an earlier version of a document:

1. **Choose File ➪ Revert to ➪ Browse All Versions.** The application disappears, and the version viewer screen appears. On the left side, you see the current version of the document, labeled Current Document. On the right side, you see a stack of all the saved versions. The date and time of the version currently being displayed is shown under the front document window. To the far right, you see the document's timeline.

2. **Click an older version of the document to bring it to the front, or use the timeline to move back to a specific version, as shown in Figure 13.8.**

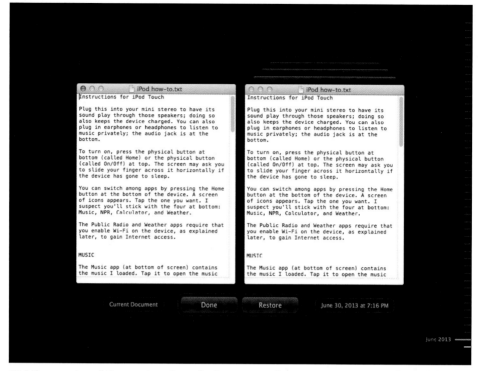

13.8 You can view all the saved versions of a document and return to a previous one if you choose.

3. **Compare the two versions of the document.** You can scroll and navigate within each document.

4. **Find the version of the document that you want to restore.**

5. **With the version you want to restore on top of the version stack on the right, click Restore.** That version of the document replaces the one you had been working on, and you return to the application. To keep the current version of the document instead of restoring an older version, click Done.

Protecting Data with Encryption

If you travel with your MacBook Pro, the data it contains is vulnerable because your computer can be carried away by other people. If you store important data on your computer, you can encrypt your data using OS X's FileVault feature so it can't be used without an appropriate password. This way, even if someone is able to mount the hard drive in your MacBook Pro, he or she must have the password to access its data.

Note

If you use your MacBook Pro in public, you should disable automatic login whether or not you use FileVault. With automatic login enabled, anyone who starts your computer can use it. With this feature disabled, a password is needed to access it, which provides some level of protection. You should also require a password to wake the computer or stop the screen saver if you leave your MacBook Pro for any period without logging out, as described earlier in this chapter.

The OS X FileVault feature encrypts your drive using a password that you create so this data can't be accessed without the appropriate password. Perform these steps to activate FileVault:

1. **Open the Security & Privacy system preference.**

2. **Unlock the system preference by clicking the Lock icon and authenticating yourself by entering your account name and password in the sheet that appears.**

3. **Go to the FileVault pane.**

4. **Click Turn On FileVault.** A sheet opens listing all the user accounts on your MacBook Pro, as shown in Figure 13.9. Each user's password must be entered for that user to be able to unlock the drive. Users who can unlock the drive are marked with a check mark. If users cannot unlock the drive, you see the Enable User button. The account under which you are working is automatically enabled.

Note

Users need a password for their accounts to access encrypted Macs; if they don't have such passwords, the Set Password button appears to the right of their names so you can assign them passwords.

5. **Click Enable User for the user you want to allow to unlock the drive.**

6. **Type that user's password, and click OK.** If you have an Administrator account, you won't be asked for the password.

7. **Repeat Steps 5 and 6 until you've enabled all the users you want to be able to unlock the drive.**

8. **Click Continue.** You see a sheet containing your recovery key. This key is needed if you forget your password. If you don't have this key and forget your password, all your data is lost. Record your recovery key by writing it down, or copying and pasting it into an iCloud-compatible application like Notes so you can get the recovery key from any Mac or iOS device using the same iCloud. Click Continue.

335

13.9 FileVault encrypts the data on your MacBook Pro to prevent unauthorized access to it. Each user needs a decryption password to access the Mac's contents.

9. **On the resulting sheet, choose to store the key with Apple by selecting Store the Recovery Key with Apple.** You can elect not to by selecting Do Not Store the Recovery Key with Apple. Click Continue.

10. **If you elected to store the key with Apple, configure your security questions on the resulting sheet, and click Continue.** If not, skip this step.

11. **Click Restart.** Your MacBook Pro restarts.

12. **Log back in to your user account.** The encryption process begins. You can work normally as your MacBook Pro encrypts itself.

While the encryption process runs, you may not notice anything. The process can take quite a while, depending on how much data you have on your MacBook Pro. To see the status of the process, open the FileVault pane again. You see that the FileVault is turned on, and if you sent a recovery key to Apple, you see a confirmation that it was sent. Below that, you see the encryption status bar.

After the process is complete, you also won't notice any difference because data is decrypted as needed when you log in. The difference occurs when someone tries to access the drive without the password; all the data on the drive is useless. For example, suppose someone steals your MacBook Pro. Although he or she can't access your user account without your login password, the thief can connect the computer to an eternal drive with OS X installed and start up from that drive. If you didn't enable encryption, the files on your MacBook startup volume are no longer protected because the OS on the external drive from which the MacBook is started is running the show, and it doesn't have a password for startup. Ditto if someone takes out your hard drive and connects it to another computer. But if FileVault is on, the MacBook Pro's files are encrypted and can't be used without the correct password.

The Security & Privacy system preference manages encryption for your internal hard drive, and Time Machine has an option to encrypt its backup drives, as described earlier in this chapter. But what about other external hard drives? OS X lets you encrypt them, too.

One way is to select a format with *Encrypted* in its name in the Disk Utility's Erase pane when you first set up an external drive. But you can enable encryption at any time by right-clicking the drive or partition in a Finder window's Sidebar or on the Desktop and choosing Encrypt from the contextual menu that appears. (The drive disappears for a few minutes while it's being encrypted.)

When you enable encryption, you are asked to provide a password. From the Finder, a dialog appears; in Disk Utility, a settings sheet appears when you click Erase, as Figure 13.10 shows.

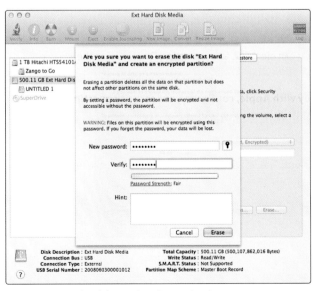

13.10 Encrypt a hard drive when formatting it so no one can access its contents without a password, even from another computer.

Both require the same information. You can change the password later in Disk Utility by choosing File ⇨ Change Password after selecting the drive there.

Using Find My iPhone to Locate Your MacBook Pro

When you sign in to the iCloud website, you can use the Find My iPhone module, which lets you (despite its somewhat misleading name) find your MacBook Pro in the event that you lose control of it, as well as any iOS devices and other Macs you may own. (Chapter 6 covers iCloud.) Because MacBook Pros are easy to move, they are also easy to lose or steal. Find My Mac provides tools for locating your MacBook Pro and limiting the damage to you should it fall into unfriendly hands.

Before you can use the Find My iPhone feature, you must enable Find My Mac on your MacBook Pro:

1. **Open the iCloud system preference.** Sign in to iCloud if you are not already signed in.

2. **Select the Find My Mac check box.**

3. **Click Allow at the prompt.**

Note To enable the find-me service for iOS devices, go to their Settings app's iCloud pane, and set the Find My iPhone, Find My iPad, or Find My iPod switch to On. You must have signed in to your iCloud account on these devices.

After you've enabled the find-me feature on your MacBook Pro and other devices, you can find them from the iCloud website's Find My iPhone application, as well as play a sound on them (in case one is hiding under a cushion), lock the device (if you think it may be stolen or lost), or erase its contents (if you're sure it's been stolen and fear sensitive information could be retrieved from it). Figure 13.11 shows the Find My iPhone web application in action.

Here's how Find My iPhone works:

1. **Sign in to the iCloud website with the same account as the missing MacBook Pro.** You can let someone else find their device, for example, by having them enter their Apple ID and password.

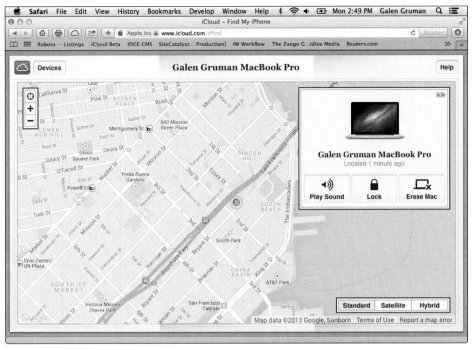

13.11 Using Find My iPhone to find and lock or erase a MacBook Pro.

2. **On the home screen, click Find My iPhone.** Provide your Apple ID's password, if prompted. All the devices for which you have enabled the Find My Device feature are shown on the map, with a green dot for each location detected. If a device is online, its dot is green; a gray dot indicates the last known location for a device not turned on or locatable. The size of the circle around a device's dot indicates how precise its location is; the larger the circle is, the less precise the device's location.

3. **Click a device's dot to open a pop-over with its name.** Or click the Devices button to open a pop-over listing all devices, and click the one you want to have the map zoom to.

Note

If Find My iPhone can't find your MacBook Pro, select it from the Devices list. Instead of seeing a map, you see a gray screen with a version of the control screen described in Step 5, offering the same controls. Of course, those actions don't take place until the MacBook is reconnected to the Internet, assuming its iCloud account is still signed in. (A thief will likely disable that account immediately.) To be notified when the MacBook is back online and located, select the Notify Me When Found check box. When the device becomes visible to Find My Mac, you receive an e-mail or text message and can then take the appropriate action to locate and secure it.

4. **Click the *i* icon in the pop-over to open a window with controls for the device.** If the *i* icon isn't visible, click the device's name, wait a second, and click it again.

5. **In the control window, select the action you want to take on the device, if any.** These actions are available:

- **Play Sound**, which plays, a loud, annoying tone until you acknowledge the prompt on the device or the battery gives out. (If the MacBook has a password enabled, as it should, the password must be entered to acknowledge the prompt.)

- **Lock**, which requires a password that you provide from the Find my iPhone application for the device to be used. You can also specify a message to appear on the screen, such as a request to call you if found.

- **Erase Mac**, which erases the Mac completely—its data and applications—and then locks it using a code you provide. (For iOS devices, Lock is called Lost Mode.) You can also specify a message to appear on the screen in case someone finds it. Note that after a MacBook is erased, it can no longer be located via Find My iPhone, so don't use this feature too quickly. If you do find your erased Mac, you can restore it from a Time Machine backup—if you've been backing it up, of course.

In the control window, you also see the power status for the device, such as battery life remaining and how long ago the device was located.

Caution

You can use the Find My iPhone app on an iOS device to do the same things as the Find My iPhone application on the iCloud website. I strongly recommend you download this free app onto your iOS devices from the App Store, because you cannot use the iCloud website from an iOS device, just from a Mac, Windows, or Linux computer.

Genius

For security, you should require a password to stop the screen saver or wake your MacBook Pro. You can set this in the General pane of the Security & Privacy system preference. You can also configure a message to appear on the screen when it's locked, such as your name and contact information. This way, if your MacBook Pro is found by someone who wants to return it, she can get in touch with you. Of course, this method is not foolproof: Someone can start the Mac from another hard drive to bypass the password requirement. Other techniques you can use to further protect a MacBook if lost or stolen are described elsewhere in this chapter.

Using Firmware Password Utility

You can make your MacBook Pro even more secure by using the Firmware Password Utility to lock its drive to the MacBook Pro itself. That way, a person who steals your MacBook Pro can't start it from any drive but the drive you specify. You could thus lock the MacBook Pro to an external drive that you store in a different location than your MacBook Pro when, say, you're on vacation. That way, if someone gets the MacBook, he or she can't start it up. If the MacBook's drives are encrypted, it's nearly impossible to access the Mac or its drives, which also means you must be sure you don't lose the drive!

To use the Firmware Password Utility, follow these steps:

1. **Start the MacBook Pro from the drive you want to lock it to.**

2. **Restart the MacBook Pro, holding ⌘+R as you do so.**

3. **The MacBook should boot into Recovery Mode.** Choose a language to use if asked.

4. **When the OS X Utilities dialog appears, choose Utilities ⇨ Firmware Password Utility.**

5. **In the dialog that appears, click Change, select the Require Password option, and type the password to use.** Confirm the password when asked.

6. **Click OK, and restart the Mac. It is now locked to that startup drive.** If someone tries to start it from a different drive, that person sees a lock symbol on the screen and cannot proceed.

Caution If you've enabled the Firmware Boot Utility and you've erased the Mac using Find My iPhone, you need to take the MacBook Pro to an Apple repair facility to reactivate it, if you get your MacBook back.

Protecting Information with Keychains

Often, you can select a check box that causes OS X to remember the passwords you type. These passwords are remembered in the keychain associated with your account. All you have to remember is the password for your user account to unlock the keychain, which in turn, applies the appropriate usernames and passwords so you don't have to type them.

Chapter 6 covers iCloud Keychain, an extension of the OS X keychain introduced in OS X Mavericks that syncs passwords and credit card information for use by the Safari browser on all Macs and iOS devices signed in to your iCloud account. But the keychains on the Mac store much more than this information, and they store it for many more applications. That Wi-Fi password you saved for automatic login? It's in the keychain. So is the sign-in information for iTunes and the App Store. And your passwords in Mail. And the logins to file shares.

Each kind of username and password is stored as a specific type in your keychain. A keychain is created automatically for each user account you create. However, you can create additional keychains for specific purposes if you need to, providing additional security while retaining the convenience of keychains.

To use a keychain, it must be unlocked. To unlock a keychain, type its password when you are prompted to do so; that's basically what happens when you are asked to authenticate yourself by entering your user account password. Although typing a keychain's password can be annoying, you should remember that at least you must remember only the keychain's password instead of remembering a separate password for each resource.

Viewing and configuring keychains

Your default keychain is called the login keychain. You also have a system keychain on your MacBook Pro.

Follow these steps to view and configure your keychain:

1. **Launch the Keychain Access application, shown in Figure 13.12, located in the Utilities folder inside the Applications folder.** In the top-left pane is a list of all keychains that your account can access. In the lower-left pane is a list of categories for all the keychains installed under your user account. Select a category, and the keychain items it contains appear in the lower-right pane of the window. You see information related to each keychain item, such as its name, kind, the date it was last modified, when it expires, and the keychain in which it is stored. When you select a keychain item, detailed information about that item appears in the upper part of the window.

2. **To see what items are included in your default keychain, select login.**

3. **Select the All Items category.** Each item in your keychain appears in the list.

4. **To get summary information about a keychain item, select it.** A summary of the item appears at the top of the window, including the kind of item it is, the user account with which it is associated, where the location to which it relates is, and the modification date.

5. **Double-click a keychain item.** Its window appears. This window has two panes: Attributes and Access Control. The Attributes pane presents information about the item, such as its name, its kind, the account, the location of the resource with which it is associated, comments you have entered, and the password (which is hidden when you first view an item). The Access Control pane lets you configure how the item is used.

6. **To see the item's password, select the Show Password check box.** You are then prompted to confirm the keychain's password.

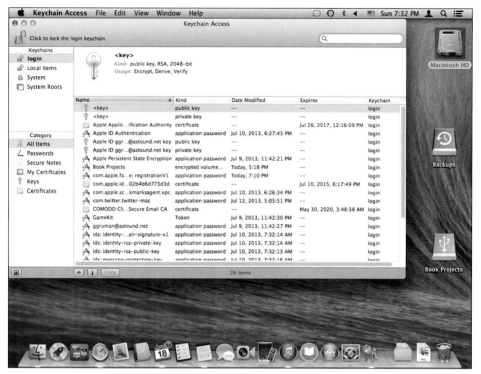

13.12 As you can see, many items are stored in my keychain.

7. **Confirm the keychain's password by typing it at the prompt and choosing to allow access to the item.** When you return to the Attributes pane, you see the item's password.

8. **Click the Access Control pane.** Use the access controls in the pane to control which applications can access this keychain item and how they can access it.

9. **To allow access to the item by all applications, select the Allow All Applications to Access This Item radio button.** If you want to configure access for specific applications, continue with the rest of these steps.

10. **To allow access by specific applications but require confirmation, select the Confirm before Allowing Access radio button.** Select the Ask for Keychain Password check box if you want to be prompted for your keychain's password before access is allowed.

11. **To enable an application not currently on the list to access the keychain item, click the Add (+) button located at the bottom of the list, and select the application to which you want to provide access.**

12. **Click Save Changes.** Your changes are saved, and you return to the Keychain Access window.

Adding keychains

Most people use just the login keychain—the one set up for their user account. But you can create additional keychains so passwords are stored separately. For example, you might use a second keychain for passwords to work accounts or for financial records.

To create an additional keychain, choose File ⇨ New Keychain in the Keychain Access application. Provide a name in the Save As field, and click Create. Now when you are asked to save a password or other information, enter that name in the prompt instead of your user account name, as well as the password for this other keychain.

Likewise, when an application asks you for a password to unlock keychain information, use this new keychain name and password if that's the keychain you used for that application. If you can't remember which keychain you used, you can try the different username and password combinations until you get it right.

Adding items to a keychain

You can add items to a keychain in any of the following ways:

- When you access a resource that can provide access to a keychain, such as a file server, select the Remember check box.
- Drag a network server onto the Keychain Access application window.
- Drag the Internet Resource Locator file for a web page onto the Keychain Access window.
- Manually create a keychain item.

Note

If a particular application or resource doesn't support keychains, you can't access that resource automatically. However, you can still use Keychain Access to store such an item's username and password for you, thus enabling you to recall that information easily.

One useful thing you can add to a keychain is a secure note. This protects the information you type with a password so it can be viewed only if the appropriate password is provided, which is the password that unlocks the keychain. Follow these steps to add a secure note to a keychain:

1. **Launch Keychain Access.**
2. **Select the keychain to which you want to add the note.**

3. **Choose File ⇨ New Secure Note Item.** The New Secure Note sheet appears, as shown in Figure 13.13.

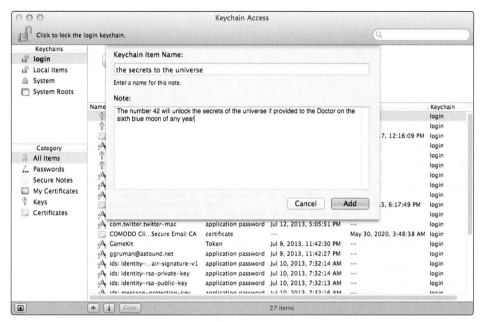

13.13 Here's a secure note containing vital information.

4. **Type a name for the note in the Keychain Item Name box.**

5. **Type the information you want to store in the Note box.**

6. **Click Add.** The note is added to your keychain, and you return to the Keychain Access window where you see the new note you added in the Secure Notes section (click Secure Notes in the lower-left pane).

Follow these steps to view a secure note:

1. **Select the Secure Notes category.** Your secure notes appear.

2. **Double-click the note you want to read.** The note opens, but the information it contains is hidden.

3. **Click the Show Note check box (if you have not displayed the note before, you need to allow keychain access to it).** Enter your password, and click Allow. You see the note in the window. You can edit if desired; click Save Changes if so.

4. **Close the note when you're finished.**

345

Caution If you click Always Allow, you no longer need to enter a password to see the note after you've signed in to your Mac, which defeats the purpose of a secure note.

Working with keychains

When an application needs to access a keychain item and it is not configured to always allow access, you see the confirm dialog that prompts you to type a keychain's password and choose an access option. When prompted, choose one of these options:

- **Deny.** Access to the item is prevented.

- **Allow.** A single access to the item is allowed.

- **Always Allow.** Access to the item is always allowed, and you don't see the prompt the next time it is used.

If you want to become a keychain master in Keychain Access, check out the following information:

- **Choose Edit ⇨ Change Settings for Keychain** *keychainname* **(where** *keychainname* **is the name of the keychain).** You can set a keychain to lock after a specified time or lock when the MacBook Pro is asleep.

- **Choose Edit ⇨ Change Password for Keychain** *keychainname* **(where** *keychainname* **is the name of the keychain) to change a keychain's password.**

- **Choose Keychain Access ⇨ Preferences.** In the General pane, select the Show Keychain Status in Menu Bar check box. This adds the Keychain Access icon to the menu bar. From this menu, you can lock or unlock keychains, and you can access security preferences and the Keychain Access application.

- **Choose Edit ⇨ Keychain List.** The Configure Keychain sheet opens, in which you can use to configure keychains for a user account or the system. For example, you can select the Shared check box to share a keychain between user accounts.

- **Choose Keychain Access ⇨ Keychain First Aid.** You see the Keychain First Aid dialog, which you can use to verify keychains or repair a damaged one.

MacBook Pro Problems?

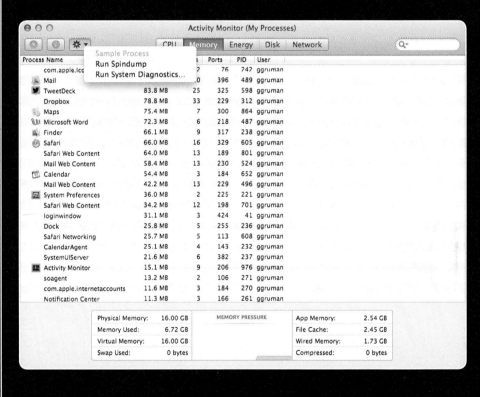

Although MacBook Pros are among the most reliable and easiest-to-use computers available, they are still complex systems that involve advanced technology, intricate software, and connections to networks, the Internet, and other devices. In other words, there are lots of moving parts. You can expect that every once in a while, something will go wrong. However, with a bit of preparation and some basic troubleshooting, you should be able to recover from most common problems easily.

Looking for Trouble

You should build a MacBook Pro toolkit to troubleshoot and solve problems. This way, you won't waste lots of time and energy trying to locate or create the tools you need to solve problems. Instead, you can simply put them into action. Here are a few of the most important tools you should have in your toolkit in case of an emergency:

- **Current backups.** Backups are a critical part of your toolkit because restoring your data is the most important task that you need to be able to do. Having a good way to restore your data limits the impact of drastic problems (like your MacBook Pro not working) and makes less significant problems (like the accidental deletion of a file) trivial to solve. Use OS X's own Time Machine application to back up your MacBook Pro to an external drive automatically, and if you use your MacBook in multiple locations, also use an online backup service, as Chapter 13 explains.

- **Alternate startup drive.** Your MacBook Pro's system software is all-important because the OS is what makes the MacBook run. If your startup drive or the system software it contains has a problem, you might not be able to start up, which reduces your MacBook Pro to being a very cool-looking piece of technology art. OS X creates the recovery partition so you can start and repair your MacBook Pro using the Disk Utility application to repair a drive or volume, reinstalling OS X, and so on. But that recovery partition is stored on your startup drive, so if the drive dies, you can't use the recovery partition. That's why you should create a separate startup drive using an inexpensive hard drive or USB flash drive; run the OS X installer from the recovery partition to create that emergency startup drive.

- **Alternate user account.** Because some problems can be related to preferences and other files specific to a user account, having an alternate user account is important for troubleshooting. If you haven't created an alternate user account for such emergencies, you should do so now. Be sure to create one with Administrator privileges, as Chapter 2 explains.

- **Application installation files.** If you purchase an application on disc, keep it where you can easily access it when necessary. If you obtain applications from the Internet, burn the installation files to a DVD or CD and keep them with your other application discs.

Note Applications that you purchase from the Mac App Store don't need to be saved on a CD or DVD because, if you need to, you can always download again from the App Store's Purchased pane, at no cost, any that you've purchased.

🔘 **A record of important information.** Consider devising a secure way to record passwords, usernames, serial numbers, and other critical data so you don't have to rely on memory. OS X's Notes application, which syncs to all your iCloud-connected devices and to the iCloud.com website (see Chapter 6), is a very convenient place to store such information; just make sure all the devices that can access Notes require a password so your secrets aren't easily taken. Although keeping such information in hard copy is usually not advised because it can be easily lost, stolen, or copied, it's a method many people prefer, especially if they have locked file drawers.

Note

You can also store this data in a keychain, because it is protected with your user account password. If you allow website and account usernames and passwords to be remembered, this information is automatically stored in your keychain. You can also store application registration information as secure notes (see Chapter 13). As long as you can get to your keychain, the information it contains is easily accessible. However, you should back up your keychains, too, to use for troubleshooting.

🔘 **System report.** Consider maintaining a system profile generated by the System Information application, as shown in Figure 14.1. This information can be very helpful when troubleshooting problems. Choose ➪ About This Mac, click More Info in the window that appears, and then click System Report in the next window that appears. You can print the report by choosing File ➪ Print. Or create a PDF copy by choosing File ➪ Print and then choosing Save As PDF from the PDF pop-up menu at the bottom left of the Print dialog.

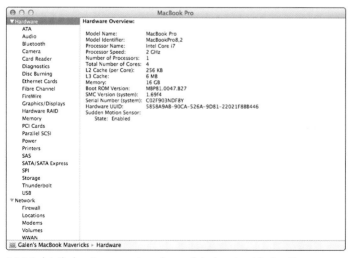

14.1 A detailed system report can be useful when troubleshooting.

Understanding and Describing Problems

When you start to troubleshoot, the most important thing you can do is understand a problem in as much detail as possible. This helps you figure out what you need to do to correct the problem, or at least it gives you ideas of things you can try. As you gain insight into your problem, you should be able to describe it in detail, so you can get help from others if you can't solve it yourself. Recognizing the symptoms of various kinds of problems also helps you identify what the problem is, which puts you in a better position to try solutions.

Recognizing user errors

One common source of problems is your own mistaken (or lack of proper) actions. Recognizing a problem that you've caused is a bit tough, because user errors can have many consequences. The most common one is software or hardware not doing what you expect it to. In such cases, a common cause is a failure to do things in the recommended way. These are some common user errors:

- **Not following instructions.** Sometimes, taking a few minutes to read directions can save minutes or hours of troubleshooting.

- **Not performing proper maintenance on your system.** Although OS X keeps itself and Mac App Store applications updated, don't forget to ensure that your other software and drives are updated too, as Chapter 13 explains.

- **Not keeping enough free space on your hard drives.** If a drive is full, or very close to it, you may have problems when you try to store more data on it. Archive to another drive files you use rarely, delete those you don't need, and consider replacing your MacBook Pro's internal hard drive with a higher-capacity model, something that is straightforward to do (Other World Computing has good instructions at www.macsales.com) or that you can find a Mac repair shop to do. (The Retina MacBook Pro model's internal SSD drive cannot be replaced.)

Recognizing software problems

Software problems manifest in many ways, but the most common symptoms are hangs and unexpected quits. A hung application is one that has stopped responding to your commands and appears to be locked up. Hangs are usually visible as a pointer that turns into spinning color wheel, which indicates that the MacBook is spinning its figurative wheels—using lots of processing power but not getting the tasks done. Let the application try to work through whatever is hanging it; if if continues in that state for more than a few minutes, consider force-quitting it.

To force-quit an application, right-click its Dock icon and choose Force Quit from the menu that appears. If the menu shows Quit rather than Force Quit, try choosing Quit. If nothing happens after a minute or so, right-click the application's Dock icon again and this time hold the Option key to force the Force Quit option to appear. Then choose Force Quit. You can also choose ⇨ Force Quit or press Option+⌘+Esc to open the Force Quit Applications dialog, shown in Figure 14.2, where you select the recalcitrant application and click Force Quit.

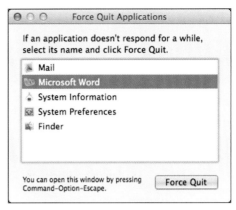

14.2 The Force Quit dialog lets you shut down a recalcitrant application.

Fortunately, because OS X has protected memory, a hung application usually affects only that application; your others continue to work normally. If you force-quit an application, you lose any unsaved data in that application, but at least your losses are limited to changes you've made there since your last save or since the last hourly Time Machine backup.

Sometimes, the application you are using suddenly quits; that's called an *unexpected quit*. The application windows that were open simply disappear. That's bad enough, but the worst part is that you lose any unsaved data with which you were working, and there's nothing you can do about it. Some of the likely causes of unexpected quits include software bugs and conflicts among applications or between applications and hardware. You should always restart your MacBook Pro after an unexpected quit.

Note

Often, when an application unexpectedly quits or is forced to quit, a window opens up with lots of computer code. It's a record of what was occurring when the application crashed, and it has a field in which you can enter more details about what you were doing before the crash. It's a good idea to provide that information, but even if you don't, click the Report button or the Send to Apple button so the details of the problem can be reviewed by Apple's engineers and passed on to the software developers or hardware developers involved. That might result in a fix being developed in a future update.

Unexpected behavior is obvious because an application starts not doing what you are telling it to or doing things you aren't telling it to. Likely causes of this problem are bugs or using the application other than how it was intended. Internet attacks and viruses can also be the cause of unexpected behavior.

Recognizing hardware problems

As odd as it might seem, the most unlikely cause of a problem is a hardware failure. Although hardware does fail now and again, it doesn't happen very often. Hardware failures are most likely to occur immediately after you start using a new piece of hardware or close to the end of its useful life. Sometimes, you can induce a hardware failure when you upgrade a machine or perform some maintenance on it.

Symptoms of a hardware problem are usually pretty obvious. You have a piece of hardware that just doesn't work as you expect it to—or not at all. (I hope that hardware isn't your MacBook Pro!) If the cause of a hardware problem is software, you can often solve the problem by updating the software for the device. If the problem is actually with the hardware, though, you probably need help solving it, such as having it repaired.

Describing problems

Being able to accurately describe a problem is one of the most fundamental skills for effective troubleshooting. To describe a problem accurately, you must take an in-depth look at the various aspects of the problem. This puts you in a better position to solve it because effectively describing your problem is critical to help someone help you. You need to answer these questions:

- Which specific applications and processes (not just the one with which you were working) were running?
- What were you trying to do (print, save, format, and so on)?
- What specifically happened? Did an application unexpectedly quit or hang? Did you see an error message?
- Have you made any changes to the computer recently (installed software or changed settings)?

The answers to these questions provide significant clues to help you figure out what is triggering the problem, which is integral to identifying its cause. As strange as this may sound, when a problem occurs, you should recover the best you can, and then immediately try to make the problem happen again. Open the same applications and follow your trail the best that you can, repeating everything that you did when the problem appeared. You can use the Activity Monitor application, shown in Figure 14.3, to see what happens when you re-create the situation that led to the problem. (The Activity Monitor application resides in the Utilities folder of the Applications folder.)

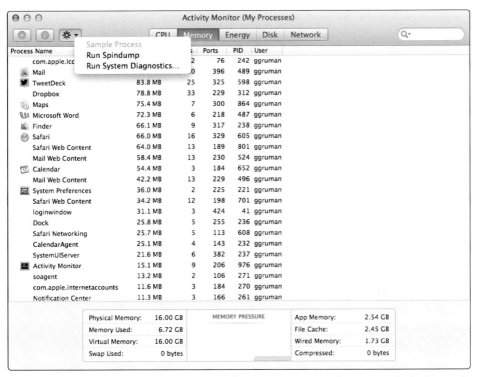

14.3 Use the Activity Monitor application to see what processes are running at any point in time, such as when you are trying to re-create a problem.

When you attempt to re-create a problem, there are two possible results—and both of them are good if you think about them correctly:

- One result is that you can't make the problem happen again. In this case, all you can do is go about your business and hope that you just got unlucky with some combination of events (if there is an underlying problem, don't worry about missing it because it will likely happen again at some point).

- The other result is that you are able to replicate a problem. Although this is painful because you don't really want to be dealing with a problem, being able to replicate it makes figuring out what is happening much easier.

The hardest problems to fix are those that occur only occasionally or intermittently. If you can re-create a problem, it is much easier to describe and also more likely that you'll be able to get help with it if you can't solve it on your own.

Trying Fast and Easy Solutions

For proper troubleshooting, you should learn to recognize and describe problems. However, in reality, your first step when solving a problem is often one of the techniques described in this section. The amazing thing is that one of these solves many of the more common problems you might encounter, at least temporarily. However, if the fast and easy solutions fail, you must move on to more complicated efforts. For each of these solutions, I also cover in what situations you should think about trying it and the steps to follow.

Forcing applications to quit

When to try: An application is hung and isn't responding to commands. The spinning color wheel appears on the screen and remains there.

What it does: The command causes the OS to forcibly stop the application and its processes. You will lose any unsaved data in the application that you force to quit. As noted earlier in this chapter, there are several ways to force-quit an application:

- **Choose ⌘ ⇨ Force Quit, or press Option+⌘+Esc.** In the Force Quit Applications dialog that appears, you see the applications that are running. The name of the application that is hung appears in red with the text *(Not Responding)* next to it. Select the application, and click Force Quit. In the warning sheet appears, click Force Quit again.
- **Right-click the Dock icon of the hung application, and choose Force Quit from the menu that appears.**

If force-quitting doesn't work, try it again. Sometimes, it can take a few times to get a hung application stopped. To be safe, save your changes in any open documents and restart your MacBook Pro before you continue working. This minimizes the chances of additional problems.

Forcing the Finder to relaunch

When to try: The Finder isn't responding to commands. The spinning color wheel pointer appears whenever you try to select or work with something in the Finder, such as a Finder window.

What it does: The command stops and starts the Finder again.

Note

Relaunching the Finder is a hit-or-miss proposition, so don't be too surprised if it doesn't work.

You force-quit the Finder the same way as any other application. But instead of seeing the Force Quit button, you'll see the Relaunch button. Click it, and a warning sheet appears. Click Relaunch again, and your MacBook Pro tries to relaunch the Finder. As with force-quitting a hung application, it can take a few tries to get the Finder to relaunch. If successful, you are able to work in the Finder again. But forcing the Finder to relaunch leaves it in an unstable condition, so save any open documents and restart your MacBook Pro before continuing to work.

Restarting or restoring

When to try: When your MacBook Pro or an application isn't working the way you expect, you've forced an application to quit, or you've relaunched the Finder.

What it does: Shuts down all applications, processes, and your MacBook Pro, and then restarts it.

1. **Perform one of the following actions:**

   - Choose ⬛ ⇨ Restart.

   - Press and hold the Power key briefly, and then click Restart (this bypasses the Restart dialog).

2. **If the Restart dialog, shown in Figure 14.4, appears and you want to restore your Desktop to its current condition (with the same applications and documents open), select the Reopen Windows When Logging Back In check box.** This is a good option to use when troubleshooting because it reopens the applications and documents open when the problem happened, making describing and diagnosing it easier.

14.4 Restart your MacBook Pro when applications aren't behaving themselves.

3. **Click Restart.** MacBook Pro shuts down, restarts, and lets you get back to work.

Note

If a restart isn't the specific cure to a problem, it is almost always one step in the process. When in doubt, restart.

Shutting down soft

When to try: When your MacBook Pro or an application isn't working the way you expect, or you've forced an application to quit or relaunched the Finder, and normal behavior isn't restored with a restart.

What it does: Shuts down all applications, processes, and your MacBook Pro. Unlike a restart, a shutdown can sometimes clear a hardware-related issue.

1. **Perform one of these actions:**

   - Choose ⇨ Shut Down.

   - Press and hold the Power key, and click Shut Down in the dialog that appears. (Just pressing Power puts the Mac to sleep, so be sure to press and hold.)

   - Press and hold the Power key briefly, and then press Return when the dialog appears.

2. **If you want to restore your Desktop to its current condition (with the same applications and documents open), select the Reopen Windows When Logging Back In check box.** This is a good option to use when troubleshooting because it returns the MacBook Pro to the condition it was in when the problem happened, making describing and diagnosing it easier.

3. **Click Shut Down.** The MacBook Pro shuts down.

Shutting down hard

When to try: When your MacBook Pro appears to be locked up and doesn't respond to any of your commands.

What it does: Shuts down the MacBook Pro, regardless of any running processes. You will lose all unsaved data in all open applications.

Press and hold down the Power key until the MacBook Pro's screen goes dark and you hear it stop running. The MacBook Pro turns off. Wait a few seconds, and then press the Power key again; your MacBook Pro starts up. It may take longer than normal to start up because the MacBook runs a diagnostic check after being shut down hard.

Using a troubleshooting user account and deleting preferences

When to try: When an application isn't performing as you expect and restarting your MacBook Pro doesn't solve the problem.

What it does: Determines whether the problem is related to your specific user account or is more general.

1. **Perform one of these actions:**
   - Choose ⌘ ⇨ Log Out *accountname* (where *accountname* is the currently logged-in account).
   - Press Shift+⌘+Q.

2. **When the Log Out dialog appears, click Log Out.** (The logout occurs automatically when the 60-second timer counts down to zero.) The Login window appears.

3. **Log in to your troubleshooting account.**

4. **Repeat what you were doing when you experienced the problem.** If the problem goes away, it is most likely related to the previous user account. In most cases, this means that a preferences file is corrupted.

5. **Log out of the troubleshooting account, and log back into your normal user account.**

Application preference files are stored in the Preferences files in the Library file in the user's Home folder. By default, the Library folder is hidden.

If the problem persists, perform these steps:

1. **In the Finder, hold the Option key down and choose Go ⇨ Library.** The Library folder opens for the current user account.

2. **Open the Preferences folder.** Locate the preferences files for the application that has the problem. Preferences files have the extension .plist and include the application name somewhere in the filename, as shown in Figure 14.5. Some preferences files are stored in the company's or application's folder inside the Preferences folder.

3. **Delete the preferences files for the application.** If asked to authenticate yourself, enter your user account name and your password.

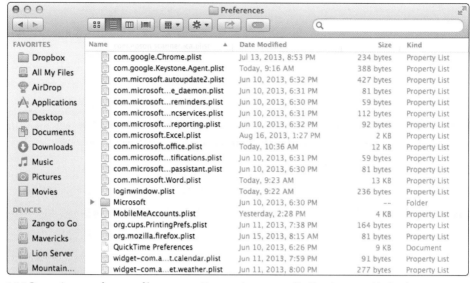

Name	Date Modified	Size	Kind
FAVORITES			
com.google.Chrome.plist	Jul 13, 2013, 8:53 PM	234 bytes	Property List
com.google.Keystone.Agent.plist	Today, 9:16 AM	388 bytes	Property List
com.microsoft.autoupdate2.plist	Jun 10, 2013, 6:32 PM	427 bytes	Property List
com.microsoft...e_daemon.plist	Jun 10, 2013, 6:31 PM	81 bytes	Property List
com.microsoft...reminders.plist	Jun 10, 2013, 6:30 PM	59 bytes	Property List
com.microsoft...ncservices.plist	Jun 10, 2013, 6:31 PM	112 bytes	Property List
com.microsoft...reporting.plist	Jun 10, 2013, 6:32 PM	92 bytes	Property List
com.microsoft.Excel.plist	Aug 16, 2013, 1:27 PM	2 KB	Property List
com.microsoft.office.plist	Today, 10:36 AM	12 KB	Property List
com.microsoft...tifications.plist	Jun 10, 2013, 6:31 PM	59 bytes	Property List
com.microsoft...passistant.plist	Jun 10, 2013, 6:30 PM	81 bytes	Property List
com.microsoft.Word.plist	Today, 9:23 AM	13 KB	Property List
loginwindow.plist	Today, 9:22 AM	236 bytes	Property List
▶ Microsoft	Jun 10, 2013, 6:30 PM	--	Folder
MobileMeAccounts.plist	Yesterday, 2:28 PM	4 KB	Property List
org.cups.PrintingPrefs.plist	Jun 11, 2013, 7:38 PM	164 bytes	Property List
org.mozilla.firefox.plist	Jun 15, 2013, 8:15 AM	81 bytes	Property List
QuickTime Preferences	Jun 10, 2013, 6:26 PM	9 KB	Document
widget-com.a...t.calendar.plist	Jun 11, 2013, 7:59 PM	91 bytes	Property List
widget-com.a...et.weather.plist	Jun 11, 2013, 8:00 PM	277 bytes	Property List

14.5 Removing a preferences file can sometimes restore an application to normal behavior.

Caution Deleting a preferences file can remove any personalized information that is stored in it, such as registration information. Make sure you have this information stored in another location before deleting an application's preferences files.

4. **Restart the application, and reconfigure its preferences.** If the problem doesn't recur, you are good to go. If it does, you need to try a more drastic step, such as reinstalling the application.

Genius An easy way to find all the files related to an application is to use AppCleaner (www. freemacsoft.net/appcleaner). When an application's icon is dropped onto the AppCleaner icon, it finds and displays all related files and allows you to delete them.

Repairing external hard drives

When to try: You see error messages relating to a hard drive, or you are unable to store data on it (and it isn't full).

What it does: Attempts to verify the drive's structure and repair any data problems.

1. **Quit all applications.**

2. **Launch Disk Utility (it's in the Utilities folder inside the Applications folder).**

3. **Select the drive you want to repair.**

4. **Check the bottom of the Disk Utility window for information about the drive you selected.** You see the drive's type, connection bus (such as ATA for internal drives or FireWire for an external drive), connection type (internal or external), capacity, write status, S.M.A.R.T. status, and partition map scheme. If you select a partition on a drive, you see various data about the volume, such as its mount point (the path to it), format, whether owners are enabled, the number of folders it contains, its capacity, the amount of space available, the amount of space used, and the number of files it contains.

5. **Go to the First Aid pane.**

6. **Click Repair Disk.** The application checks the selected drive for problems and repairs any it finds. When the process is complete, a report of the results appears.

If Disk Utility can repair any problems it found, you're finished and the drive should work normally. If the problems can't be fixed, you can try a different drive maintenance application, such as Alsoft's Disk Warrior (www.alsoft.com) or Prosoft's Drive Genius (www.prosofteng.com). In some cases, you might need to reformat the drive, which erases all its data.

Repairing the internal hard drive

When to try: You see error messages relating to the internal hard drive, or you cannot store data on it even though it isn't full.

What it does: Tries to verify the drive's structure and repair any data problems.

1. **Start your MacBook Pro from the Recovery HD partition by pressing and holding ⌘+R during startup.**

2. **Select the main language you want to use, and click the → button.**

3. **Click Disk Utility, and then click Continue.** The Disk Utility application opens.

4. **Select the MacBook Pro's internal hard drive in the Disk Utility application.**

5. **Follow Steps 4 through 6 in the previous section's instructions for repairing an external drive.**

Repairing permissions

When to try: When you get an error message stating that you don't have permission to do something for which you should have permission, or when you are experiencing unexpected behavior.

What it does: Repairs the security and access permissions associated with applications and files on a selected drive.

1. **Quit all applications.**

2. **Launch Disk Utility (it's in the Utilities folder inside the Applications folder).**

3. **Select the drive for which you want to repair permissions.**

4. **Go to the First Aid pane.**

5. **Click Repair Disk Permissions.** The application starts searching for permission problems and repairs those that it finds. When the process is complete, you see the results in the information window in the First Aid pane, as shown in Figure 14.6.

Reinstalling applications

When to try: You're using the current version (all patches and updates have been applied) of an application, but it's not working correctly, and you've tried restarting and shutting down soft.

What it does: Restores the application to like-new condition.

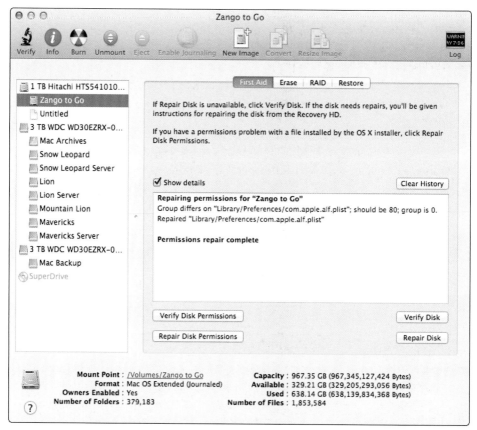

14.6 If you see odd security errors, try repairing a drive's permissions.

Caution

You will lose any updates or patches that were released after the installer you have was produced. You may also lose all your preferences for that application, including registration information, so make sure you have it stored elsewhere. Also, some applications such as Adobe's Creative Suite and Quark's QuarkXPress use registration schemes meant to deter software piracy; you must de-authorize the software from your Mac before or as part of uninstalling it. Otherwise, you may use up your two-computer license allotment and not be allowed to run the reinstalled copy.

How you do this depends on how you installed the application on your MacBook Pro. Perform these steps if you installed the application through the Mac App Store:

1. **Delete the application by dragging it to the Trash.** Or open the Launcher, click and hold the application's icon, and click the Close (X) box that appears in its upper left corner. If asked, authenticate yourself.

2. **Launch the Mac App Store.**

3. **Go to the Purchased pane.**

4. **Click the Install button for the application you deleted.**

5. **Type the Apple ID and password under which the application was purchased, and click Sign In.** The application is downloaded and installed. The benefit of this option is that you always get the most current version of the application you purchased.

Follow these steps to reinstall an application that wasn't installed through the Mac App Store:

1. **Perform one of the following actions to delete the application:**

   - Run the uninstall application (if one was provided) for the application you want to remove.

   - Drag the application's files and its preferences files to the Trash, and then empty it.

2. **Restart the Mac, so it can clean up any stray active processes from the removed application.**

3. **Run the application's installer.**

4. **Update the application to its latest version.**

5. **Reset your preferences.** If the application still doesn't work normally, the cause is likely a conflict between the application and either the version of OS X you are using or some other part of your system—or the application might just be buggy. Possible solutions are to use a different application, avoid the functionality of the application that causes the problem, or live with the problem until an update fixes it.

Starting up from the Recovery HD partition

When to try: When you start your MacBook Pro and the normal startup sequence stops with a flashing folder icon on the screen, or the MacBook Pro behaves oddly and you want to isolate the problem to your current startup drive.

What it does: Starts up your MacBook Pro from the Recovery HD partition.

OS X includes a Recovery HD partition that you can use when your primary system software has an issue or you need to perform a repair on your startup hard drive. Follow these steps to start the MacBook Pro from its Recovery HD partition:

1. **Restart your MacBook Pro.**

2. **As it restarts, hold down ⌘+R to boot into the Recovery HD partition.**

3. **In the window that appears, select one of these options, and click Continue:**

   - **Restore From Time Machine Backup.** This option lets you recover data from your Time Machine backup or even restore the entire system.

   - **Reinstall OS X.**

   - **Get Help Online.** This option lets you access the web to find a solution to the problem you are having.

   - **Disk Utility.** This launches the Disk Utility application so you can repair your startup drive.

4. **Use the selected tool to try to solve the problem.** For example, try to repair your startup drive with the Disk Utility application.

Note

Additional options appear in the Utilities menu. These are Firmware Password Utility (covered in Chapter 13), Network Utility (for running network diagnostics), and Terminal (for running the Unix operating system that undergirds OS X).

Starting up from an alternate external drive

When to try: When you try to start up your MacBook Pro and the normal startup sequence stops with a flashing folder icon on the screen, or the MacBook Pro is behaving oddly and you want to isolate the problem to your current startup drive.

What it does: Starts up your MacBook Pro from the system software installed on the external drive.

1. **Connect the external startup drive to your MacBook Pro.**

2. **Restart your MacBook Pro.**

3. **As it restarts, hold down the Option key.** After a few moments, each valid startup drive appears, as well as their Recovery HD partitions.

4. **Select the external hard drive from which you want to start up.**

Genius

To set the default startup drive to something other than your internal drive, so you don't have to keep selecting the desired drive at startup, use the Startup Disk system preference. In it, select the drive that you want to be the default. That drive is used the next time you restart or start your computer. You can, of course, change that default startup drive to a different drive, including the internal hard drive, later in the Startup Disk system preference.

5. **Press Return, or click the arrow icon pointing to the drive you selected.** Your MacBook Pro starts up, using the OS installed on the selected drive.

6. **Use the MacBook Pro.** If things work as expected, you know the problem is related to the previous startup drive, in which case, you must take more drastic action, such as reinstalling OS X on your normal startup drive. If the problem recurs, you know it is related to a specific application, hardware device, or the MacBook Pro itself, in which case the likely solutions are to reinstall the application or get help with the problem.

Note

If you ever start up your MacBook Pro and it displays a gray screen with a flashing disk icon, it means that the computer can't find a valid startup drive. This either means there is a problem with the drive itself or something has happened to critical OS X files, which is preventing the system from operating. If using Disk Utility from the Recovery HD partition or an external startup drive doesn't repair the drive, and if the drive still won't start, try reinstalling OS X via the Recovery HD partition or from an external startup drive in which you download the OS X installer from the Mac App Store. In a worst case, you may need to replace the hard drive and reinstall your OS X environment on it from your Time Machine backup.

Getting Help with MacBook Pro Problems

We all need a little help once in a while. When it comes to your MacBook Pro, there's a wealth of assistance available to you.

Using the Mac Help system

OS X includes a sophisticated Help system that you can use to find solutions to problems or to get help with a specific task. In addition to OS X, many other applications use the same Help system. Follow these steps to search for help:

1. **Choose Help in the menu bar.** The Help menu opens.

2. **Type the term for which you want to search in the Search box.** As you type, matches are shown on the menu, as shown in Figure 14.7. These are organized into two sections. In the Menu Items section, you see menu items related to your search. In the Help Topics section, you see links to articles about the topic. (If there are no entries for a section, that section does not appear.)

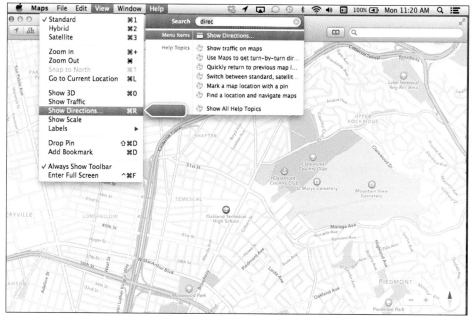

14.7 The OS X Help system can show you where menu commands are as well as open detailed instructions on application functions you seek help with.

3a. **To see where a menu item is located, select it.** The menu opens, and the item is highlighted. Figure 14.7 shows the Show Directions menu item being selected in the Maps application.

3b. **To read an article, click its link.** The Help Center window opens, and you see the selected article in the window. Figure 14.8 shows a help article about getting driving directions in Maps.

Genius

When you move away from the Help menu, it closes. However, your most recent search is saved so you can return to the results just by opening the menu again. To clear a search so you can perform a new one, click the Clear (X) button in the Search bar when it contains a search term. By contrast, the Help Center window stays on-screen on top of everything else no matter what you click or open; close or minimize it to get it out of your way.

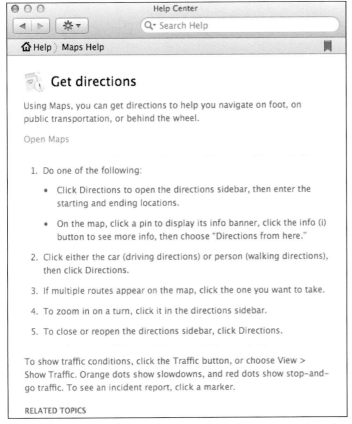

14.8 The Help Center displays articles that explain how to use a selected feature in an application.

Describing a problem in detail

If none of the fast and easy solutions presented earlier result in a problem being solved, you may have to create a more detailed description. This increases the odds that someone can help you. This section covers tools that can help you increase the level of detail in your problem descriptions.

Profiling a MacBook Pro

Your MacBook Pro is a complex system of hardware and software, in which each element has numerous technical specifications. Fortunately, you can use the System Information application to capture all the details about your system so you have them when you need to get help, as described earlier in this chapter (and shown in Figure 14.1).

Monitoring MacBook Pro activity

When a problem occurs, OS X doesn't provide lots of direct feedback. However, you can use the Activity Monitor application to get a closer look at what's happening in the background. Follow these steps to do so:

1. **Open Activity Monitor (it's in the Utilities folder inside the Applications folder).**

2. **Go to the CPU pane.** In the upper part of the window, you see a list of all running processes on the MacBook Pro. For each process, you see a variety of information, such as how many CPU resources it is using and the amount of memory. At the bottom of the window, you see a graphical representation of the current thread and process activity in the processor, as shown in Figure 14.9.

3. **Click the % CPU column heading to sort the list of processes by the amount of processor activity.**

4. **Click the Sort triangle so it is pointing down, indicating that the processes consuming more resources appear at the top of the list.** When a process is consuming a large amount of CPU resources or lots of drive activity over a long period, it can indicate that the process is having a problem or is the cause of problems you are experiencing. In most cases, problems you are experiencing are caused by applications. You can limit the processes shown in the window to just applications, which can make the information easier to interpret.

5. **Choose View ⇨ Windowed Processes to show only processes associated with applications.**

6. **Use the panes at the top of the window to explore other areas of the system.** You can use the Disk pane to assess how much free space your drives have, the Network pane to monitor network activity, the Energy pane to monitor power consumption (this is new to OS X Mavericks), and the Memory pane to assess the status of the MacBook Pro's RAM and its virtual memory.

Note

When you select a process and click the Inspect button (the *i* icon), the Inspect window opens and you see several panes of process information, such as memory use, statistics about how a process is working, and the files and ports it has open. This information is sometimes useful when troubleshooting. You can also stop a process by clicking Quit in its Inspect window, which is similar to a force quit.

Process Name	% CPU ▼	CPU Time	Threads	Idle Wake Ups	PID	User
Activity Monitor	1.0	1.29	11	2	663	ggruman
TweetDeck	1.0	13.34	25	18	598	ggruman
Microsoft Word	0.7	1:39.68	7	29	487	ggruman
distnoted	0.1	2.10	11	0	212	ggruman
Microsoft Database Daemon	0.0	0.99	2	3	497	ggruman
SystemUIServer	0.0	4.45	5	0	237	ggruman
Dropbox	0.0	11.56	33	0	312	ggruman
Dock	0.0	2.96	5	0	236	ggruman
xpcd	0.0	0.48	5	0	222	ggruman
fontd	0.0	2.04	3	0	243	ggruman
Mail	0.0	42.43	15	1	489	ggruman
PTPCamera	0.0	0.23	5	0	285	ggruman
PTPCamera	0.0	0.33	5	0	345	ggruman
com.apple.iCloudHelper	0.0	0.35	6	0	611	ggruman
loginwindow	0.0	1.69	3	1	41	ggruman
launchd	0.0	0.61	2	0	207	ggruman
Image Capture Extension	0.0	0.44	3	0	355	ggruman
com.apple.dock.extra	0.0	0.27	3	0	287	ggruman
recentsd	0.0	0.11	2	0	391	ggruman
sharingd	0.0	0.25	3	0	244	ggruman
identityservicesd	0.0	0.40	4	0	280	ggruman
ShareKitHelper	0.0	0.31	3	0	273	ggruman
Mail Web Content	0.0	2.26	12	0	524	ggruman

Activity Monitor (My Processes)

CPU | Memory | Energy | Disk | Network

System:	0.50 %	CPU LOAD	Threads:	687
User:	0.41 %		Processes:	151
Idle:	99.08 %			

14.9 If CPU activity is maxed out for a long period, a process is hung. You probably need to force it to quit and then restart your MacBook Pro.

Capturing screenshots

When you experience a problem, capturing a screenshot is a great way to describe and document it. It's even more useful when you ask for help because you can give the person helping you all the detailed information she needs. For example, if an error message appears on the screen, you can capture it in a screenshot. There are two built-in ways to capture a screenshot in OS X. You can use keyboard shortcuts or the Grab application.

Perform these steps to use a keyboard shortcut to capture the screen:

1. **When you want to capture the entire screen, press Shift+⌘+3.** A PNG-format image file is saved to the Desktop. Move to Step 3.

2. **When you want to capture part of the screen, press Shift+⌘+4.** The captured PNG-format image file is saved to the Desktop. You can select what you want to capture in two ways:

   - **To capture a window, press the space bar.** Move the pointer to the window you want to capture. When it is shaded in blue, click to capture a screenshot containing only that window.

   - **Drag the pointer over the area of the screen you want to capture, and release the trackpad button when the area is highlighted.**

3. **Use the image file you created.** The screenshot is named Screen Shot *X* (where *X* is the date and time at which the screenshot was captured). The file is now ready to use, such as to attach to an e-mail message or text chat. (Double-click the image to open it in Preview.)

OS X also includes the Grab application, which lets you capture screenshots in a slightly more sophisticated way.

Follow these steps to capture a screen with Grab:

1. **Organize your screen so what you want to capture is visible.** Open and close applications and document windows so there's nothing extraneous to confuse people and to ensure you're showing what you want to show.

2. **Launch the Grab application (it's in the Utilities folder inside the Applications folder).** The application opens, but you don't see any windows until you capture a screenshot. But you do see the Grab menu.

3. **Capture the screen. There are three methods, depending on what you want to capture:**

   - **Choose Capture ⇨ Timed Screen.** The Timed Screen Grab dialog appears, as shown in Figure 14.10. Click Start Timer to begin the countdown. You have 10 seconds in which to adjust what appears on-screen; after those 10 seconds, the screen is captured in its then-current state.

   - **Choose Capture ⇨ Selection.** The pointer turns into a + symbol, and you click and drag the pointer to create a rectangle (called a *marquee*) whose contents you want to capture. Release the trackpad button to capture the selection.

- **Choose Capture ⇨ Window.** The Choose Window dialog appears. Click Choose Window, and then click in the window you want to capture.

- **Choose Capture ⇨ Screen.** The Screen Grab dialog appears. Click outside it to capture the entire screen (the Screen Grab dialog is not captured with the screen).

14.10 After you click Start Timer, you have 10 seconds until the screen is captured.

4. **Save the image file.** After you capture the screen or a portion of it, Grab opens a window with the image. Choose File ⇨ Save to save the image as a TIFF file.

Genius

If you are serious about screenshots, you should consider using Ambrosia Software's Snapz Pro X (www.ambrosiasw.com/utilities). It gives you lots of control over the screenshots you take, such as deciding when to include the pointer. You can even capture motion and make movies of your MacBook Pro's on-screen activities, similar to what QuickTime Player can do.

Getting help from others

After you've tried the fast and easy solutions and the various Help systems on your MacBook Pro, your next stop should be the Internet. Check out these helpful websites:

- www.apple.com/support. The Apple support pages are a great source of information. You can also download system and software updates from Apple. You can search for specific problems by product or application or just by running a general search. You can also read manuals and have discussions about problems in the forums. If the problem you are having seems to be related to OS X, Apple hardware, or an Apple application, this should be your first stop.

- www.google.com. Type a description of the problem you are having. The odds are good that someone else has had, and maybe solved, the same issue. Explore the results until you find the help you need.

- www.macintouch.com. This site offers lots of news that can help you solve problems, especially if they can be solved by a software update of which you may be unaware.

Caution Many companies appear in Google and other search results promising to help with Mac support needs. Many appear to be official Apple support sites, but they are not. Scammers run many of these sites and will do things like have you run Activity Monitor to show "problems" that do not exist, and then they try to get your credit card information and/or have you download "repair" software that's actually malware. Always start at apple.com for support, or go to your local Apple Store or to an independent Mac repair store in your town.

Starting Over

I hope you never need to perform any of the tasks described here because they apply only when you have a significant problem. They also either take lots of time and effort or can be expensive. Still, you have to do what you have to do.

Reinstalling OS X

If you discover that your system has major problems, such as when your internal drive is no longer recognized as a valid startup drive, you might need to reinstall OS X. Because it takes a while, and you might lose some of the installation and configuration you've done, you shouldn't make this decision lightly.

Caution If you don't have your data backed up, be aware that reinstalling the operating system can damage or delete your data. That doesn't usually happen, but you should always have a good backup just in case. Chapter 13 explains how to do that.

If you determine that you do need to reinstall OS X, follow these steps to go about it:

1. **Back up your data, as described in Chapter 13.** Make sure it backed up by trying to recover a file or two if you can. Some problems prevent you from doing this verification. In those cases, you just have to trust that your backup system has worked.

2. **Start up from the Recovery HD partition by pressing and holding ⌘+R during startup.** When your Mac starts up, you see the OS X Utilities screen.

3. **Select Reinstall OS X, and click Continue.**

Genius When you are installing OS X, you can click Customize to choose specific options to install. For example, to save some drive space, you can deselect languages you don't use. When you've selected or deselected options, click OK, and the files you excluded won't be installed.

4. **Click Continue again.**

5. **Click Continue at the prompt.** This sends your MacBook Pro's serial number to Apple to verify your OS X license. (If your Mac is not online, connect it to the Internet via an Ethernet cable or use the Wi-Fi menu in the menu bar to select an available wireless network.)

6. **Follow the on-screen instructions to complete the installation.** When the process is complete, your MacBook Pro restarts.

7. **Update your software (see Chapter 13) so you are running the most current version of OS X.**

8. **Reinstall any applications that don't work correctly.** Mostly, these are applications that install software into the system. They need to be reinstalled because their software was removed when OS X was reinstalled.

I hope your MacBook Pro has returned to prime condition and is working like you expect. Because the installer doesn't change the contents of your Home folder, the data you had stored there should be intact, including your application preferences and iTunes content, so you can get back to what you were doing quickly. In rare cases, these data might have been disturbed, in which case you need to restore them from your backups.

Starting completely over

Sometimes, things get so bad that you just need to start over. This goes even farther than simply reinstalling OS X because you need to erase the internal hard drive. This means that all the data on it is deleted, including the system and all the files stored on it. This is drastic action and should be taken only if you really must do it. Also expect the initial process to take a long time.

Caution If you follow these steps, all the data on your hard drive is erased. If you don't have it backed up, it's gone forever. Don't do this unless you are sure your data is protected.

Follow these steps to wipe your hard drive and start over:

1. **Back up your data, and test your backups to make sure they work if you can.** In some cases, you won't be able to do this—for example, if you can't start up your MacBook Pro. In those cases, you must rely on your existing backups. If they are out of date, you shouldn't perform these steps unless it is your only recourse.

2. **Start up from the Recovery HD partition by pressing and holding ⌘+R during startup.** After your Mac starts up, you see the OS X Utilities screen. If there is no Recovery partition and your Mac is from 2011 or later, you have the option to download OS X from Apple.

3. **Choose Disk Utility, and click Continue.** The Disk Utility application opens.

4. **Use Disk Utility to erase the internal hard drive.** (See Chapter 11 for the details.) When the process is complete, quit Disk Utility. You return to the OS X Utilities window.

5. **Select Reinstall OS X, and click Continue.**

6. **Follow the on-screen instructions to complete the installation.** When the process is complete, your MacBook Pro restarts. When it does, it is in the same condition as when you first took it out of its box and turned it on.

7. **Follow the on-screen instructions to perform the initial configuration.** Again, this is just like the first time you started your MacBook Pro.

8. **If you used Time Machine for your backups, you can restore your data into the appropriate user accounts when prompted in the Transfer Information to This Mac window.**

9. **After the MacBook Pro has started up in the Finder, update your software (see Chapter 13).**

10. **Reinstall your applications.** You can use the Mac App Store application to reinstall any you purchased from the store. For your other applications, user the installers you downloaded from the web or the discs on which the software came.

11. **Restore your data from your backups, if you didn't do that during setup.** Your MacBook Pro should be back to its old self, but without the problems you were having.

Professional Repairs by Apple

If your MacBook Pro has hardware problems, you probably need to have it repaired by Apple. You can do this by taking it to a local Apple Store or using Apple's website to arrange technical support. Follow these steps to get started with the web approach:

1. **Go to** https://selfsolve.apple.com/GetWarranty.do.

2. **Type your MacBook Pro's serial number.** This number is on the MacBook Pro case and in your system report document. You can also get your serial number in OS X by choosing ➪ About This Mac and clicking the OS X version information twice in the window that appears.

3. **Select your country, and click Continue.** On the resulting screen, you see warranty information about your MacBook Pro, along with links to various resources you can use to have Apple repair it for you.

Index